Inhalt

Vorwort

Das PONS Reisewörterbuch Japanisch ist ein „Verständigungs-
führer". Mit ihm lernen Sie nicht nur einzelne Wörter, sondern wie
Sie sich tatsächlich im Ausland verständigen können.

Für Alltagssituationen, in die Sie bei Ihrer Reise geraten, sind die
gebräuchlichsten Redewendungen aufgeführt. Diese sind dialo-
gisch aufgebaut, so daß Sie nicht nur wissen, was Sie zu sagen
haben, sondern auch die entsprechenden Antworten verstehen
können.
Beachten Sie die blauen Punkte. Sie markieren Äußerungen oder
Sätze, mit denen Sie auf Ihrer Auslandsreise am häufigsten kon-
frontiert werden.

Das PONS Reisewörterbuch Japanisch ist in 11 Themenbereiche
gegliedert. Es begleitet Sie auf allen Etappen Ihrer Auslandsreise:
auf der Anreise oder bei der Ankunft im Hotel, am Strand genauso
wie bei einem Treffen mit Geschäftsfreunden.
Zu jedem dieser Themenbereiche finden Sie die wichtigsten Redewendungen mit thematisch geordneten Wortlisten. In ihnen sind
die wichtigsten Begriffe aufgeführt, die in den jeweiligen Situationen vorkommen können.
Mit Hilfe dieser Wortlisten sowie des zusätzlichen Wörterbuch-
teils am Ende des Buches können Sie die aufgeführten Beispiel-
sätze den konkreten Situationen individuell anpassen.

Die in den Kapiteln 1-11 verwendete einfache, dem deutschen
angepaßte Lautschrift erleichtert die korrekte japanische Aussprache. Bei modernen Fremdwörtern, die ins Japanische übernommen wurden, lehnt sich die Lautschrift an die Original-
schreibweise an, z. B. wird zwischen „r" und „l" unterschieden:
Mineralwasser – mineralu-sui, Kristall – kurisutalu.

Die international gebräuchliche Hepburn-Umschrift, die eng an
die englische Aussprache angelehnt ist, wurde in den Länderinformationen, der Kurzgrammatik sowie im Wörterbuchteil verwendet, um einen Vergleich mit Nachschlagewerken zu vereinfachen.

Die Kurzgrammatik hilft Ihnen, sich rasch über den Aufbau der japanischen Sprache zu orientieren.

Bilder und nützliche Tips informieren Sie und stimmen Sie auf kulturelle Besonderheiten und die landschaftlichen Reize Japans ein.

Die Schrift

Im 5. Jahrhundert kamen buddhistische Mönche aus Korea nach Japan und brachten mit der buddhistischen Lehre die chinesische Schrift mit. Japan verfügte damals noch nicht über eine eigene Schrift, und so wurde mit der buddhistischen Lehre auch die Schrift übernommen.

Die chinesischen Schriftzeichen sind keine Lautzeichen wie z. B. unsere Schrift, sondern ein Zeichen entspricht einem Wort. Daher gab es zwei Möglichkeiten: entweder konnte man ein japanisches Wort mit dem bedeutungsgleichen chinesischen Schriftzeichen darstellen, oder mit dem chinesischen Schriftzeichen auch das zugehörige chinesische Wort als Lehnwort übernehmen. Die Konsequenzen sind ein Reichtum der Sprache, aber auch große Schwierigkeiten für die Lernenden.

Ein chinesisches Schriftzeichen, genannt **Kanji,** kann verschieden gelesen werden, und zwar auf die chinesische und auf die japanische Lesart. In zusammengesetzten Worten tritt vorwiegend die chinesische Lesart auf, bei isolierten Worten die japanische. Das heißt: ein und dasselbe **Kanji** klingt je nach Zusammenhang so verschieden wie „gai" (chinesische Lesart) und „soto" (japanische Lesart).

Schwierig ist das übrigens nicht nur für uns. Japaner lernen während der ganzen Schulzeit bis hin zum Studium neue Schriftzeichen.

Eine weitere Schwierigkeit besteht darin, daß die japanische Sprache eine völlig andere als die chinesische ist. Das Japanische ist eine agglutinierende Sprache, d. h. es gibt grammatikalische Endungen, Vorsilben, Partikel, die jeweils an das Wort angehängt werden können. Nicht so das Chinesische: für diese Sprache gilt – salopp gesagt: eine andere Bedeutung – ein anderes Zeichen. Genau hierin ist wohl der Grund zu suchen, warum im Japanischen neben den **Kanjis** noch zwei Silbenalphabete existieren, die im Mittelalter entwickelt wurden. Mit diesen Silbenalphabeten, deren Zeichen aus den Kanjis durch Vereinfachung entwickelt wurden, konnte der japanischen Sprache Rechnung getragen werden.

Das runder aussehende Silbenalphabet heißt **Hiragana.** Es wurde vor vielen hundert Jahren vorwiegend von Frauen benutzt. Das eckiger aussehende Silbenalphabet **Katakana** entstand zur selben Zeit. Es wurde vorwiegend von Mönchen benutzt, um sich schnell Notizen machen zu können. Heute wird **Katakana** für die Schreibung von Fremdwörtern verwendet.

Diese beiden Silbenalphabete sind rein phonetische Schriften, d. h. man kann sie lesen wie unsere Schrift. Die offizielle Zahl der Silben beträgt je 46. Sie werden von oben nach unten und von rechts nach links geschrieben. Mithilfe dieser Silbenalphabete kann man japanische Wörter und auch ganze Texte wiedergeben.
Für diese beiden Silbenalphabete existieren zwei von der Regierung gebilligte Umschriftsysteme in unsere lateinischen Buchstaben, genannt **Romaji.** Das für uns geeignetere, weil unserer Aussprache näher kommende Umschriftsystem ist das **Hepburn-System,** so genannt nach einem Missionar und Sprachforscher, der Ende des 19. Jahrhunderts ein japanisch-englisches Wörterbuch erstellte.
Man könnte also fragen: Warum schreiben die Japaner nicht einfach ihre Sprache mit unserer lateinischen Schrift?
Und wieder begegnen wir einerseits dem Reichtum und auch der Schwierigkeit, die durch das Chinesische ins Japanische kommt.
Die chinesische Sprache verfügt über ein anderes Lautinventar als das Japanische. Z. B. existiert für 6 verschieden ausgesprochene chinesische Wörter aufgrund der mangelnden lautlichen Möglichkeiten des Japanischen nur ein japanisches Wort. Die Folge davon ist, daß es unglaublich viele gleichlautende Wörter gibt, die jedoch sehr Unterschiedliches bedeuten. Nur durch die chinesischen Schriftzeichen läßt sich eindeutig ausdrücken und klären, was gemeint ist. Man kann häufig Japaner im Gespräch miteinander sehen, die Kanjis in die Luft oder auf die Handfläche malen. Dies tun sie, um sich präzise verständlich zu machen.

Das Japanische ohne die chinesischen Schriftzeichen wäre wohl sehr unpräzise. Die Schönheit dieser Schriftzeichen und die Geschicklichkeit, mit der Japaner diese komplizierten Zeichen aufschreiben, gehören mit zur japanischen Kultur.
Die relativ schnell erlernbaren Silbenalphabete ermöglichen es einem, sich in Japan verständigen zu können. Die Kanjis zu erlernen ist dagegen fast ein Lebenswerk.

Japanische Silbenschriften und lateinische Umschriften

Konsonant	Vokal	Hiragana	Katakana	Hepburn	Lautschrift
-	A	あ	ア	a	a
	I	い	イ	i	i
	U	う	ウ	u	u
	E	え	エ	e	e
	O	お	オ	o	o
K	A	か	カ	ka	ka
	I	き	キ	ki	ki
	U	く	ク	ku	ku
	E	け	ケ	ke	ke
	O	こ	コ	ko	ko
S	A	さ	サ	sa	sa
	I	し	シ	shi	schi
	U	す	ス	su	su
	E	せ	セ	se	se
	O	そ	ソ	so	so
T	A	た	タ	ta	ta
	I	ち	チ	chi	tchi
	U	つ	ツ	tu	tu
	E	て	テ	te	te
	O	と	ト	to	to
N	A	な	ナ	na	na
	I	に	ニ	ni	ni
	U	ぬ	ヌ	nu	nu
	E	ね	ネ	ne	ne
	O	の	ノ	no	no

Konsonant	Vokal	Hiragana	Katakana	Hepburn	Lautschrift
H	A	は	ハ	ha	ha
	I	ひ	ヒ	hi	hi
	U	ふ	フ	fu	hu
	E	へ	ヘ	he	he
	O	ほ	ホ	ho	ho
M	A	ま	マ	ma	ma
	I	み	ミ	mi	mi
	U	む	ム	mu	mu
	E	め	メ	me	me
	O	も	モ	mo	mo
Y	A	や	ヤ	ya	ja
	U	ゆ	ユ	yu	ju
	O	よ	ヨ	yo	jo
R	A	ら	ラ	ra	la
	I	り	リ	ri	li
	U	る	ル	ru	lu
	E	れ	レ	re	le
	O	ろ	ロ	ro	lo
W	A	わ	ワ	wa	wa
	O	を	ヲ	wo	wo
N	-	ん	ン	n	n

- Die Reihen für die Konsonanten K, S, T, H kann man durch Anführungsstriche rechts oben erweichen und erhält die Reihen für G, Z, D, B.
- Die Reihe „HA ..." kann man durch einen kleinen Kreis rechts oben zu der Reihe „PA ..." erhärten.

Konsonanten gefolgt von einem „y"

Konsonant Vokal		Hiragana	Katakana	Hepburn	Lautschrift	Konsonant Vokal		Hiragana	Katakana	Hepburn	Lautschrift
K	YA	きゃ	キャ	kya	kja	R	YA	りゃ	リャ	rya	lja
	YU	きゅ	キュ	kyu	kju		YU	りゅ	リュ	ryu	lju
	YO	きょ	キョ	kyo	kjo		YO	りょ	リョ	ryo	ljo
S	YA	しゃ	シャ	sha	scha	G	YA	ぎゃ	ギャ	gya	gja
	YU	しゅ	シュ	shu	schu		YU	ぎゅ	ギュ	gyu	gju
	YO	しょ	ショ	sho	scho		YO	ぎょ	ギョ	gyo	gjo
T	YA	ちゃ	チャ	cha	tcha	J	YA	じゃ	ジャ	ja	dja
	YU	ちゅ	チュ	chu	tchu		YU	じゅ	ジュ	ju	dju
	YO	ちょ	チョ	cho	tcho		YO	じょ	ジョ	jo	djo
N	YA	にゃ	ニャ	nya	nja	B	YA	びゃ	ビャ	bya	bja
	YU	にゅ	ニュ	nyu	nju		YU	びゅ	ビュ	byu	bju
	YO	にょ	ニョ	nyo	njo		YO	びょ	ビョ	byo	bjo
H	YA	ひゃ	ヒャ	hya	hja	P	YA	びゃ	ビャ	pya	pja
	YU	ひゅ	ヒュ	hyu	hju		YU	びゅ	ビュ	pyu	pju
	YO	ひょ	ヒョ	hyo	hjo		YO	びゅ	ビュ	pyo	pjo
M	YA	みゃ	ミャ	mya	mja						
	YU	みゅ	ミャ	myu	mju						
	YO	みょ	ミョ	myo	mjo						

Aussprache

In den Kapiteln 1-11 wird eine dem Deutschen angepasste Lautschrift verwendet.

Besonderheiten:

- „·" steht für einen Stimmabsatz wie in *dt.* Bade·insel.

Vokale:
- Ein Strich über einem Vokal bedeutet, daß der Vokal lang ausgesprochen wird, z. B. „ō" wie in *dt.* Lob.
  Ansonsten sind die Vokale kurz, z. B. „u" wie in *dt.* Runde.
- „u" hört man nur, wenn betont langsam gesprochen wird. In der normalen Aussprache verschwindet es fast völlig.
- „i" ist wie „u" ein schwacher Vokal, den man oft kaum hört; z. B. klingt deschita und -maschita wie „deschta" bzw. „-maschta", wenn nicht betont langsam gesprochen wird.
- Die anderen Vokale (vor allem „a" und „e") werden immer deutlich ausgesprochen.
- Diphtonge (Doppelselbstlaute) werden in der Regel getrennt gesprochen. Der erste Vokal wird betont. Auch „ei" wird wie ein langes **e** und angehängtes, unbetontes **i** gesprochen!

Konsonanten:
- Doppelkonsonanten werden als zwei Laute gesprochen, wie **tt** in *dt.* Rottanne. Eine flüchtige Aussprache kann zu Bedeutungsverwechslungen führen: z. B. ite = bleib, itte = geh.
- Im Japanischen gibt es keine Laute, die den deutschen Buchstaben „r" und „l" entsprechen. Wo in der Lautschrift „r" oder „l" steht, ist ein Laut gemeint, der etwa wie das *dt.* **l** gebildet wird. Dabei streicht aber der Luftstrom nicht seitlich an der Zunge vorbei, sondern wie bei einem weich gesprochenen **d** zwischen Zungenspitze und vorderem Gaumen hindurch. Bei Lehnwörtern aus europäischen Sprachen wurde das „r" beibehalten, während in japanischen Wörtern stets das phonetisch ähnlichere „l" steht.
- „f" wird mit gerundeten Lippen gehaucht und klingt wie ein **h**. Die japanischen Silbenschriften machen keinen Unterschied zwischen „h" und „f"; nur bei Fremdwörtern wurde das „f" in der Lautschrift beibehalten: Graphik – gurafikku.
- „g" wird in der Wortmitte wie **ng** in A**ng**el ausgesprochen.

- „sch" wird stimmlos, mit leicht gespreizten Lippen ausgesprochen. Der Laut kann erzeugt werden, indem man versucht, **sch** und (i)**ch** zugleich zu sprechen, ähnlich wie in manchen *dt*. Dialekten, in denen beide Laute zusammenfallen.
- „dj" ist ein Laut, der zwischen einem stimmhaften **dsch** und **dj** ausgesprochen wird.
- „w" wird wie im Englischen mit zum „u" gerundeten Lippen gesprochen.
- „z" steht für ein stimmhaftes **s** wie in *dt*. Mu**s**ik.

Die Hepburn-Umschrift

In der Kurzgrammatik, im Wörterbuch und in den Länderinformationen ist die international gebräuchliche Hepburn-Umschrift verwendet worden, um den Vergleich mit anderen Schriften zu erleichtern.

- Die Hepburn-Umschrift ist eng an die englische Aussprache angelehnt.
- Die Hepburn-Umschrift ist eine direkte Trankription der japanischen Silbenschriften (Hiragana und Katakana), und unterscheidet daher z. B. nicht zwischen „l" und „r"; z. B. Rollschuhe (*engl.* roller-skates): „rōrā-sukēto".
- Die japanischen Silbenzeichen für „hu" werden mit „fu" transkribiert; ansonsten gibt es in der Hepburn-Umschrift kein „f".
- Einige Buchstaben werden gleich oder ähnlich wie im Englischen ausgesprochen:
    - j   wie „dsch" in **Dsch**ungel.
    - y   wie „j"
    - sh   wie „sch" (s. o.)
    - ch   wie „tsch"

Betonung

Die Betonung spielt keine so große Rolle wie im Deutschen. Nur die längeren Silben werden etwas stärker betont, wie auch die Fall-Partikel **wa, ga, ni, o** (Ausnahme: die Genitiv-Partikel **no**) und andere Partikel (**wo, made ...**). Die Betonung drückt sich dabei eher durch eine höhere Tonlage als durch lauteres Sprechen aus.
Auch wird im Fragesatz die Fragepartikel **ka** am Satzende durch ein Ansteigen der Tonhöhe betont.

Abkürzungen im Reisewörterbuch

adv.	Adverb, Umstandswort
adj.	Adjektiv, Eigenschaftswort
buddh.	buddhistisch
dt.	deutsch
etw.	etwas
el.	Elektrotechnik, Elektrizität
ev.	evangelisch
f	Femininum, weiblich
jdm	jemandem
jdn	jemanden
kath.	katholisch
m	Maskulinum, männlich
med.	Medizin
n	Neutrum, sächlich
präp	Präposition
s.	sich
subst	Substantiv, Hauptwort
u.	und

1 **Auf einen Blick**
初対面

Oft gesagt und oft gehört

Joku hanasu kotoba, joku kiku kotoba

Ja.	Hai.
Nein.	ĩe.

ĩe (nein) wird von Japanern als sehr abrupt empfunden und selten gebraucht. **Chotto muzukashii desu** „Es ist ungünstig" sagt man, wenn man etwas ablehnen möchte.

Bitte.	Dōzo.
Danke.	Aligatō.
Keine Ursache!	Dō itaschimaschite!
Wie bitte?	Nan des^u ka? / E, nan to osschaima-schita ka?
Selbstverständlich!	Motchilon!
Einverstanden!	Wakalimaschita!
In Ordnung!	Wakalimaschita!
Verzeihung!	Sumimasen!
Einen Augenblick, bitte.	Tchotto matte kudasai.
Genug!	Djūbun des^u!
Hilfe!	Tas^{u}kete!
Achtung!	Kiotsukete!
Vorsicht!	Kiotsukete!
Wer?	Dale?
Was?	Nani?
Welcher/Welche/Welches?	Dole?
Wo?	Doko?
Wo ist, sind …?	Doko ni … ga imas^u ka? *(Lebewesen)* Doko ni … ga alimas^u ka? *(Dinge)*
Woher?	Doko kala?
Wohin?	Doko e?
Warum?	Naze?

Weshalb?	Dōschite?
Wofür? Wozu?	Nan no tameni?
Wie?	Dono-jōni?
Wieviel?	Dono kulai?
Wie viele?	Ikutsu?
Wie lange?	Dono kulai nagaku?
Wann?	Itsu?
Gibt es …?	… ga alimas^u ka?

Zahlen/Maße/Gewichte

Sūdji/Ljō/Omosa

0	zero, lē
1	itchi
2	ni
3	san
4	schi, jon
5	go
6	loku
7	schitchi, nana
8	hatchi
9	kjū
10	djū
11	djū-itchi
12	djū-ni
13	djū-san
14	djū-schi, djū-jon
15	djū-go
16	djū-loku
17	djū-schitchi, djū-nana

18	djū-hatchi
19	djū-kjū
20	ni-djū
21	nidjū-itchi
22	nidjū-ni
23	nidjū-san
24	nidjū-schi, nidjū-jon
25	nidjū-go
26	nidjū-loku
27	nidjū-schitchi, nidjū-nana
28	nidjū-hatchi
29	nidjū-kjū
30	san-djū
31	sandjū-itchi
32	sandjū-ni
40	jon-djū
50	go-djū
60	loku-djū
70	nana-djū
80	hatchi-djū
90	kjū-djū
100	hjaku
101	hjaku-itchi
200	ni-hjaku
300	san-bjaku
1000	sen
2000	ni-sen
3000	san-zen
10000	itchi-man
100000	djū-man

1 000 000	hjaku-man
1/2	nibun no itchi
1/3	sanbun no itchi
1/4	jonbun no itchi
3/4	jonbun no san
3,5 %	san-ten-go pāsento
27 °C	nidjū nana do
−5 °C	mainasu go do
1994 *(Jahr)*	sen kjūhjaku kjūdjū jo nen
Millimeter	milimētoru
Zentimeter	sentchimētoru
Meter	mētoru
Kilometer	kilomētoru
Meile	mailu
Seemeile	kaili
Quadratmeter	hēhō-mētoru
Quadratkilometer	hēhō-kilomētoru
Hektar	hekutālu
Liter	littoru
Gramm	guramu
100 Gramm	hjaku guramu
Pfund	pondo
Kilogramm	kiloguramu
Dutzend	itchi dāsu

Zeitangaben

Djikoku-hjōdji

Uhrzeit	Djikan
Wieviel Uhr ist es?	Nandji des^u ka?
Es ist (genau/gegen) …	Tchōdo/golo … *(nur bei Zeitangaben)*
3 Uhr.	san-dji des^u.
5 nach 3.	san-dji go-hun sugi des^u.
4 Uhr 10.	jo-dji djupp^{u}n sugi des^u.
Viertel nach 4.	jo-dji djū-go-hun sugi des^u.
halb 5.	jo-dji han des^u.
Viertel vor 6.	loku-dji djūgo-hun mae des^u
5 vor 7.	schitchi-dji go-hun mae des^u.
12 Uhr (mittag).	djūni-dji des^u.
Mitternacht.	majonaka des^u.
Geht diese Uhr richtig?	Kono toke·i wa atte imas^u ka?
Diese Uhr geht vor/ nach.	Kono toke·i wa s^{u}s^{u}nde imas^u/okulete imas^u.
Es ist zu spät/zu früh.	Ososugimas^u/Hajasugimas^u.
Um wieviel Uhr?	Nandji ni?
Wann?	Itsu?
Um 3 Uhr.	San-dji ni.
Gegen 4 Uhr.	Jo-dji golo.
In einer Stunde.	Itchi-dji kan go ni.
In zwei Stunden.	Ni-dji kan go ni.
Nach 8 Uhr abends.	Jolu, hatchi-dji sugi ni.
Gegen 7 Uhr.	Schitchi-dji golo.
Zwischen 3 und 4 Uhr.	San-dji to jo-dji no aida ni.
Wie lange?	Dono kulai?
Drei Stunden (lang).	San-dji kan.
Von 10 bis 11 Uhr.	Djū-dji kala djū-itchi-dji made.
Bis 5 Uhr.	Go-dji made.

Seit wann?	Itsu kala?
Seit 10 Uhr morgens.	Asa no djū-dji kala.
Seit einer halben Stunde.	San-djupp^{u}n mae kala.
Seit acht Tagen.	Isschūkan mae kala.

Sonstige Zeitangaben — Sonohoka no djikoku-hjōdji

abends	jolu
alle halbe Stunde	han-dji-kan goto ni
alle zwei Tage	itchi-nitchi oki ni
am Wochenende	schūmatsu ni
bald	sugu ni, mamonaku
letzte/diese/nächste Woche	senschū/konschū/laischū
letzten/diesen/nächsten Monat	sengetsu/kongetsu/laigetsu
letztes/dieses/nächstes Jahr	kjonen/kotoschi/lainen
gegen Mittag	hilu golo
gestern	kinō
heute	kjō
heute morgen/abend	kesa/konban, kon·ja
in 14 Tagen	nischū-kan go ni
innerhalb einer Woche	isschū-kan inai ni
täglich	mainitchi
jetzt	ima
kürzlich	saikin
letzten Montag	senschū no getsujōbi
manchmal	tokidoki
mittags	hilu
morgen	aschita

morgen früh/abend	aschita no asa/aschita no jolu
morgens	asa
nachmittags	gogo
nachts	jolu
stündlich	itchidjikan-goto ni
täglich	mainitchi
tagsüber	hiluma no aida
übermorgen	assatte
vor zehn Minuten	djuppun mae ni
vorgestern	kinō ototoi
vormittags	gozentchū ni

Wochentage — Jōbi

Montag	getsu-jōbi
Dienstag	ka-jōbi
Mittwoch	sui-jōbi
Donnerstag	moku-jōbi
Freitag	kin-jōbi
Samstag	do-jōbi
Sonntag	nitchi-jōbi

Monate — Tsuki

Januar	itchi-gatsu
Februar	ni-gatsu
März	san-gatsu
April	schi-gatsu
Mai	go-gatsu
Juni	loku-gatsu
Juli	schitchi-gatsu

August	hatchi-gatsu
September	ku-gatsu
Oktober	djū-gatsu
November	djūitchi-gatsu
Dezember	djūni-gatsu

Jahreszeiten — **Schiki**

Frühling	halu
Sommer	natsu
Herbst	aki
Winter	huju

Feiertage (dt. Kalender) — **Doitsu no saidjitsu**

Neujahr	schin·nen
Ostern	hukkatsusai, īsᵘtā
Weihnachten	kurisᵘmasᵘ

Feiertage (jap. Kalender) — **Nihon no saidjitsu**

Neujahrstag, 1. Januar	Gantan, Gandjitsu
Tag der Volljährigkeit, 15. Januar	Se·idjin no hi
Gründungstag des Staates, 11. Februar	Kenkoku-kinen bi
Frühlingsanfang, 21. oder 20. März	Schunbun no hi
Tag des Grüns, 29. April	Midoli no hi
Tag der Verfassung, 3. Mai	Kenpō-kinen bi

*Beim „Knabenfest" am
5. Mai wird für jeden
männlichen Familien-
nachwuchs ein Karpfen-
banner gehißt – Karpfen
symbolisieren Stärke,
Ausdauer und Mut.*

Tag der Kinder, 5. Mai	Kodomo no hi
Tag der Ehrerbietung für die älteren Mitmenschen, 15. September	Lōdjin no hi
Herbstbeginn, 23. oder 24. September	Schūbun no hi
Tag des Sports und der Gesundheit, 10. Oktober	Tai·iku no hi
Tag der Kultur, 3. November	Bunka no hi
Arbeits-Danktag, 23. November	Kinlō-kanscha no hi
Geburtstag des Kaisers, 23. Dezember	Ten·nō-tandjō bi

Datum

Hizuke

Den Wievielten haben wir heute?	Kjō wa nan-nitchi des^u ka?
Heute ist der 1. September.	Kjō wa ku-gatsu tsuitatchi des^u.
Heute ist der 10. Oktober.	Kjō wa djū-gatsu tōka des^u.
Morgen ist der 2. Mai.	Aschita wa go-gatsu hutsuka des^u.

Wetter

Tenki

Das Klima in Japan entspricht in etwa dem in Südeuropa, außer, daß im Sommer eine hohe Luftfeuchtigkeit herrscht und es eine Regenzeit im Juni und Juli gibt.

In Japan fangen die meisten Gespräche über das Wetter an.

Wie wird das Wetter heute?	Kjō wa don·na tenki ni nali̅ mas^u ka ne?
Wir bekommen… schönes schlechtes unbeständiges Wetter.	o-tenki ga joku nalisō des^u. o-tenki ga waluku nalisō des^u. o-tenki ga kawalijasui des^u.
Es bleibt schön/schlecht.	i̅ o-tenki/warui o-tenki ga tsuzuki-mas^u.
Es wird wärmer/kälter.	Atsuku/Samuku nalisō des^u.
Es wird regnen/schneien.	Ame/Juki ga hulisō des^u.
Es ist schwül.	Muschiatsui des^u.
Wir bekommen ein Gewitter/einen Sturm.	Jūdatchi ga kisō des^u./Taifū ni nalisō des^u.
Es ist windig.	Kaze ga tsujoi des^u.
Die Sonne scheint.	Halete imas^u.
Es ist wolkenlos/bedeckt.	Kaisē/Kumoli des^u.

Wieviel Grad haben wir heute?	Kjō wa nan-do des^u ka?
Es ist 20 Grad Celsius.	Nidjū-do des^u.

Wieviel Grad haben wir heute?

Kjō wa nan-do des^u ka?

Es ist 20 Grad Celsius.

Nidjū-do des^u.

Die Kirschblütenzeit wird in Japan als Frühlingsbote gefeiert.

Wortliste Wetter

Barometer	baromētā
bewölkt	kumoli
Blitz	inazuma
Donner	kaminali
Ebbe	hikischio
Eis	kōli
Erdbeben	djischin

Das Inselreich Japan wird häufig von (überwiegend leichten) Erdbeben erschüttert. Strenge Baubestimmungen sorgen dafür, daß die Gebäude nahezu erdbebensicher sind und die meisten Beben nur geringfügig wahrgenommen werden.

feucht-warm	muschi atsui
Flut	mitchischio
Frost	schimo

Gewitter	laiu
Glatteis	tōketsu
Graupel	alale
Hagel	hjō
heiß	atsui
heiter	kaise·i
Hitze	atsusa, nekki
Hoch	kōkiatsu
kalt	samui
Klima	kikō
Luft	kūki
~druck	kiatsu
naß	schimetta
Nebel	kili
neblig	kili no kakatta
Niederschlag	ame ja juki
Regen	ame
~zeit	tsuju
Schnee	juki
schwül	muschiatsui
Sonne	taijō, hi, nikkō
Sonnen|aufgang	hinode
~untergang	hinoili
sonnig	haleta
Sturm	alaschi
Taifun	taihū
Temperatur	ondo
Tief	te·ikiatsu
trocken	kansō
warm	atatakai
Wetter|bericht	kischō-tsūhō
~vorhersage	tenkijohō
Wind	kaze
~stärke	hūsoku
Wolke	kumo

Wortliste Farben

beige	bēdju-ilo
blau	ao
dunkel~	kon-ilo
hell~	mizu-ilo
braun	tscha-ilo
kastanien~	kuli-ilo
farbig	ilo no tsuita
ein~	mudji no
mehr~	kalafulu na
gelb	ki-ilo
golden	kin-ilo
grau	nezumi-ilo
grün	midoli-ilo
lila	hudji-ilo
orange	orendji-ilo
rosa	pinku-ilo
rot	aka
schwarz	kulo
silbern	gin-ilo
violett	mulasaki-ilo
weiß	schilo

2 Kontakte
コンタクト

Begrüßung/Vorstellung/Bekanntschaft

Aisatsu/Schōkai/Kōljū

Westliches Händeschütteln ist in Japan nicht populär. Man verbeugt sich voreinander, wobei die Tiefe der Verbeugung die Tiefe des entgegengebrachten Respekts widerspiegelt.
Sich umarmen oder küssen in der Öffentlichkeit wäre völlig fehl am Platze. Derlei Dinge sind der Privatsphäre vorbehalten.

Guten Morgen!	Ohajō gozaimasu!
Guten Tag!	Kon·nitchiwa!
Guten Abend!	Kon banwa!
Wie ist Ihr Name, bitte?	Anata no o-namae o oschiete kudasai?
Mein Name ist …	Wataschi no namae wa … desu.
Es freut mich, Sie kennenzulernen.	Hadjimemaschite. Dōzo joloschiku.
Wie heißen Sie?	Anata no o-namae wa nanto osschai masu ka?

Ich heiße …	Wataschi wa … to mōschimasᵁ.
Ich möchte bekannt machen.	Goschōkai itaschimasᵁ.

Das ist …	Kotchila wa …
Herr …	…-san desᵁ.
Frau …	…-san desᵁ.
Mein Mann.	Schudjin desᵁ.
Meine Frau.	Kanai desᵁ.
Meine Tochter.	Musume desᵁ.
Mein Sohn.	Musuko desᵁ.
Mein Bruder.	Ani *(älter)* / Otōto *(jünger)* desᵁ.
Meine Schwester.	Ane *(älter)* / Imōto *(jünger)* desᵁ.
Mein Freund/Meine Freundin.	Wataschi no tomodatchi desᵁ.
Mein Kollege/Meine Kollegin.	Wataschi no dōljō desᵁ.

*Herr, Frau, Fräulein heißt im Japanischen **san**, das entweder nach dem Familiennamen oder auch dem Vornamen steht. Niemals wird ein Name **ohne nachfolgendes san** genannt, mit Ausnahme seines eigenen Namens. Frau Müller wäre also **Mura**-san, Herr Müller ebenfalls **Mura**-san. Spricht man eine Freundin mit Vornamen an, so sagt man z. B. **Hiroko**-san. Geschwister reden sich untereinander nicht mit Vornamen, sondern mit Titel an, z. B. „ältere Schwester", „jüngerer Bruder" usw. (s. a. Kurzgrammatik).*

Wie geht es Ihnen?	Gokigen ikaga desᵁ ka?
Danke. Und Ihnen?	Okagesamade. Anata wa?
Woher kommen Sie?	Doko kala iraschaimaschita ka?
Ich komme …	
aus Deutschland	Doitsu kala kimaschita.
aus Österreich.	Ōstoria kala kimaschita.
aus der Schweiz.	Suisᵁ kala kimaschita.
Sind Sie schon lange hier?	Kotchila wa nagai desᵁ ka?
Wie lange bleiben Sie?	Dono kulai taizai schimasᵁ ka?
Sind Sie zum ersten Mal hier?	Koko wa hadjimete desᵁ ka?
Gefällt Ihnen Japan?	Nihon wa kini·itte·imasᵁ ka?
Ja, sehr gut.	Hai, totemo.

Sind Sie allein hier oder mit einer Gruppe?	Anata wa o-hitoli desᵘ ka? Soletomo gurūpᵘ de kite·imasᵘ ka?
Alleine.	Hitoli desᵘ.
Mit einer Gruppe.	Gurūpᵘ to isschoni.
Mit der Familie.	Kazoku to isschoni.
Sind Sie mit Ihrer Familie hier?	Anata wa go-kazoku to go-isscho desᵘ ka?
Nein, alleine.	Ie, hitoli desᵘ.
In welchem Hotel wohnen Sie?	Doko no hotelu ni otomali desᵘ ka?

Alleine unterwegs/Verabredung

Hitolitabi/Jakusoku

Warten Sie auf jemanden?	Dale ka o matte imasᵘ ka?
Haben Sie für morgen etwas vor?	Aschita, nanika jotē ga alimasᵘ ka?
Wollen wir zusammen hingehen?	Isscho ni ikimasen ka?
Wollen wir heute abend miteinander ausgehen?	Isscho ni konban dokoka e ikimasen ka?
Darf ich Sie zum Essen einladen?	Schokudji ni go-schōtai schitai no desᵘ ga …?
Wann treffen wir uns?	Nan-dji ni oaischimaschō ka?
Soll ich Sie abholen?	Wataschi ga mukaeni ikimaschō ka?
Wann soll ich kommen?	Nan-dji ni kimaschō ka?
Morgen um 9 Uhr.	Asa ku-dji ni.
Treffen wir uns …	
in der Hotellobby?	Hotelu no lobī de oaischimaschō ka?
am Bahnhof vor dem Informationsbüro?	Eki no an·naischo no mae de oaischimaschō ka?
Holen Sie mich bitte im Hotel ab.	Hotelu e mukaeni kite kudasai.

Sind Sie verheiratet?	Kekkon schite ilasschaimasᵘ ka?
Darf ich Sie nach Hause begleiten/fahren?	Utchi made ōkuli itaschimaschō ka?
Ich bringe Sie bis zum/zur …	… made ōkuli itaschimasᵘ.
Möchten Sie auf einen Kaffee hereinkommen?	Otcha demo nonde ikimasen ka?
Wann sehen wir uns wieder?	Kondo wa itsu aemasᵘ ka?
Ich freue mich, Sie bald wiederzusehen.	Mata tchikai utchini oaidekileba, uleschī desᵘ.
Vielen Dank für den netten Abend.	Tanoschī jolu deschita. Dōmo aligatō gozaimaschita.
Lassen Sie mich bitte in Ruhe!	Hotte, oite kudasai!
Hau ab!	Ike!
Jetzt reicht's!	Mō djūbunda!

Besuch

Hōmon

Entschuldigen Sie, wohnt hier Herr/Frau/Fräulein …?	Sumimasenga …-san wa koko ni sunde imasᵘ ka?
Nein, er/sie ist umgezogen.	īe, sono kata wa hikkoschimaschita.
Wissen Sie, wo Herr/Frau … jetzt wohnt?	…-san wa ima doko ni sunde iluka gozondji desᵘ ka?
Verstehen Sie diese Adresse?	Kono djūscho ga wakalimasᵘ ka?
Kann ich mit Herrn/Frau/Fräulein … sprechen?	… san o onegai schimasᵘ?
Ja, einen Augenblick bitte.	Hai, tchotto omatchi kudasai.

Nein, Herr/Frau … ist nicht da.	…-san wa ima tchotto imasenga.
Wann ist Herr/Frau … zu Hause?	…-san wa itsu utchi ni ilassaimasu?
Geben Sie ihm/ihr bitte diese Nachricht.	Dōzo kono koto o kale ni/kanodjo ni tsutaete kudasai.
Ich komme später noch einmal vorbei.	Atode mō itchido kimasu.
● Kommen Sie herein.	Dōzo ohaili kudasai.
● Nehmen Sie bitte Platz.	Dōzo okake kudasai.

*Das **Familienbesuchsprogramm (Home Visit)** bietet die Möglichkeit, für einige Stunden ein privates Heim zu besuchen und sich mit Familienmitgliedern zu unterhalten.*
Japaner haben gerne Kontakt mit Ausländern. Auf diesem Weg können internationale Kontakte gepflegt werden, und Sie haben die Chance, für ein paar Stunden in eine original japanische Atmosphäre einzutauchen.
Sowohl die Vermittlung (TIC, s. S. 46) als auch die Einladung verstehen sich auf freiwilliger Basis.
Dieses Familienbesuchsprogramm wird in folgenden Städten organisiert: Sapporo, Tokyo, Narita, Yokohama, Nagoya, Kyoto, Osaka, Otsu, Kobe, Kuraschiki, Okayama, Hiroshima, Shirahama, Fukuoka, Nagasaki, Miyazaki und Kagoshima. Die jeweiligen Adressen können Sie entweder beim TIC in Tokyo erfahren oder in den Informationszentren vor Ort. Mindestens einen Tag vor dem Besuch sollten Sie Ihren Antrag stellen.

Wenn man in ein japanisches Privathaus eingeladen wird, eignet sich als Gastgeschenk ein Mitbringsel aus der Heimat – oder man bringt Obst, Blumen oder Süßigkeiten mit. Dies ist selbst unter guten Freunden üblich.

Beim Betreten eines japanischen Heims zieht man seine Schuhe aus. Meist stehen am Eingang Hauspantoffeln bereit.
Betritt man einen Tatamiraum, so geht man auf Strümpfen.

In Privathäusern wechselt man für die Toilette die Schuhe. Sie stehen vor der Toilettentüre bereit. Vergessen Sie nicht, diese Schuhe nachher wieder auszuziehen.

Ich soll Sie von Paul grüßen.	Paulu-san kala joloschiku to no koto desu.
● Darf ich Ihnen etwas zu trinken/essen anbieten?	Nanika onomimono/tabemono wa ikaga desu ka?
Ja, bitte.	Hai, itadakimasu.
Nein, danke.	Īe, kekkō desu.
Auf Ihr/dein Wohl!	Kanpai!
● Bleiben Sie doch noch ein bißchen.	Motto jukkuli schite itte kudasai.
Es tut mir leid, aber ich muß gehen.	Zannen desu ga, schitsulei schinakeleba nalimasen.
Vielen Dank für den netten Abend/Tag.	Konja/kjō wa dōmo aligatō gozaimaschita.
Vielen Dank für die Einladung.	Go-schōtai aligatō gozai maschita.

Abschied

Wakale

Auf Wiedersehen!	Sajōnala!

*Verabschiedet man sich von der Familie, von Freunden oder der Arbeitsgruppe, sagt man **itte kimasu** („ich gehe und komme wieder"). Kommt man zurück, sagt man **tadaima** (dem Sinn nach: „ich bin jetzt wieder da"). Der/die Zu-Hause-Gebliebene antwortet mit **itterasshai** („machs gut") bzw. mit **okaerinasai** („schön, daß du wieder da bist").*

Bis bald!	Djā mata!
Bis später!	Mata atode!
Bis morgen!	Mata aschita!
Gute Nacht!	Ojasuminasai!
Alles Gute!	Ogenkide!
Viel Vergnügen!	Tanoschinde kudasai!
Gute Reise!	Joi goljokō o!
Grüßen Sie Herrn/Frau … von mir.	…-san ni dōzo joloschiku.

Bitte und Dank

Onegai to olei

Möchten Sie noch etwas … haben?	… o mō sukoschi ikaga desu ka?
Ja, bitte.	Hai, itadakimasu.
Nein, danke.	ĭe, kekkō desu.
Ich habe eine Bitte.	Onegai ga alimasu.
Gestatten Sie?/Darf ich?	Joloschĭ deschō ka?
Ist das in Ordnung?	Kamaimasen ka?/ĭdesu ka?
Können Sie mir bitte helfen?	Otetsudai itadake masu ka?
Danke. *(Wenn es sich auf etwas Vergangenes bezieht)*	Aligatō gozaimaschita.
Danke!	Aligatō!
Das ist nett, danke.	Goschinsetsu ni aligatō gozaimasu.
Gerne geschehen./Keine Ursache.	Dō itaschimaschite.

Entschuldigung/Bedauern

Owabi

Hallo, Entschuldigung! *(Wenn man z. B. etwas fragen möchte)*	Tchotto sumimasen!
Entschuldigung! *(Bedauern, Verzeihung)*	Gomen·nasai!
Es tut mir sehr leid.	Dōmo sumimasen.
Es war nicht so gemeint.	Sōjū imide wa alimasen.
Schade!	Zan·nen!
Es ist leider nicht möglich.	Zan·nen·nagala, mulino jō desu.
Das ist ungünstig.	Tchotto tsugō ga walui no desu ga …
Vielleicht ein andermal.	Kono tsugi no kikai ni.

Glückwunsch

Ojuwai

Herzlichen Glück- wunsch … !	*(Geburt)* Go-schussan … *(Hochzeit)* Go-kekkon … *(Geburtstag)* O-tandjōbi … *(Neujahr)* Akemaschite … *(bestandene Prüfung)* Gōkaku … … omedetō gozaimas^u!
Viel Erfolg!	Go-sēkō o oinoliitaschimas^u!
Viel Glück!	O-schiawase ni!
Gute Besserung!	O-daijini!
Schönes Wochenende!	Joi schūmatsu o!
Ein glückliches Neues Jahr!	Schin·nen akemaschite omedetō go- zaimas^u!
Frohe Weihnachten!	Tanoshī kuris^{u}mas^u o!

Verständigungsschwierigkeiten

Kikikaeshi no kotoba

Wie bitte?	E? Nan to osshaimaschita ka?
Ich verstehe Sie nicht. Bitte, wiederholen Sie es.	Joku wakalimasen. Dōzo mō itchido itte kudasai.
Bitte sprechen Sie etwas langsamer/lauter.	Mō sukoschi jukkuli hanaschite ku- dasai.
Ich verstehe./Ich habe verstanden.	Wakalimas^u./Wakalimaschita.

Sprechen Sie …?
  Deutsch?
  Englisch?
  Französisch?
	Anata wa … o hanaschimas^u ka?
	  doitsu-go
	  e·i-go
	  hulansu-go

Ich spreche nur wenig …	… o sukoschi dake hanaschimas^u.
Kennen Sie jemanden, der vom Deutschen/Eng- lischen ins Japanische übersetzen kann?	Daleka doitsu-go/E·i-go kala nihon- go ni Hon·jaku dekilu kata o schitte imas^u ka?

Was heißt … auf japanisch?	Kole wa nihon-go de nanto īmasu ka?
Was bedeutet dieses Kanji *(chines. Schriftzeichen)*?	Kono kandji wa dōjū imi desu ka?
Was bedeutet das?	Kole wa don·na imi desu ka?
Wie spricht man dieses Wort aus?	Kole wa nan to jomimasu ka?
Schreiben Sie es mir bitte auf!	Dōzo kami ni kaite kudasai!
Schreiben Sie das bitte in lateinischer Schrift.	Rōmadji de kaite kudasai.
Könnten Sie mir diesen Satz bitte übersetzen?	Dōzo kono bun o jakuschite kudasai masenka?
Übersetzen Sie bitte!	Jakuschite kudasai!

Meinungsäußerung

Iken o nobelu

Das gefällt mir.	Kole ga kini itte·imasu.
Das gefällt mir nicht so ganz.	Amali kini ilimasen.
Ich möchte lieber …	… no hōga ī desu.
Am liebsten wäre mir …	Itchiban ī no wa …
Das wäre nett!	Sole dattala, uleschī desu.
Mit Vergnügen!	Tanoschinde kudasai!
Prima!	Subalaschii!
Ich habe keine Lust dazu.	Sole o sulu ki ni nalimasen.
Das kommt nicht in Frage!	Sole wa mondai gai desu!
Auf gar keinen Fall!	Keschite nai desu!
Ich weiß noch nicht.	Mada, wakalimasen.
Vielleicht.	Tabun, hjotto schitala.
Wahrscheinlich.	Osolaku.

Angaben zur Person

Hito ni tsuite

Alter	Nenlē

Wie alt sind Sie	Anata wa nan-sai desᵘ ka?
Ich bin 40 Jahre alt.	Watakuschi wa jondju-ssai desᵘ.
Wann haben Sie Geburtstag?	Anata no tandjōbi wa itsu desᵘ ka?
Ich bin am 12. April 1954 geboren.	Wataschi wa sen kjū-hjaku godjū jonen schi-gatsu, djū-ni nitchi ni umale maschita.

Beruf/Studium/Ausbildung	Schokugjō/Gakugjō/Kjōiku

Was sind Sie von Beruf?	Anata no go-schokugjō wa nan desᵘ ka?

In Japan ist es weniger üblich, seinen Beruf zu nennen, sondern sich vielmehr als Mitglied der Firma, für die man arbeitet, vorzustellen.

Ich bin Arbeiter/in.	Wataschi wa lōdō-scha desᵘ.
Ich bin Angestellte/r.	Wataschi wa kaischa-in desᵘ.
Ich bin Beamter/Beamtin.	Wataschi wa kōmu-in desᵘ.
Ich bin selbständig.	Wataschi wa djiēgjō desᵘ.
Ich bin Hausfrau.	Wataschi wa schuhu desᵘ.
Ich bin Rentner/in.	Wataschi wa nenkin-sēkatsu o schite imasᵘ.
Ich bin arbeitslos.	Wataschi wa schitsugjō-scha desᵘ.
Ich arbeite bei …	… ni tsutomete imasᵘ.
Ich gehe noch zur Schule.	Wataschi wa mada gakkō e itte imasᵘ.
Ich gehe ins Gymnasium.	Wataschi wa kōkō e itte imasᵘ.
Ich bin Schüler/in.	Wataschi wa sēto desᵘ.

Ich bin Student/in.	Wataschi wa gakusē des^u.
Wo/Was studieren Sie?	Doko de/nani o benkjō schite imas^u ka?
Ich studiere … in Heidelberg.	Heidelberg no daigaku ni itte imas^u.
Was für Hobbies haben Sie?	Anata no schumi wa nan des^u ka?

Wortliste Berufe/Studium/Ausbildung

Akademie	akademī, daigaku
Angestellte/r	kaischa-in
Anglistik	ēbun-gaku
Apotheker/in	jakuzai-schi
Arbeiter/in	lōdō-scha
Archäologie	kōko-gaku
Architekt/in	kentchiku-ka
Architektur	kentchiku
Arzt/Ärztin	ischa
Auszubildende/r	minalai
Automechaniker	djidōscha-kikai-kō
Bäcker/in	pan-ja
Bankkaufmann/frau	ginkō-in
Beamter/Beamtin	kōmu-in
Berufsschule	schokugjō-gakkō
Betriebswirtschaft	kēē-gaku
Bibliothekar/in	toschokan-in, schischo
Biologe/in	sēbutsu-gakuscha
Biologie	sēbuts-gaku
Briefträger/in	jūbin-haitatsu-nin
Buchhalter/in	kēli-schi
Buchhändler/in	hon-ja
Chemie	kagaku
Chemiker/in	kagaku-scha
Designer/in	dezainā
Dolmetscher/in	tsūjaku
Dozent/in	sensē
EDV-Fachmann/frau	konpjūtā-gischi
Eisenbahner	tetsudō-schoku in
Elektriker/in	denki-gidjutsu-scha
Erzieher/in	kjōiku-scha

Fischer/in	Ljō-schi
Florist/in	hana-ja
Förster/in	schinlin-kanli-nin
Fotograf/in	kamera-man, schaschin-ka
Friseur, Friseuse	bijō-schi
Gärtner/in	ueki-ja, niwa-schi
Gastwirt/in	sābisᵘ-gjō
Geographie	tchili-gaku
Geologie	tchischitsu-gaku
Germanistik	doitsu-bun-gaku
Geschäftsführer/in	tolischimali-jaku, schihai-nin
Geschichte	lekischi
Glaser	galasu-schokunin
Handelsschule	schogjō-gakkō
Handwerker/in	schokunin
Haus|frau	schuhu
~mann	schuhu
~meister/in	kanli-nin
Hebamme	djosanpᵘ, sanba-san
Hochschule	daigaku
Informatik	djōhō-gaku
Ingenieur/in	gischi, endjinia
Installateur/in	gasu-ja, suidō-ja, denki-ja
Institut	kenkjūdjo
Journalist/in	kischa, djānalisᵘto
Jurist	hōlitsu-ka
Juwelier	hōseki-schō

Kassierer/in	kaikē-gakali
Kaufmann/frau	sēlusuman
Kellner/in	uētā *(m)*, uētolesu *(f)*
Koch/Köchin	tchōli-schi
Konditor/in	kēki-ja
Kraftfahr|er	unten-schu
~zeugmechaniker/in	djidōscha-kō
Kranken|pfleger	kango-nin
~schwester	kango-hu
Künstler/in	gēdjutsu-ka
Kunst	gēdjutsu
~geschichte	bidjutsuschi
~handwerk	kōgēhin
Laborant/in	kenkjū-in
Landwirt/in	nōgjō
Lehrer/in	sensē, kjōschi
Lehrling	minalai, djissjūsē
Leiter/in	sekinin-scha
Makler/in	tchūkai-gjō
Maler/in	gaka
Mannequin	modelu
Maschinenbau	kikai-kōgaku
Masseur/in	massādji-schi
Mathematik	sūgaku
Matrose	hunanoli
Maurer	sekkō, sakan
Mechaniker/in	kikai-gischi
Medizin	igaku
Meteorologe/in	kischō-gakuscha
Metzger/in	niku-ja
Missionar	senkjō schi
Monteur	kumitate-in
Musik	ongaku
Musiker/in	ongaku-ka
Naturwissenschaft	schizen-kagaku
Notar/in	kōschō-nin
Optiker/in	megane-ja
Pfarrer/in	bokuschi
Philologie	bungaku-gogaku-kenkjū
Pförtner/in	schuē
Pharmazie	kusuli-ja
Philosophie	tetsugaku
Physik	butsuli
Physiker/in	butsuli-gakuscha

Pilot/in	pailotto
Politikwissenschaft	sēdji-gaku
Polizist/in	kēsatsu-kan
Postbeamter/beamtin	jūbinkjoku-in
Professor/in	daigaku-kjōdju
Psychologe/in	schinlī-gakuscha
Psychologie	schinli-gaku
Rechtsanwalt/anwältin	bengo-schi
Redakteur/in	henschū-scha
Reiseleiter/in	tendjō-in
Rentner/in	nenkin-sēkatsu-scha
Restaurator/in	resutolan-kē·ē·scha
Richter/in	handji, saiban-kan
Sachbearbeiter/in	djimu-in
Schauspieler/in	djojū
Schlosser/in	djōmae-ja
Schneider/in	jōsai-schi, schitate-ja
Schreiner/in	kagu-schoku nin
Schriftsteller/in	sakka
Schuhmacher/in	kutsu-ja
Schule	gakkō
Grundschule	schōgakkō
Realschule	tchūgakkō
Gymnasium	kōtōgakkō
Schüler/in	sēto
Sekretär/in	hischo
Sozialarbeiter/in	sōschalu-wākā
Soziologie	schakai-gaku
Steuerberater/in	zēli-schi
Steward/eß	sᵘtchuwādo/sutchuwādesᵘ
Student/in	gakusē
Studienfach	senmon
Studium	gakugjō
Taxifahrer/in	takuschī-untenschu
Techniker/in	kōin
Technische Hochschule	gidjutsu-daigaku
Technische(r) Zeich-ner/in	sēzu-kō, torēsᵘ
Theologie	schingaku
Therapeut/in	ljōhō-schi
Tierarzt/ärztin	djūi
Übersetzer/in	honjaku-scha
Uhrmacher/in	tokē-ja
Universität	daigaku

Verkäufer/in	ten-in
Vertreter/in	daili-nin
Vorlesung	kōgi
Werkzeugmacher/in	kōsaku-kikai-kō
Wirtschafts|prüfer/in	kōnin-kaikē-schi
~wissenschaftler/in	kēzai-gakuscha
Wissenschaftler/in	kagaku-scha
Zahnarzt/ärztin	ha-ischa
Zahntechniker/in	gikō-schi
Zimmermann	daiku

3 **Unterwegs**
出先で

*Stadtpläne und Landkarten, die sowohl japanisch als auch la-
teinisch beschriftet sind, erleichtern Ihnen die Orientierung er-
heblich.*

Um den Touristen das Zurechtfinden in der fremden, durch Lesen
und Sprechen kaum erschließbaren Umgebung zu erleichtern, bietet das **Tourist Information Center (TIC)** viele kostenlose Dienst-
leistungen an. (Reservierungen und Buchungen werden allerdings
nicht vorgenommen.)

Büro Tokyo
Kontani Bldg., 1-6-6, Yurakucho, Chiyoda-ku, Tokyo 100,
Tel.: (03) 33502-1461

Büro New Tokyo International Airport
Airport Terminal Bldg., Narita, Chiba Pref. 282, Tel.: (0476) 32-8711

Büro Kyoto
Kyoto Tower Bldg., Higashi-Shiokojicho, Shimogyo-ku, Kyoto 600,
Tel: (075) 371-5649

Japan Travel Phone: Über diesen landesweiten englischsprachi-
gen Telefondienst für Touristen können Sie täglich von 9.00 – 17.00
Uhr Informationen und Tips per Telefon erfragen.
Wählen Sie
im Stadtgebiet Tokyo 33502-1461 (TIC),
in Kyoto-Stadt 371-5649 (TIC).
(Ein Ortsgespräch kostet jeweils 10 Yen für 3 Minuten.)
Unter der Nummer 0120-222800 erhalten Sie Informationen über
Ostjapan, über Westjapan unter 0120-444800.
Diese Anrufe sind gebührenfrei. Nach dem Telefonat erhalten Sie
das Geld aus dem Automaten zurück.

Ortsangaben

Hōkō-hjodji

links	hidali
rechts	migi
geradeaus	mass^{ugu}
vor	mae
hinter	uschilo
neben	tonali
gegenüber	hantai-gawa
hier	koko
dort	asoko
nah	tchikai

weit	tōi
Straße	mitchi
Kreuzung	djūdjilo
Kurve	kābu, magalikado

Auto/Motorrad/Fahrrad

Kuluma/Baiku/Djitenschia

Auskunft   **Tōtchaku**

Entschuldigung, wie komme ich bitte nach …?	Sumimasen, … e wa dō ittala ī desᵘ ka?
Können Sie mir den Ort/ die Strecke bitte auf der Karte zeigen?	Tchizu no ue de kono bascho/kono mitchi o oschiete kudasaimasen ka?

In Japan herrscht wie in England Linksverkehr. Es gelten die internationalen Verkehrszeichen.
Es ist nicht leicht, Straßenkarten zu bekommen, auf denen die Orte in japanischen Schriftzeichen und in lateinischer Schrift angegeben sind. (Solche Karten gibt es beim Japanischen Automobilklub.) Autobahnen sind immer auch in lateinischer Schrift beschildert. Da dies auf Landstraßen nicht der Fall ist, empfiehlt es sich, die Schriftzeichen auf der Landkarte mit den vorhandenen Hinweisschildern zu vergleichen.

Wie weit ist das?	Kjoli wa dono kulai alimasᵘ ka?
Bitte, ist das die Straße in Richtung …?	… e iku mitchi wa kole desᵘ ka?
Wie komme ich zur Autobahn in Richtung …?	… e iku kōsoku-dōlo e wa dō ittala ī deschō ka?

Autobahnen sind in Japan gebührenpflichtig.
Die Geschwindigkeitsbegrenzungen liegen auf der Autobahn bei 80 km/h, auf der Landstraße 60 km/h, oft auch nur 40 km/h. Die Straßen sind in Japan sehr schmal. Auch beim Überlandfahren kann man kaum mehr als 40 km pro Stunde zurücklegen.
*Informationen: **JAF** (englisch: Japan Automobil Federation)*
3-5-8, Shiba Park, Minato-ku, Tokyo; Tel: (03)3436-2881

- Immer geradeaus bis …   … made zutto massᵘgu itte kudasai

- Dann …   Soschite …
  - bei der Ampel   mittsᵘme no schingō o
  - an der nächsten Ecke   tsugi no kado o

links/rechts abbiegen.   hidali/migi ni magatte kudasai.

- Sie sind hier falsch.   Koko wa matchigatte imasᵘ.
  Bitte zurückfahren bis …   … made modotte kudasai.

Folgen Sie den Schildern.   Hjōschiki dōli ni itte kudasai.

Können Sie diese japanischen Zeichen in lateinischen Buchstaben aufschreiben?   Kono nihon-go o rōmadji de kaite kudasai masen ka?

Können Sie diese lateinischen Buchstaben in japanischen Schriftzeichen wiedergeben?   Kono rōmadji o nihon-go de kaite kudasai masen ka?

注意	chuui	Achtung/Vorsicht
危険	kiken	Gefahr
高速道路	kousoku-douro	Autobahn
一方通行	ippou tsuukou	Einbahnstraße
迂回路	ukairo	Umleitung
工事中	koujichuu	Baustelle

An der Tankstelle   Gasolin-Sutando de

An Tankstellen wird man äußerst zuvorkommend bedient. Der Tankwart füllt Ihnen auf jeden Fall das richtige Benzin ein, Scheiben werden gewischt, Aschenbecher geleert, und mit Hilfe des Tankwarts, der sich zum Abschied höflich verbeugt, werden Sie wieder in den Verkehr eingeschleust.
Sonntags sind die Tankstellen meist geschlossen.

Wo ist bitte die nächste Tankstelle?   Koko kala itchiban tchikai gasolin-sᵘtándo wa doko desᵘ ka?

Ich möchte … Liter	… littoru ilete kudasai.
Normalbenzin.	gasolin
Super.	sūpā
Diesel.	dīselu
bleifrei mit … Oktan	muen … okutan

Super bitte, für 2000 Yen. Sūpā o nisen-en bun onegai schimas^u.

Volltanken, bitte. Mantan ni schite kudasai.

Bezahlen Sie bar oder mit Karte? Schihalai wa kuredjitto-kādo des^u ka, soletomo genkin des^u ka?

Prüfen Sie bitte … Sumimasenga …
  den Ölstand.   oilu no djōtai o schilabete kudasai.
  den Reifendruck.   taija no kūkiatsu o schilabete kuda-sai.
  das Kühlwasser.   lēkjakusui o schilabete kudasai.

Füllen Sie bitte Öl nach. Oilu o taschite kudasai.

Könnten Sie mir einen Ölwechsel machen? Oilu-kōkan o schite itadake mas^u ka?

Waschen Sie den Wagen, bitte. Senscha o onegaischimas^u.

Ich möchte eine Landkar-te dieser Gegend, bitte. Kono atali no tchizu ga hoschī no des^u ga.

Wo sind bitte die Toilet-ten? Toile wa doko des^u ka?

Parken   Tchūscha

In Japan ist es schwierig, Parkplätze zu finden. Wer falsch parkt, wird abgeschleppt, die Bußgelder sind sehr hoch. Also: Parkhäuser benutzen, auch wenn Warteschlangen die Regel sind.
Auf Stadtplänen sind Parkplätze, z.B. bei Tempeln, eingezeichnet. Hier haben Sie eine reelle Chance. Noch besser: öffentliche Ver-kehrsmittel benutzen.

Gibt es hier in der Nähe eine Parkmöglichkeit? Kono tchikaku ni tchūscha dekilu tokolo ga alimas^u ka?

Darf ich den Wagen hier abstellen? Koko ni kuluma o tometemo ī des^u ka?

| 駐車場 | chuushajou | Parkplatz |
| 駐車禁止 | chuushakinshi | Parkverbot |

Wir sind leider voll besetzt. — Zan·nen·nagala koko wa ippai des^u.

Wie lange kann ich hier parken? — Dono kulai koko ni tchūscha deki mas^u ka?

Wie hoch ist die Parkgebühr pro … — Tchūscha-ljō wa … o-ikula des^u ka?

Stunde? — itchi-djikan ni tsuki
Tag? — nittchū wa
Nacht? — jolu wa

Ist das Parkhaus die ganze Nacht geöffnet? — Tchūscha-djō wa hitobandjū aite imas^u ka?

Bis wann ist das Parkhaus geöffnet? — Tchūscha-djō wa nan-dji made aite imas^u ka?

Eine Panne — Koschō

Ich habe eine Panne. — Kuluma ga koschō schimaschita.

Könnten Sie bitte den Pannendienst anrufen? — Koschō-sābis^u ni denwa o schite kulemasenka?

Meine Auto-/Motorradnummer ist … — Wataschi no kuluma/baiku no bangō wa …

Würden Sie mir bitte einen Abschleppwagen schicken? — Rekkā-scha o okutte kudasai masenka?

Könnten Sie mir mit Benzin aushelfen? — Sumimasen ga, gasolin o sukoschi wakete itadake masen ka?

Könnten Sie mir beim Reifenwechsel helfen? — Taija-kōkan o tas^{u}kete kudasai masen ka?

Würden Sie mich bis zur nächsten Werkstatt/Tankstelle abschleppen? — Sumimasen ga, tchikaku no djidōscha schūli-kōdjō/gasolin-sutando made hippatte itte kudasai masen ka?

In der Werkstatt

Kōdjō de

Wo ist hier in der Nähe eine Werkstatt?	Itchiban tchikai djidōscha schüli-kōdjō wa doko des^u ka?
Mein Wagen ist kaputt.	Kuluma ga ugokanaku nalimaschita.
Ich weiß nicht, woran es liegt.	Doko ga kowalete·ilu no ka wakali-masen.
Können Sie mit mir kommen/mich abschleppen?	Wataschi to isschoni kite molaema-sen ka?/Hippatte mola e masen ka?
Mit … stimmt was nicht.	… ga okaschī no des^u ga.
Die Bremsen funktionieren nicht.	Burēki ga okaschī des^u.
… ist/sind defekt.	… ga kowalete imas^u.
Der Wagen verliert Öl.	Oilu ga molemas^u.
Können Sie mal nachsehen?	Itchido mite kudasai masen ka?
Wechseln Sie bitte die Zündkerzen aus.	P^{u}lagu o kōkan schite kudasai.
Haben Sie Ersatzteile für diesen Wagen?	Kono kuluma no buhin ga alimas^u ka?
Machen Sie bitte nur die nötigsten Reparaturen.	Kinkjū-schotchi dake schite kudasai.
Wann ist der Wagen/das Motorrad fertig?	Itsu kuluma/baiku ga dekiagalimas^u ka?
Was wird es kosten?	Schüli-hi wa dono kulai kakalimas^u ka?

Verkehrsunfall

Kōtsū-djiko

Es ist ein Unfall passiert.	Djiko ga okolimaschita.
Kann ich bei Ihnen telefonieren?	Otaku de denwa o kalitemo ī des^u ka?
Rufen Sie bitte schnell … einen Krankenwagen.	Dōzo sugu ni … kjūkjū-scha o jonde kudasai.

| die Polizei. | kēsatsu o jonde kudasai. |
| die Feuerwehr. | schōbō-scho ni lenlaku schite kudasai. |

| 警察 | keisatsu | Polizei |
| 案内所 | annaijo | Auskunft |

Können Sie sich um die Verletzten kümmern?	Sumimasen ga keganin no mendō o mite kudasai masen ka?
Haben Sie Verbandszeug?	Kjūkjū-bako o motte imas^u ka?
Es ist meine Schuld.	Wataschi no sekinin des^u.
Es ist Ihre Schuld!	Anata no sekinin des^u!
Sie haben …	
die Vorfahrt nicht beachtet.	Jūsen-tsūkō o tchūi schimasen deschita.
die Fahrspur gewechselt, ohne zu blinken.	Uinkā o agezu ni losen o kaemaschita.
Sie sind zu schnell gefahren.	Anata wa s^{u}pĬdo o daschis^{u}gite imaschita.
Sie sind zu dicht aufgefahren.	Anata wa kanali schakan-kjoli o tsumete haschitte imaschita.
Sie sind bei Rot über die Kreuzung.	Djūdjilo o aka no toki ni watalimaschita.
Ich bin … km/h gefahren.	Wataschi wa djisoku … kilo de haschlimaschita.
Sollen wir die Polizei holen, oder können wir uns so einigen?	Kēsatsu o jobimaschōka, soletomo djidan ni schimaschō ka?
Ich möchte mir zuerst einen Dolmetscher nehmen.	Mazu tsūjaku o jonde hoschĬ no des^u ga.
Ich muß mich erst mit meiner Firma in Verbindung setzen.	Mazu wataschi no kaischa ni lenlaku schinakeleba nalimasen.
Geben Sie mir bitte Ihre Anschrift.	Anata no djūscho o oschiete kudasai.

Ich gebe Ihnen meine Anschrift.	Kole ga wataschi no djūscho des^u.
Können Sie für mich Zeuge sein?	Wataschi no schōnin ni natte kulemas^u ka?
Vielen Dank für Ihre Hilfe.	Otetsudai kudasaimaschite aligatō gozaimaschita.

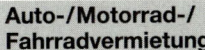

Auto-/Motorrad-/Fahrradvermietung

Kuluma/Baiku/Djitenscha rentalu

Staatsangehörige Deutschlands, Österreichs und der Schweiz können in Japan nicht mit dem internationalen Führerschein Auto fahren, wenn sie dort für längere Zeit leben. Man kann jedoch einen japanischen Führerschein erwerben, ohne noch einmal eine Fahrprüfung machen zu müssen. (Auskunft beim japanischen Automobilverband.)

Für kürzere Aufenthalte genügt eine internationale Fahrerlaubnis, ebenso für das Mieten oder Leihen eines Wagens.

Sie übernehmen das Auto mit gefülltem Tank und geben es so auch wieder ab. Die Preise sind Tages- oder Stundenpauschalen, unabhängig von der Kilometerzahl, die Sie zurücklegen (außer auf Hokkaido, wo Sie nach Zeit und zurückgelegten Kilometern bezahlen). Automieten ist teuer; Campmobile sind noch nicht zu haben.

Wo kann ich ein Auto mieten?	Kuluma wa doko de kalilalemas^u ka?
ein Motorrad	baiku
ein Fahrrad	djitenscha
Wie hoch ist die Tages-/Wochenpauschale?	Rentalu-ljōkin wa itchi-nitchi/isschūkan ni tsuki ikula des^u ka?
Wieviel verlangen Sie pro gefahrenen km?	Sōkō-kjoli itchi-kilo ni tsuki ikula des^u ka?
Was soll ich im Falle eines Unfalls tun?	Djiko no toki wa dō schitala ī des^u ka?
Ich nehme den .../das ...	Wataschi wa ... ni schimas^u.
Ist das Fahrzeug versichert?	Kono kuluma wa hoken ga kakete aimas^u ka?
● Möchten Sie eine Zusatzversicherung?	Hosoku-hoken o kaketai des^u ka?

Darf ich Ihren Führerschein sehen?

Anata no menkjoschō o misete kudasai masen ka?

Kann ich den Wagen gleich mitnehmen?

Suguni kuluma ga kalilale masᵘ ka?

Ist es möglich, das Fahrzeug in … abzugeben?

… de nolisᵘte wa dekimasᵘ ka?

Der aktive Vulkan Sakurajima bringt bei Ostwind Asche nach Kagoshima. Auf dieser fruchtbaren Asche wird intensiver Gemüseanbau betrieben.

Wortliste Auto/Motorrad/Fahrrad

abbiegen	magalu
abblenden	heddo-laito o genkou sulu
Abblendlicht	hikali o jowaku sulu
Abschleppdienst	Rekkā scha-sābisu
abschleppen	ken·in sulu
Achse	schadjiku
Hinter~	kōlin
Vorder~	zenlin
Alarmanlage	alāmu-sōtchi
Allradantrieb	jonlin-kudō
Ampel	schingōki

Anlasser	sutātā
anspringen	schidō sulu
Auspuff	haikikō
Autobahn	kōsoku-dōlo
~gebühren	kōsoku-ljōkin

Kobe, Stadtautobahn in mehreren Etagen

Automatik(getriebe)	ōtomatchikku
Autoreifen	taija
Baustelle	kōdji-genba
Benzin	gasolin
~kanister	gasolinkan
~pumpe	gasolin jō ponp[u]
blenden	telas[u]
Blinker	bulinkā
Bremsbelag	burēki-raining[u]
Bremse	burēki
bremsen	burēki o kakelu
Brems|flüssigkeit	burēki-oilu
~hebel	burēki-lebā
~licht	burēki-lanp[u]
Bußgeld	ihan-ljokin
Defekt	koschō
Dichtung	mippū
Düse	nozulu
Einspritzpumpe	hunscha-ponpu

Ersatz|rad	jobi-taija
~teile	jobi-buhin, supea
Fahrrad	djitenscha
~kette	tchēn
Fahrradweg	djitenscha-dō
Fahrspur	schasen
Federung	bane
Fehlzündung	huhats^u
Felge	rimu
Fernlicht	hai-bĭmu
Flickzeug	tchūbu
Frostschutzmittel	hutōeki
Führerschein	unten-menkjoschō
Fußbremse	aschi-burēki
Gang	gia
erster ~	fās^{u}to
Leerlauf	kala-unten
Rückwärts~	kōschin
Gangschaltung	gia
Gas geben	akuselu o humu
Gaspedal	akuselu
Gebläse	sōhūki
gebrochen	kowaleta, waleta
Gepäckträger	pōtā
Getriebe	unten-sōtchi
Handbremse	hando-brēki
Hebel	lebā, handolu, teko
Heizung	danbō
Hinterrad	kōlin
Hupe	kēteki, kulakschon
Kabel	kēbulu
Karosserie	schatai
Keilriemen	v-beluto (bui-beluto)
Kette	tschēn
Klingel	belu
klopfen *(Motor)*	nokking^u
Kofferraum	toranku
Kolben	pis^{u}ton
Kotflügel	fendā
Kugellager	bōlu-bearing^u
Kühler	radjiētā
Kühlwasser	lēkjakusui
Kupplung	kulattchi

Kurzschluß	schōto
Landstraße	kokudō, kendō
Lastwagen	torakku
Lenker *(Zweirad)*	handolu
Lenkrad	handolu
Lichtmaschine	tenkajō-hatsᵘdenki
Luft|filter	eā-filutā
~pumpe	kūki-ponpᵘ
Motor	mōtā, endjin
~haube	bon·netto
~rad	baiku
Nabe	habu
Notrufsäule	kinkjū-lenlaku-sōtchi
Nummernschild	nanbā-pᵘlēto
Oktanzahl	okutan-ka
Öl	oilu. abula
~meßstab	oilu-kē
~wechsel	oilu-kōkan
Panne	panku
Pannendienst	koschō-sābis
Papiere	scholui
Park|haus	pākingᵘ
~platz	tschūscha-djo
Pedal	pedalu
Plattfuß	panku schita taija
Promille	pāmiru

Die Promillegrenze liegt in Japan bei 0,0.

PS	baliki
Rad	schalin
Radarkontrolle	rēdā-kontorōlu
Raststätte	kjūkē-djo
Reifen	taija
Reserverad	jobi-taija
Rück|licht	bakku-laito
~spiegel	back-mirā
Sattel	sadolu
Schalthebel	hensoku-lebā
Scheibenwischer	waipā
Scheinwerfer	heddo-laito
Schiebedach	san-rūhu
Schlauch *(Reifen)*	tchūbu

Schnellstraße	kōsoku-dōlo
Schraube	nedji
Schrauben|mutter	natto
~schlüssel	spana
~zieher	nedjimawaschi
Sicherheitsgurt	anzen-bel^{u}to
Sicherung	hjūzu
Speiche	s^{u}pōku
Ständer	s^{u}tando
Standlicht	tchūscha-tō
Stau	djūtai
Stoßstange	banpā
Straßen|benutzungs- gebühr	tsūkō-ljōkin
~karte	dōlō-tchizu
Sturzhelm	helumetto
Tachometer	sokudokē, takomētā
Tankstelle	gasolin-s^{u}tando
trampen	hittchi haiku
Tramper	hittchi haikā
überholen	oikos^u
Umleitung	ukailo
Ventil	balubu
Vergaser	kjaburetā
Verteiler	haidenki
Vorder|licht	fogg^u lanp^u
~rad	zenlin
~radantrieb	zenlin-kudō
Wagen|heber	djakki
~wäsche	senscha
Warn|blinker	kēkoku-tō
~dreieck	tēschi-hjōdjiki
Wegweiser	mitschi-schilube
Werk|statt	schūli-kodjō
~zeug	kōgu
Windschutzscheibe	kazejoke
Winterreifen	huju jō taija
Zündkerze	s^{u}pāku-p^{u}lagu
Zündung	tenka
Zylinder	schilindā

Flugzeug

Hikōki

JAL Japan Airlines

> *Auf japanischen Flughäfen ist alles auch in Englisch ausge-schildert. Ansagen erfolgen sowohl auf japanisch als auch auf englisch.*
> *Bei der Paßkontrolle reihen Sie sich in die Schlange der „Aliens" ein, bei der Gepäckkontrolle gehören Sie zu den „Non Resedents".*

Im Reisebüro/Am Flughafen

Ljokō-gaischa de/Kūkō de

Wo ist der Schalter der …-Fluggesellschaft?	… no hikōki-gaischa no kauntā wa doko desu ka?
Wann fliegt die nächste Maschine nach …?	Tsugi no … iki no hikōki wa nan-dji ni tobimasu ka?

| 出発 | shuppatsu | Abfahrt/Abflug |
| 到着 | touchaku | Ankunft |

Ich möchte einen einfachen Flug/Hin- und Rückflug nach … buchen.	… e no katamitchi/ōhuku-tchiketto o jojaku schitai no desu ga.
Sind noch Plätze frei?	Mada seki ga alimasu ka?
Gibt es auch Charterflüge?	Tchātā-bin mo alimasu ka?
Was kostet der Flug Touristenklasse/1. Klasse?	Ekonomī/Fāsuto-kulasu wa ikula desu ka?
Wieviel Gepäck ist frei?	Nimotsu wa nan-ko made ī desu ka?
Was kostet das Kilo Übergepäck?	Tchōka-tenimotsu wa itchi-kilo ni tsuki ikula desu ka?

Ich möchte diesen Flug stornieren/umbuchen.	Kono hikōki no jojaku o tolikeschitai no desu ga.../jojaku o henkō schitai no desu ga.
Wann muß ich am Flughafen sein?	Nan-dji made ni kūkō ni ittala ī desu ka?
Wo ist der Informationsschalter?	An·nai-scho wa doko desu ka?
Kann ich das als Handgepäck mitnehmen?	Kole wa tenimotsu ni dekimasu ka?
Hat die Maschine nach ... Verspätung?	... iki no hikōki wa okulete imasu ka?
Wieviel Verspätung hat sie?	Dono kulai okulete imasu ka?
Ist die Maschine aus ... schon gelandet?	... kala no hikōki wa mō tōtchaku schimaschita ka?
• Letzter Aufruf. Die Passagiere nach ..., Flug-Nr. ..., werden gebeten, sich zum Ausgang ... zu begeben.	... iki ... bin no o-kjaku-sama ni saigo no go-tōdjō no go-an·nai o mōschi agemasu.

出口	deguchi	Ausgang

An Bord   Kinai de

• Bitte das Rauchen einstellen! Anschnallen, bitte!	O-tabako wa goenljo negai masu. Schīto-beluto o oschime kudasai.

シートベルトを締めて下さい	
shīto bēruto wo shimete kudasai	bitte anschnallen

Was ist das für ein Fluß/ See/Gebirge?	Kono kawa/mizu umi/sanmjaku wa nan to īmasu ka?
Wo sind wir jetzt?	Ima dono atali o tonde imasu ka?

Der winterliche Vulkan Yolei-zan auf Hokkaido, über den Toya-ko hinweg betrachtet

Wann landen wir in ...?	... ni wa nan-dji ni tōtchaku schimasu ka?
● Wir landen in etwa ... Minuten.	Jaku ... pun go ni tchakuliku itaschimasu.
Wie ist das Wetter in ...?	... no tenki wa dō desu ka?

Ankunft — Tōtchaku

▶ auch Kap. 9 – Fundbüro

Ich finde mein Gepäck/ meinen Koffer nicht.	Wataschi no nimotsu ga mitsukalanai no desu ga.
Mein Gepäck ist verlorengegangen.	Wataschi no nimotsu ga nakunalimaschita.
Mein Koffer ist beschädigt worden.	Wataschi no kaban ga hason schimaschita.
An wen kann ich mich wenden?	Dale ni/Doko de tazunetala ī deschō ka?
Von wo fährt der Bus zum Air Terminal ab?	Eā-tāminalu e iku basu wa doko kala demasu ka

Wortliste Flugzeug ▶ auch Wortliste Eisenbahn

Abflug	liliku
Air Terminal	eā-tāminalu
Anflug	tchakuliku
Anhänger *(am Koffer)*	nahuda
Ankunft	tōtchaku
Ankunftszeit	tōtchaku-djikan
Anschluß	setsuzoku
anschnallen, sich	schimelu
Anschnallgurt	schĭto-beluto
Auslandsflug	kokusai-sen
Besatzung	djōmu-in
an Bord	kinai de
Bordkarte	tōdjō-ken
buchen	jojaku sulu
Buchung	jojaku
Business class	bisines^u-kulas^u
Charterflug	tchātā-bin
Direktflug	tchokkō-bin
Düsenmaschine	djettoki
Economy class	ekonomĭ-kulas^u
einchecken	tchekku in
Fenstersitz	mado-gawa no seki
Flug	hikō
~gast	djōkjaku
~gesellschaft	kōkū-gaischa
~hafen	kūkō
~hafenbus	kūkō-bas^u
~hafengebühr	kūkō-schijōrjō
~plan	(hikōki no) djikokuhjō
~schein	kōkū-ken
~strecke	kūlo
~zeug	hikōki
Gang *(im Flugzeug)*	tsūlo-gawa
Gepäck	nimots^u
~ausgabe	tenimotsu-hikitolidjo
Handgepäck	tenimots^u
Hubschrauber	helikop^{u}tā
Inlandsflug	kokunai-sen
Kapitän	kjap^{u}ten, sōdjū-schi
Kofferkuli	te nimotsu jō wagon
landen	tchakuliku sulu

Landung	tchakuliku
Linienflug	tēki-bin
Nichtraucher	hi-kitsuen-scha
Not|ausgang	hidjō-gutchi
~landung	hudji-tchakuliku, kinkjū-tchakuliku
Passagier	djōkjaku
Pilot/in	pailotto
planmäßiger Abflug	djikokudōli no liliku
Raucher	kitsuen-scha
Reiseziel	ikisaki, mokutekitchi
Rollfeld	kassōlo
Schalter	kauntā
Schwimmweste	kjūmē-dōgi
Sicherheitskontrolle	sekjuriti-tchekku
Steward/eß	sᵘtchuwādo, sᵘtchuwādesᵘ
stornieren	tolikesu
umbuchen	henkō
Verspätung	okule
zollfreier Laden	menzē-ten
Zwischenlandung	totschū-tchakuliku

Eisenbahn

Tetsudō

Im Reisebüro/ **Auf dem Bahnhof**	**Ljōkō-gaischa de/Eki de**
Eine einfache Fahrt 2. Klasse/1. Klasse nach …, bitte.	… iki no katamitchi-kippᵘ o nitō-seki/ittō-seki de onegai schimasᵘ.

Die Preistabellen auf den Fahrkartenautomaten sind nur auf japanisch. Am besten, man fragt nach dem Preis.
Expreßzüge, die nur an wenigen Stationen halten, haben meist eine rote Plakette, Personenzüge nicht.
*Für Touristen gibt es den **Japan Railpass**, der unserem Interrail-Paß vergleichbar ist. Diesen Paß kann man **nicht in Japan** kaufen, man muß sich ihn schon aus Deutschland mitbringen (erhältlich über ein Japan-Airline-Büro oder eine Reiseagentur). Mit diesem Paß kann man sämtliche Strecken des JR-Netzes benutzen, auch den Shinkansen, den japanischen Hochgeschwindigkeitszug. Solch ein Tikket lohnt sich, auch wenn man die Bahn nicht ständig benutzt.*

中央口	chuou-guchi	Haupteingang/-ausgang
東口	higashi-guchi	Ein-/Ausgang Ost
南口	minami-guchi	Ein-/Ausgang Süd
西口	nishi-guchi	Ein-/Ausgang West
北口	kita-guchi	Ein-/Ausgang Nord
改札口	kaisatsu-guchi	Fahrkartenentwerter (Eingang)
出札口	shussatsu-guchi	Fahrkartenabgabe (Ausgang)
待合室	machiai shitsu	Wartesaal
コインロッカー	koin-roka	Münzschließfach

Zweimal … hin und zurück, bitte.	… e ouhuku ni-mai kudasai.
Gibt es eine Ermäßigung für Kinder/Familien/Studenten?	Kodomo/Kazoku/Gakusē walibiki ga alimasu ka?
Gibt es verbilligte Wochenendkarten?	Schūmatsu jo walibiki-ken ga alimasu ka?
Bitte eine Platzkarte für den Zug um … Uhr nach …	…-dji hatsu … iki no zaseki-schitē-ken o itchi-mai onegai schimasu.
● Einen Fensterplatz?	Mado-gawa no seki desu ka?
Ich möchte einen Schlafwagenplatz für den Zug um 20 Uhr nach … reservieren.	Hatchi-dji hatsu … iki no schindai-scha o jojaku schitai no desu ga.
Wo kann ich mein Fahrrad aufgeben?	Doko de djitenscha o azuke lalemasu-ka?
Wann kommt es in … an?	Nan-dji ni … ni tōtchaku schimasu ka?
Hat der Zug aus … Verspätung?	… kala no denscha wa okulete imasu ka?
Wann habe ich Anschluß nach …?	… iki no setsuzoku wa nan-dji ni alimasu ka?

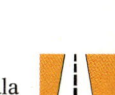

Wo muß ich umsteigen?	Doko de nolikaenakeleba nalimasu ka?
Welches Gleis bitte?	Nan-ban noliba desu ka?
Von welchem Gleis fährt der Zug nach … ab?	… iki no denscha wa nan-bansen kala demasu ka?
Gleis 1	itchi-bansen
Gleis 2	ni-bansen
Ist das ein Shinkansen?	Kole wa schinkansen desu ka?

Bahnstationen wie Shin-Osaka oder Shin-Kobe weisen darauf hin, daß hier eine Shinkansen-Station ist. Der **Shinkansen** (s. S. 45) fährt nur tagsüber. Von Tokyo aus legt er die 1181 km bis Hakata auf Kyushu in 5 Stunden 50 Minuten zurück. Er verkehrt auch auf den Strecken Tokyo–Morioka, ganz im Norden von Honshu und Tokyo–Niigata am japanischen Meer. **Nozomi** (Hoffnung) heißt der schnellste, der seit März 1993 zwischen Tokyo und Hakata verkehrt. **Hikari** (Blitz) und **Kodama** (Echo) sind die etwas langsameren, halten dafür etwas häufiger. Es gibt reservierte und nichtreservierte Plätze. Die nichtreservierten sind meist im ersten Wagen. In den Bahnhöfen der größeren Städte werden an grün markierten Schaltern (midori-no-madogutschi) Platzkarten für Shinkansen und Schnellzüge sowie Liegewagenkarten verkauft oder vorgebucht.

Hält der Zug in …?	Kono denscha wa … ni tomalimasu ka?
• Der Zug Nr. … aus … hat 10 Minuten Verspätung.	… hatsu … gō no denscha wa djuppun okulete imasu.
• Achtung, die Türen schließen.	Doa ga schimalimasu node gotchūi kudasai.

Im Zug | Densha no naka de

Verzeihung, ist dieser Platz frei?	Sumimasen, kono seki wa aite imasu ka?
Können Sie mir bitte helfen?	Sumimasen ga, tchotto tasukete kudasaimasen ka?
Darf ich das Fenster öffnen/schließen?	Mado o aketemo/schimetemo ī desu ka?

Entschuldigen Sie, das ist mein Platz. Ich habe eine Platzkarte.	Schitsulē des^{u}ga, koko wa wataschi no seki des^u. Zaseki-schitēken ga ali-mas^u.
Wann kommen wir in … an?	… ni nan-dji ni tōchaku schimas^u ka?
Wo sind wir jetzt?	Koko wa doko des^u ka?
Wie lange haben wir hier Aufenthalt?	Koko ni dono kulai tomalimas^u ka?
Kommen wir pünktlich an?	Djikan dōli ni tōtchaku schimas^u ka?

Wortliste Eisenbahn ▶ auch Wortliste Flugzeug

Abfahrt	schuppatsu
Abfahrtszeit	schuppatsu-djikan
Abteil	schaschitsu
ankommen	tōtchaku sulu
Aufenthalt	taizai
aussteigen	olilu
Bahn|hof	eki
~hofsrestaurant	eki no resutoran
~steigkarte	njūdjō-ken
einsteigen	nolu
Eisenbahn	tetsudō
Ermäßigung	walibiki
Fahr|karte	djōscha-ken
~kartenkontrolle	djōschaken-kensa
~kartenschalter	djōschaken-kaisatsu
~plan	djikoku-hjo
~preis	djōscha-ljōkin
Fensterplatz	mado-gawa no seki
Gang *(im Zug)*	tsūro-gawa
Gepäck	nimotsu
~aufbewahrung	itchidji-azukali-scho
~schalter	tenimotsu-toliatsukai-madogutchi
~schein	azukari-hjō
~schließfach	koin-lokkā
~träger	pōtā, akabō
~wagen	wagon

Gleis	denscha no noliba
Hauptbahnhof	tchūō-eki
Hochgeschwindigkeit	kōsoku-dō
Kinderfahrkarte	kodomo jō djōscha-ken
Lokomotive	djōki-kikanscha
nachlösen	sēsan sulu
Nichtraucherabteil	kin·en-scha

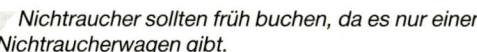

Nichtraucher sollten früh buchen, da es nur einen Nichtraucherwagen gibt.

Notbremse	hidjō-burēki
Platzkarte	schitēseki-ken
Raucherabteil	kitsuen-scha
Reisebegleiter *(Broschüre)*	gaido-bukku
Reservierung	jojaku
Rückfahrkarte	ōhuku-djōscha-ken

Rückfahrkarten sind in Japan nicht günstiger.

Rundreisefahrschein	schūjū-djōscha-ken
Schaffner	schaschō
Schlafwagenkarte	schindai-ken
Speisewagen	schokudō-scha
Toilette	toile
Wagennummer	schaljō-bangō
Wartesaal	matchiai-schitsu
Waschraum	senmen-djo
Zug	denscha
~begleitpersonal	djōmuin
Zuschlag	walimaschi-ljōkin, tokkjū-ljōkin
zuschlagpflichtig	walimaschi-ljōkin no kakalu

Schiff

Hune

Auskunft	An·nai
Welche ist die beste Schiffsverbindung nach …?	… iki no hune no lenketsu ga itchi-ban joi no wa dole desᵘ ka?

Welche ist die beste
Schiffsverbindung
nach …?

… iki no hune no lenketsu ga itchiban joi no wa dole desᵘ ka?

Wann fährt …
  das nächste Schiff
  die nächste Fähre
nach … ab?

Tsugi no … iki no
  hune
  felĩ
wa itsu demasᵘ ka?

Wie lange dauert die
Überfahrt?

Watalu no ni wa dono kulai djikan ga
kakalimasᵘ ka?

Wie lange dauert die
Rundfahrt?

Jūlan sᵘlu no ni wa dono kulai djikan
ga kakalimasᵘ ka?

Welche Häfen werden
angelaufen?

Doko no minato ni kikō schimasᵘ
ka?

Wann legen wir in … an?

… ni wa nan-dji ni tsukimasᵘ ka?

Wie lange haben wir Auf-
enthalt in …?

… ni wa dono kulai tēhaku schimasᵘ
ka?

Ich möchte eine Schiffs- karte nach …	… made no djōsen-ken o itchi-mai onegaischimasᵁ.
1. Klasse	ittō-seki
Touristenklasse	nitō-seki
eine Einzelkabine	koschitsu
eine Zweibettkabine	hutali jō senschitsu
Ich möchte eine Karte für die Rundfahrt um … Uhr.	… dji no jūlan-sen no djōsen-ken o itchi-mai onegaischimasᵁ.
Wann kommen wir zu- rück?	Nan-dji ni modotte kimasᵁ ka?

An Bord Sendjō de

Bitte, ich suche Kabine Nr. …	…-gōschitsu wa doko desᵁ ka.
Kann ich eine andere Ka- bine haben?	Betsu no senschitsu ni kaete motae- masᵁ ka?
Wo ist mein Koffer/mein Gepäck?	Wataschi no kaban/nimotsu wa doko desᵁ ka?
Wo ist der Speisesaal/der Aufenthaltsraum?	Schokudō/Laundji wa doko desᵁ ka?
Wann wird gegessen?	Schokudji wa nan-dji desᵁ ka?
Bringen Sie mir bitte …	… o mottekite kudasai.
Ich fühle mich nicht wohl.	Kibun ga walui no desᵁ ga.
Rufen Sie bitte …!	… o jonde kudasai!
Geben Sie mir bitte ein Mittel gegen Seekrank- heit.	Dōzo hunajoi no kusuli o kudasai.

Wortliste Schiff ▶ auch Wortlisten Flugzeug, Eisenbahn

Anker	ikali
anlaufen	schidō sulu
anlegen in	ni tsukelu
Anlegeplatz	tē haku
auslaufen	nagale delu

ausschiffen	schuppan sulu
Backbord	sagen
an Bord	sendjō
Buchung	jojaku
Bug	senschu
Dampfer	kisen
Deck	dekki
einschiffen	djōsen sulu
Fähre	ferĭ
Auto~	kā-ferĭ
Fahrkarte	djōsen-ken
Festland	tailiku

Am Kamo-Fluß in Kyoto

Hafen	minato
~gebühr	tē haku-ze
Heck	senbi
Jacht	jotto
Kabine	senschitsu
Kai	hutō
Kajüte	senschitsu
Kapitän	sentchō
Knoten	notto
Kreuzfahrt	kurūzu
Kurs	kōsu
Küste	kaigan

Leuchtturm	tōdai
Matrose	hunanoli
Motorboot	mōtā-bōto
Passagier	djōkjaku
Promenadendeck	dekki
Rettungs|boot	kjūmē-bōto
~ring	kjūmē-ukiwa
Ruder	kadji
~boot	kadji-bōto
Rundfahrt	schūjū
Schwimmweste	kjūmē-dōi
Seegang	nami no jōsu
seekrank	hunajoi
Segelboot	jotto
Steuerbord	ugen
Tragflächenboot	suitchū-jokusen
Überfahrt	tokō
Ufer	kischi
Verbindung	setsuzoku, lenketsu
Welle	nami

Bei der Einreise

Njūkoku no sai

Paßkontrolle **Ljoken-kensa**

- Ihren Paß, bitte! — Pasupōto/Ljoken o misete kudasai!

- Ihr Paß ist abgelaufen. — Pasupōto ga kilete imasu.

Für die Einreise nach Japan benötigen Sie einen gültigen Reisepaß und ein Visum, wenn Sie dort arbeiten. Reisende aus Deutschland, Österreich und der Schweiz können sich bis zu 6 Monaten ohne Visum in Japan aufhalten, allerdings nur als Touristen. Ein Impfpaß wird nicht benötigt, ebenfalls keine speziellen Impfungen.

Werden Ihnen Fingerabdrücke abgenommen, so nicht deshalb, weil man Sie für einen Verbrecher hält, sondern weil die japanische Behörde Ihre Fingerabdrücke benötigt, um Ihnen einen japanischen Personalausweis ausstellen zu können. Dieses – wahrscheinlich einmalige – Vergnügen wird Ihnen aber nur zuteil, wenn Sie für längere Zeit in Japan bleiben.

Ich gehöre zu der Reise-
gesellschaft aus …

… kala no ljokō-gurūpᵘ ni zokuschite
imasᵘ.

● Haben Sie ein Visum?

Biza ga alimasᵘ ka?

Zollkontrolle

Zēkan-kensa

● Haben Sie etwas zu ver-
zollen?

Nanika schinkoku sulu mono ga alimasᵘ ka?

Nein, ich habe nur ein
paar Geschenke.

īe, omijage o sᵘkoschi motte ilu dake
desᵘ.

● Öffnen Sie bitte diesen
Koffer/diese Tasche.

Kono toranku/bakku o akete kudasai.

Muß ich das verzollen?

Kole ni kanzē o schihalawanakeleba
nalimasen ka?

Wie hoch sind die Zoll-
gebühren?

Kanzē wa ikula kakalimasᵘ ka?

Wortliste Grenze

Ausfuhr	juschutsu
Ausreise	schukkoku
Bestimmungen	kitē
Einfuhr	junjū
Einreise	njūkoku
Familien|name	sē, mjōdji
~stand	kazoku-kōsē
ledig	dokuschin
verheiratet	kikon, kekkon schite ilu
Witwe	mibōdjin
Witwer	jamome
Führerschein	unten-menkjo-schō
Geburts|datum	sēnen-gappi
~name	kjūsē
~ort	schussētchi
Grenzübergang	kokkjō
gültig	jūkō
internationaler Impfpaß	kokusai-jobōsesschu-schōmē-scho
Paßkontrolle	pasᵘpōto-kensa, ljoken-kensa
Personalausweis	mibun-schōmē-scho
Reisepaß	pasᵘpōto, ljoken

Sichtvermerk	biza, saschō
Staatsangehörigkeit	kokuseki
Visum	biza
Vorname	namae
Wohnort	djūscho
Zoll	kanzē
~frei	muzē
~gebühren	tsūkan-tesūljō
~kontrolle	tsūkan-kensa
~pflichtig	kanzē no kakalu

Nahverkehrsmittel

Kōtsū-kikan

Bitte, wo ist die nächste Bushaltestelle/U-Bahn-station?	Sumimasen, itchi ban tchikai tēljūdjo/tchikatetsu no eki wa doko desu ka?
Welcher Bus fährt nach …?	… iki no basu wa dole desu ka?

⟋ *Die Busbenutzung ist nicht so einfach, da die Zielorte jeweils*
nur in Japanisch angeschrieben sind.
⇨ *Zum Lösen von Fahrscheinen siehe Info Seite 80.*

Gibt es Bus-/Tagestouren von hier aus?	Koko kala basu tsuā/higaeli tsuā ga demasu ka?
Wann/Wo fährt der Bus ab?	Basu wa itsu/doko kala demasu ka?
Welche U-Bahn fährt nach …?	… iki no tchikatetsu wa dole desu ka?
Wann fährt die erste/letzte Bahn nach …?	… iki no schihatsu/saischū wa nan-dji desu ka?
Wo muß ich aussteigen/einsteigen?	Doko de olitala/nolikaetala ī desu ka?
Sagen Sie mir bitte, wenn wir dort sind.	Soko ni tsuitala, oschiete kudasai.
Wo kann ich den Fahrschein kaufen?	Doko de kippu ga kaemas ka?
Bitte, einen Fahrschein nach …	… iki no djōscha-ken o itchi-mai kudasai.

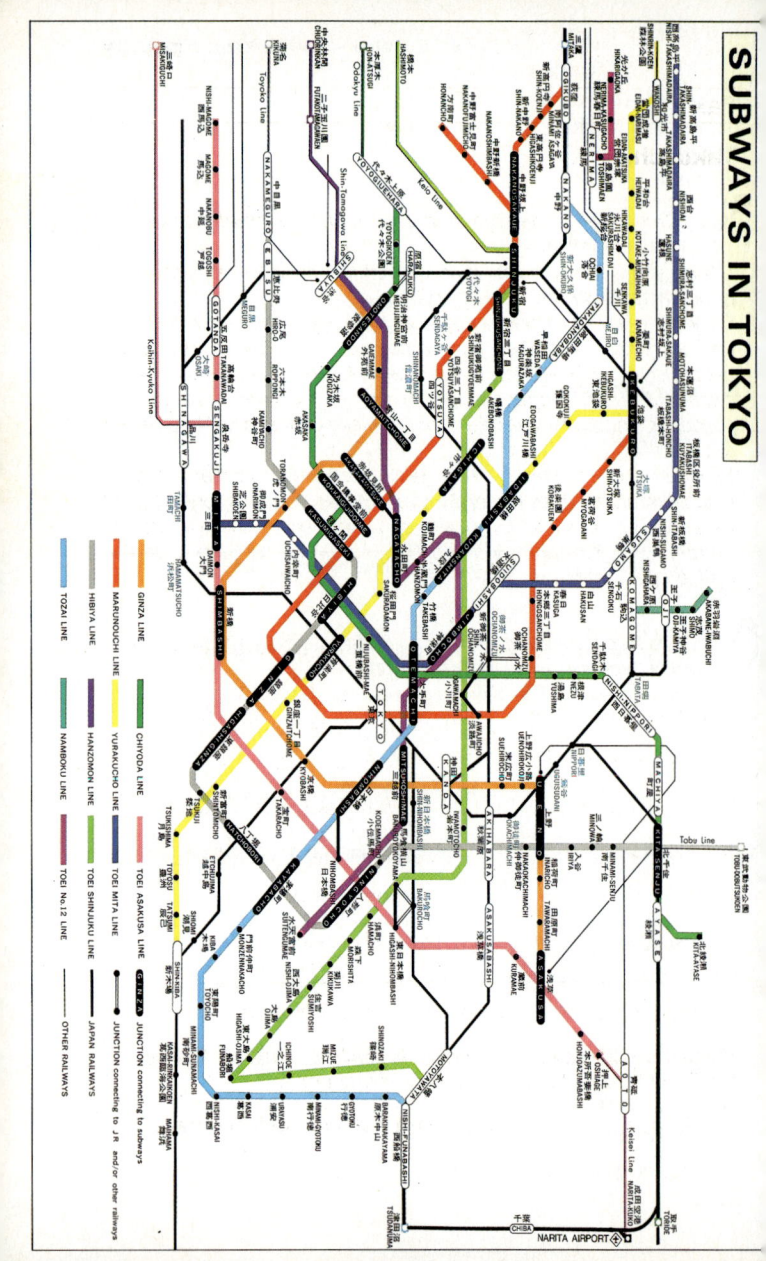

SUBWAYS IN TOKYO

Taxi

Takuschī

Taxis gibt es genügend in Japan. Der Taxameter zeigt den Preis deutlich an.

Trinkgeld gibt man nicht, es sei denn, der Taxifahrer hat sich aus irgendeinem Grund besondere Mühe gegeben.

Sie winken ein Taxi heran, indem Sie die ausgestreckte flache Hand im Handgelenk von oben nach unten bewegen. Diese Bewegung gleicht eher einem Abwehren als einem Heranwinken. Mit dem ausgestreckten Zeigefinger zu sich herwinken gilt in Japan als ausgesprochen unhöflich. Taxitüren springen automatisch auf und gehen automatisch zu.

Es ist empfehlenswert, sich die gesuchte Adresse immer auf japanisch aufschreiben zu lassen bzw. eine japanische Visitenkarte, auf deren Rückseite meist ein Ministadtplan aufgedruckt ist, mit sich zu führen. Auch Taxifahrer können sich mit einem solchen Lageplan besser zurechtfinden.

Wo ist der nächste Taxistand?	Itchi ban tchikai takuschī-noliba wa doko desᵘ ka?
Zum Flughafen, bitte.	Kūkō made onegai schimasᵘ.
Zum Bahnhof, bitte..	Eki made onegai schimasᵘ.
Zum ...-Hotel, bitte.	... hotelu made onegai schimasᵘ.
In die ...-Straße.	... dōli made onegai schimasᵘ.
Nach ..., bitte.	... made onegai schimasᵘ.
Wieviel kostet es nach ...?	... made o-ikula desᵘ ka?
Halten Sie bitte hier.	Koko de tomatte kudasai.
Warten Sie bitte hier. Ich bin in 5 Minuten zurück.	Koko de matte ite kudasai. Go-hun go ni modotte kimasᵘ.
Das ist für Sie.	Kole wa anata ni saschiage masᵘ.

Zu Fuß

Aluite

Japanische Adressen folgen keinem linearen Prinzip nach Straßen, sondern einem Flächenprinzip nach Bezirken. Straßennamen gibt es so gut wie keine, ausgenommen einige besonders große Straßen. Die kleinste Flächeneinheit heißt **chome** und besteht meist nur aus wenigen Häuserblocks. Jedes Gebäude innerhalb eines solchen chome hat eine einstellige oder durch einen Bindestrich verbundene zweistellige Nummer, z.B. 16-6. Da das keine Hausnummern sind, können Sie nicht davon ausgehen, daß sie fortlaufend sind wie bei uns. Diese Zahlen haben etwas mit dem Erbauungsdatum des jeweiligen Hauses zu tun. Tauchen drei durch Bindestrich verbundene Zahlen auf, so gibt die erste dieser Zahlen das chome an. 1-16-6 wäre also 1-chome.

Die nächstgrößere Einheit hat verschiedene Bezeichnungen: **cho, machi,** oder manchmal auch gar keine.

Darüber gibt es das **-ku,** was soviel wie Stadtteil heißt. **Higashinada-ku** wäre also der Stadtteil in östlicher Richtung. **Chuo-ku** führt Sie ins Stadtzentrum. Bei **Minato-ku** wissen Sie, daß Sie sich Richtung Hafen bewegen müssen. Mit Hilfe eines kleines Wörterbuches können Sie enträtseln, was vor **-ku** steht.

Die Städtenamen erhalten in Anschriften die Endung **-shi,** was so viel wie „Stadt" heißt und zur Unterscheidung von **-ken,** der Präfektur mit gleichem Namen, dient:

Okayama-shi, Okayama-ken

Bei Osaka und Kyoto wird **-fu** (nicht -shi) gebraucht, bei Tokyo **-to.** Die Orte auf dem Land heißen **mura** „Dorf". Das Wort **gun,** das mitunter auch vorkommt, bedeutet die nächstkleinere Verwaltungseinheit nach dem **ken.**

Bitte, wo ist …?	Sumimasen, … wa doko des^u ka?
Wie komme ich am besten nach …?	… ni wa dō ittala ī des^u ka?
Ich möchte nach … In welche Richtung muß ich gehen?	… e ikitai nodes ga, dotchila no hōkō e ittala ī deschō ka?
Wie weit ist es zum/ zur …?	… made dono kulai hanalete imas^u ka?

● Es ist weit.	Tōi desᵘ.
● Es ist ganz in der Nähe.	Sugu tchikaku desᵘ.
● Gehen Sie geradeaus.	Massugu itte kudasai.
Gehen Sie nach links/rechts.	Hidali ni/Migi ni itte kudasai.
● Biegen Sie die erste/zweite Straße links/rechts ab.	Hadjime no/Nibanme no tōli o hidali/migi ni magatte kudasai.
● Auf der rechten/linken Seite.	Migi-gawa/hidali-gawa.

● Gehen Sie über …
    die Brücke.   Haschi o watatte kudasai.
    den Platz.   Hiloba o tōlisugite kudasai.
    die Straße.   Mitchi o watatte kudasai.

● Dann fragen Sie noch einmal.	Soschite mō itchido tazunete kudasai.
● Sie können den Bus Nr. …/die U-Bahn nehmen.	…-ban no basᵘ/tchikatetsu ni notte kudasai.

Wortliste Unterwegs in der Stadt

abfahren	schuppatsu sulu
Abfahrt	schuppatsu
ausrufen	jobidasᵘ
aussteigen	olilu
Bus	basᵘ
~bahnhof	basᵘ-tāminalu
einsteigen	nolu
Endstation	schūten
Fahr|er/in	unten-schu
~kartenautomat	djōschaken-djidōhanbaiki
~plan	djikoku-hjo
~preis	untchin
~schein	djōschaken
Fußgängerzone	hokōschā-tengoku
Gasse	lodji
Gebäude	tatemono
Gehsteig	hodō

Takadanobaba

Waseda Univ.

CHUO MAIN LINE

Tokyo Globe

National Hospital

Tokyo Int'l Youth Ho
Iidaba

Okubo   Shin-Okubo

kyo Hilton Int'l

Seibu-Shinjuku
Shinjuku Prince Hotel

Isetan Dept. Store

Century
t Tokyo
o Plaza Hotel
Shinjuku
Vashington Hotel

Odakyu
Dept. Store
Keio
Dept.
Store

SHINJUKU

Marui Dept. Store

Mitsukoshi Dept. Store

Ichigaya

Ki

Yotsuya

Diamond Ho

Sophia Univ.

Hotel Sunroute
Tokyo

Yoyogi

Keio Line

Odakyu Line

Shinjuku Gyoen
National Garden

Sendagaya

Shinanomachi

Hotel New Otani

anese Sword
seum

Sangubashi

Yoyogi Youth Hostel

Meiji Shrine

National Noh Theater
National Stadium

Meiji Shrine
Outer Garden

Akasaka Prince Hotel

Akasaka Palace

Akasaka

Meiji Shrine
Inner Garden

HARAJUKU

Capitol Tokyu Hotel

Yoyogi-Hachiman

Yoyogi Sports Center

Hotel Tokyukanko

Aoyama
Cemetery

ANA Hotel Tokyo
Ark Hills

NHK

Oriental Bazaar

Roppongi Prince Hotel

Suntor

Shibuya Tobu Hotel
Marui Dept. Store
Seibu Dept. Store
Tokyu Dept. Store
Tokyo Univ.
iberal Arts Dept.

Aoyama Gakuin Univ.

Nezu Institute of
Fine Arts

SHIBUYA

shira
Line

Tokyu Dept. Store

Tokyo Tow

Tamagawa Line

Red Cross Central Hospital

S

Keio

Ebisu

Naka-Meguro

Toyoko Line

YAMANOTE LINE

National Park
for Nature Study

Hotel Tokyo

Miyako Hotel Tokyo   Hotel Takanawa

TOKYO

halten	tomalu
Haltestelle	tēljūdjo
Hauptstraße	menuki-dōli
Haus	ie, uchi
~nummer	bantchi
Innenstadt	toschin
Kilometerpreis	kilomētā-ljōkin
Kirche	kjōkai
Knopf drücken	botan o os^u
Kontrolleur	kensa-kan
lösen *(Fahrschein)*	kippu o kau

Fahrscheine werden auf zweierlei Weise gelöst.

1. In Tokyo und in anderen Städten herrschen Einheitspreise. Man bezahlt beim Einsteigen. Rechts neben der Kasse ist ein Wechselautomat, der 100-Yen-Münzen in 10-Yen-Münzen umtauscht. Manche Kassen haben oben 2 Öffnungen. Die linke ist für die Fahrscheine, die rechte für das Kleingeld.

2. Oft berechnen sich die Fahrpreise nach der zurückgelegten Strecke. Man steigt an der hinteren Wagentüre ein und zieht einen Fahrschein aus dem Automaten rechts neben der Treppe. Das Ticket gibt die Nummer der Tarifzone an, in der man zugestiegen ist. Auf der Anzeigetafel vorne im Bus sieht man, wieviel man zu bezahlen hat.

Nebenstraße	ula-dōli
Netzkarte	kin·itsu-schūjū-ken
Park	kōen
Pauschalpreis	ikkatsu-ljōkin, kin·itsu-ljōkin
Quittung	ljōschūscho
Richtung	hōkō
Schaffner	schaschō
Stadt|bus	schinai-bas^u
~rundfahrt	schinai-kankō-bas^u
~teil	matchi no ikkaku
~zentrum	hankagai
Straße	mitchi
Straßenbahn	schiden
Tageskarte	itchinitchi-ken
Taxi|fahrer/in	takuschī, no untenschu
~stand	takuschī-noliba
Trinkgeld	tchipp^u
U-Bahn	tchikatetsu
Überlandbus	tchōkjoli-bas^u
Vorort	kōgai
Zeitkarte	tēki-djōschaken

4 Unterkunft
宿

Auskunft

An·nai

Die **Japan National Tourist Organisation** (JNTO) vermittelt und bucht Übernachtungen, außer für Love Hotels und Tempel. Das Büro in Tokyo kann Ihnen die Adressen der jeweiligen Büros in anderen Städten nennen. Auskünfte können Sie dort auf Englisch erhalten.
JNTO Tokyo: 6-6, Yurakucho 1-chome, Chiyoda-ku, Tokyo 100
Tel.: (03) 3502-1461

ホテル **Business-Hotels:** westlicher Stil, d.h. entsprechen unseren Lebensgewohnheiten. Es gibt sie in jeder größeren Stadt. Sie sind allerdings nicht billig, haben aber den Vorteil, daß Sie sich am Abend ohne Einstellen auf die fremde Kultur erholen können.

旅館 **Ryokan:** Japanischer Stil, Futonbetten. Es gibt kein westliches Badezimmer , sondern ein japanisches Furo. Das Frühstück besteht aus Reis und Suppe. Zum Trinken gibt es grünen Tee. Frühstück und Abendessen sind inklusiv. Meist teuer.

民宿 **Minshuku:** Einrichtung und Essen sind gleich wie im Ryokan. Der Unterschied ist, daß man sich seinen Futon selbst herrichtet und ihn morgens auch selbst aufräumt. Das Minshuku ist wesentlich billiger als das Ryokan. Man bezahlt nicht das Zimmer, sondern die benutzten Futons. Frühstück und Abendessen sind inklusive. Die erste Übernachtung dient sicher weniger der Entspannung, als daß sie selbst spannend ist (Verständigungsprobleme, Zurechtfinden im Zimmer, im Badezimmer, in der Toilette usw.). Im Minshuku wird man wie ein Familienmitglied behandelt und handelt auch selbst, als wäre man ein Familienmitglied.

ペンション **Pension:** Ähnlich wie Minshuku. Nicht mehr so traditionell japanisch. Wird meist von jungen Leuten geführt.

Love Hotels (Rabu Hoteru): Hinter diesem Namen verbirgt sich nicht etwa ein Bordell. Love Hotels sind Häuser – man erkennt sie häufig an ihrem Äußeren (Disney-Schlösser im Stil von Neuschwanstein, Ritterburgen usw.) –, in denen sich Paare ein Zimmer mieten, um ein paar Stunden in ungestörter Atmosphäre verbringen zu können (japanische Häuser mit ihren Papiertüren sind sehr hellhörig). Da Love Hotels nur tagsüber besucht werden, kann man dort mitunter billiger übernachten als irgendwo anders. Allerdings erst ab 22.00 Uhr.

*In manchen **Tempeln** kann man übernachten. Ein besonderes Vergnügen für Ästheten. Das vegetarische Essen wird im Zimmer serviert. Köstlich für Augen und Gaumen.*

Können Sie mir bitte ein Hotel empfehlen?	Doko-ka hotelu o oschiete kudasaimasen ka?
Können Sie mir eine günstige Übernachtungsmöglichkeit empfehlen?	Doko-ka jasᵘku schukuhaku dekilu tokolo o oschiete kudasaimasen ka?
Liegt es zentral/ruhig?	Sole wa hanka-gai ni/schizukana tokolo ni alimasᵘ ka?
Ist es in der Nähe des Bahnhofs gelegen?	Sole wa eki no tchikaku ni alimasᵘ ka?
Was wird eine Übernachtung etwa kosten?	Ippaku daitai o-ikula desᵘ ka?
Gibt es hier eine Jugendherberge?	Koko ni jūsᵘ-hosᵘtelu ga alimasᵘ ka?
Wie komme ich am besten dorthin?	Soko e wa dono-jō ni ittala ˊ desᵘ ka?

Camping und Ferienwohnungen sind in Japan noch nicht üblich.

Hotel/Gasthof

Hotelu/Ljokan

An der Rezeption | **Uketsuke de**

Ich habe bei Ihnen ein Zimmer reserviert. Mein Name ist …	Wataschi no namae wa … desᵘ. Hito-heja jojaku o schimaschita.
Haben Sie noch Zimmer frei?	Mada hito-heja aite imasᵘ ka?
für eine Nacht	hito-ban, ippaku
für zwei Tage/eine Woche	nihaku, Huta-ban/Isshū-kan
• Nein, wir sind leider vollständig belegt.	Zan·nen·nagala, manschitsu desᵘ.

Können Sie mir ein anderes Hotel empfehlen?	Doko-ka hoka no hotelu o oschiete kudasaimasen ka?
Können Sie für mich dort anrufen?	Soko ni denwa o kakete kudasaimasen ka?
● Was für ein Zimmer wünschen Sie?	Don·na heja o onozomi desᵘ ka?
Ein Einzelzimmer	Schingulu, hitoli-beja
Ein Doppelzimmer	Tsuin, hutali-beja
Ein ruhiges Zimmer	Schizukana heja

Ein Zimmer …
  mit Bad.
  mit Balkon/Terrasse.
  mit Blick aufs Meer.
	Basᵘ-tsuki no heja.
	Balukōni/Terasᵘ tsuki no heja.
	Umi ga mielu heja.

Können Sie noch ein zusätzliches Bett ins Zimmer stellen?	Kono heja ni betto o mō hitotsu ilete kudasaimasen ka?
Was kostet das Zimmer?	Ikula ni nalimasᵘ ka?
Ist das Frühstück inklusive?	Tchōschoku-tsuki desᵘ ka?
Halbpension	Nischoku-tsuki
Vollpension	Sanschoku-tsuki
● Würden Sie bitte den Anmeldeschein ausfüllen?	Dōzo kono mōschikomi-jōschi ni kinjū schite kudasai?
● Darf ich Ihren Paß sehen?	Pasᵘpōto o misete kudasai masen ka?
Bitte lassen Sie das Gepäck auf mein Zimmer bringen.	Nimotsu o wataschi no heja ni hakonde kudasai.
Wo kann ich den Wagen abstellen?	Doko ni tchūscha dekimasᵘ ka?
● In unserer Tiefgarage.	Tchika no tchūscha-djō ni tomete kudasai.
Auf unserem Parkplatz.	Wataschi domo no tchūscha-djō ni.
Bitte geben Sie mir Zimmerschlüssel Nr. …	…-gō schitsu no kagi o kudasai.

Gibt es Zimmerservice?	Rūmu-sābisu ga alimasu ka?
Kann ich mein Gepäck hier lassen, bis ich wiederkomme?	Wataschi ga mata kulu made, nimotsu o koko ni oite oite mo ī desu ka?
● Wie viele Futons benötigen Sie?	Huton wa nan-kumi ilimasu ka?
Zeigen Sie mir bitte, wie ich den Futon hinlegen soll.	Huton o dono-jōni schiku no ka oschiete kudasaimasen ka.

Tatami: Reisstrohmatten mit genormter Größe. Auch in modernen Wohnungen ist mindestens ein Zimmer mit diesen Reisstrohmatten ausgelegt, die man nur auf Strümpfen betritt. Tatamiräume sind meist in traditionell japanischem Stil eingerichtet: Papierschiebetüren, Rollbild, darunter ein Ikebanagesteck auf einem kleinen Tischchen, in einer Ecke noch ein kleiner Hausschrein. Japanische Wohnungen enthalten sehr viel weniger Möbel und sonstige Dinge als unsere.

Futon: Das japanische Bett, das unseren Betten in keiner Weise gleicht. Der etwas härtere Teil ist die Matratze, der weichere die Zudecke. Futons werden tagsüber in Wandschränken aufbewahrt, abends werden sie dort ausgebreitet, wo tagsüber gelebt, gegessen und gearbeitet wird. Morgens wird alles zuerst auf dem Balkon gelüftet und dann wieder verstaut.

Furo: Das Furo ist das japanische Bad. Im Ryokan oder im Minshuku gibt es ein solches. Es liegt ein Baumwollkimono (Yukata) im Zimmer bereit (nicht im Minshuku). Im Zimmer kleidet man sich um und geht im Yukata ins Bad. Das Wasser ist schon in der Badewanne und meist sehr heiß. Begehen Sie nicht den Fehler und setzen Sie sich hinein, um mit Ihren Waschaktivitäten zu beginnen. Das japanische Furo dient der Entspannung und nicht der Säuberung. Im Badezimmer finden Sie Plastikschüsseln, mit denen Sie Wasser aus der Badewanne schöpfen. Sie seifen sich außerhalb der Badewanne ab, spülen die Seife gut weg, indem Sie sich – je nach Beschaffenheit des Badezimmers – mit Wasser übergießen. Jetzt können Sie sich in die Wanne setzen. Lassen Sie das Wasser nicht ab, wenn Sie Ihr Bad beendet haben. Nach Ihnen werden alle Gäste und alle Familienmitglieder noch darin baden. Morgens geht man nicht ins Furo.

Kotatsu: Traditionelle und moderne japanische Häuser verfügen über keine Zentralheizung. Im Winter wird es manchmal unangenehm kalt in den Wohnungen. Um dem entgegenzuwirken, verkriecht man sich unter den Kotatsu. Das ist eine in den Boden eingelassene, mit Heizschlangen versehene Vertiefung unter dem Eßtisch. Die Familie versammelt sich um den Tisch und streckt die Beine in die Vertiefung. Ein Tischtuch, das bis zum Boden reicht, sorgt dafür, daß die Wärme nicht entweicht. Der Nachteil dieser „Spot-Heating" ist, daß Füße und Beine fast geröstet werden, während Rücken und Oberkörper sich im Kalten befinden.

Könnten Sie mir bitte ein Leintuch/eine Decke geben?	Sumimasen ga, schikihu/kakebuton o kudasai masen ka?
Ab wann gibt es Frühstück?	Tchōschoku wa nan-dji kala dekimasu ka?
Könnte ich bitte heißes Wasser/grünen Tee haben?	Sumimasen ga, atsui oju/otcha o itadakemas^u ka?

Gespräche mit dem Hotelpersonal	**Hotelu de no kaiwa**
Ab wann gibt es Frühstück?	Tchōschoku wa nandji kala dekimas^u ka?
Wann sind die Essenszeiten?	Schokudji no djikan wa nan-dji des^u ka?
Wo ist der Speisesaal?	Schokudō wa doko des^u ka?
Wo ist der Frühstücksraum?	Tchōschoku no heja wa doko des^u ka?
Schicken Sie mir bitte das Frühstück um … Uhr aufs Zimmer.	Hatchi-dji ni tchōschoku o heja made motte kite kudasai.
Zum Frühstück hätte ich gerne …	Tchōschoku ni wa … o onegai schimas^u.
schwarzen Tee.	kōtcha
Kaffee.	kōfī
Tee mit Milch/Zitrone.	miluku-tī/lemon-tī
Schokolade.	kokoa

einen Fruchtsaft.	djūsu
ein gekochtes Ei.	jude-tamago
Rühreier.	nama-tamago
Spiegeleier.	medamajaki
Brot.	pan
Butter.	batā
Käse.	tchĩzu
Wurst.	sōsēdji
Schinken.	hamu
Honig.	hatchimitsu
Marmelade.	djamu
ein Joghurt.	jōguruto
Obst.	kudamono

Wecken Sie mich bitte morgen früh um … Uhr.	Aschita no asa … dji ni mōningu-kōlu o onegai schimasu.

In den japanischen Alpen

Würden Sie mir bitte … bringen?	
ein Handtuch	Taolu …
eine Seife	Sekken …
Kleiderbügel	Hangā …
	… o mottekite kudasaimasen ka?

Bitte geben Sie mir meinen Schlüssel.	Wataschi no kagi o kudasai.
Hat jemand nach mir gefragt?	Dale-ka, wataschi o tazunete kimaschita ka?
Ist Post für mich da?	Wataschi-ate ni jūbinbutsu ga todoite imasu ka?
Ich möchte ein Telefax schicken.	Fakkusu o okulitai no desu ga.
Wo kann ich telefonieren?	Doko de denwa ga kakelalemasu ka?
Haben Sie Ansichtskarten/Briefmarken?	Ehagaki/Kitte ga alimasu ka?
Wo kann ich diesen Brief einwerfen?	Doko de tegami ga dasemasu ka?
Wo kann ich … mieten/ausleihen?	Doko de … o kalilalemasu ka?
Kann ich meine Wertsachen bei Ihnen in den Safe geben?	Wataschi no kitchō-hin o sēfutī-bokkusu ni azukelu koto ga dekimasu ka?

Beanstandungen   Kudjō o iu

Das Zimmer ist nicht gereinigt worden.	Heja ga sōdji salete imasen.
Die Dusche …	Schawā ga demasen.
Die Spülung …	Suisen-toile no mizu ga nagale masen.
Die Heizung …	Danbō ga kikimasen.
Die Kühlanlage …	Lēbō ga kikimasen.
Das Licht …	Denki ga tsukimasen.
Das Radio …	Radjio ga kakalimasen.
Der Fernseher … funktioniert nicht.	Mado ga ugokimasen.
Der Wasserhahn tropft.	Djagutchi ga umaku schimalimasen.
Es kommt kein (warmes) Wasser.	Omizu (oju) ga demasen.

Die Toilette/Das Waschbecken ist verstopft.	Toile/Senmendai ga tsumatte imas^u.
Das Fenster schließt nicht/geht nicht auf.	Mado ga schimalimasen/akimasen.
Der Schlüssel paßt nicht.	Kagi ga aimasen.

Abreise   Schuppatsu

Ich reise heute abend/ morgen um … Uhr ab.	Wataschi wa kon·ja/aschita … dji ni schuppatsu schimas^u.
Bis wann muß ich das Zimmer räumen?	Nan-dji made ni heja o akenakeleba nalimasen ka?
Machen Sie bitte die Rechnung fertig.	Sēsan o onegai schimas^u.
Getrennte Rechnungen bitte.	Sēsan wa betsubetsu ni onegai schimas^u.
Kann ich mit Kreditkarte bezahlen?	Kuredjitto-kādo ga tsukaemas^u ka?
Bitte senden Sie meine Post an diese Adresse nach.	Wataschi no jūbin-butsu o kono djūscho ni okutte kudasai.
Lassen Sie bitte mein Gepäck herunterbringen.	Wataschi no nimotsu o schita ni hakonde kudasai.
Kann ich meine Sachen hier abstellen bis zu meiner Abreise?	Schuppatsu made wataschi no mono o koko ni oite oitemo ī des^u ka?
Lassen Sie bitte mein Gepäck zum Bahnhof/Air Terminal bringen.	Wataschi no nimotsu o eki/eātāminalu made todokete kudasai.
Rufen Sie mir bitte ein Taxi.	Takuschī o jonde kudasai.
Vielen Dank für alles! Auf Wiedersehen!	Iloilo aligatō gozaimaschita! Sajōnala!

ホテル	hoteru	Hotel
フロント	furonto	Rezeption
受付	uketsuke	Rezeption
浴室	yokushitsu	Bad
ユースホステル	jūsu-hosuteru	Jugendherberge

Wortliste Hotel/Gasthof

Abendessen	jūschoku
Animationsprogramm	manga-bangumi
Anmeldung	todokede, schinkoku
Aschenbecher	haizala
Aufenthaltsraum	danwa-schitsu
Aufzug	elebētā
Bade|wanne	hulo-oke
~zimmer	basᵘ-rūmu, huloba
Balkon	balukonĭ
Bett	betto
~decke	kakebuton
~laken/~wäsche	schĭtsu, schikihu
Cafeteria	kissaten
Dusche	schawā
Empfangshalle	genkan-hōlu, lobĭ
Etage	kai
Fenster	mado
Fernseher	telebi
Fernsehraum	telebi-schitsu
Frühstück	tchōschoku, asagohan
Frühstücks|büfett	bjuffe
~raum	schokudō
Futon	huton
Halbpension	ni-schoku-tsuki
Handtuch	taolu
Heizung	danbō
Kategorie	kategorĭ
Kinder|betreuung	bebĭ-schittā, komoli
~bett	bebĭ-betto
~spielplatz	jūentchi, asobi-ba
Kleiderbügel	hangā
Klimaanlage	eakon

Kopfkissen	makula
Lampe	lanpu
Lichtschalter	suitchi
Matratze	mattoresu
Mittagessen	tchūschoku, hilu gohan
Nachttisch	dezāto
Papierkorb	kamikuzu-ile
Pension	penschon
Portier	schuē
Radio	radjio
reinigen	kulīningu sulu
Reservierung	jojaku
Rezeption	uketsuke
Safe	kinko se·ifutī-bokkusu
Schlüssel	kagi
Schrank	todana, tansu
Sessel	āmu-tcheā
Speisesaal	schokudō
Spiegel	kagami
Steckdose	konsento saschikomi
Stecker	pulagu

Die elektrische Spannung beträgt 100 Volt. Rasierapparate, die man auf 110 Volt umschalten kann, funktionieren einigermaßen. Die Steckkontakte entsprechen nicht der europäischen Norm. Man braucht einen Vorsatzstecker. Will man in Japan seine elektrischen Geräte benützen, kann man dies mit Hilfe eines Transformators tun.

Terrasse	terasu
Toilette	toile
Toilettenpapier	toiletto-pēpā
Übernachtung	schukuhaku
~ mit Frühstück	tchōschoku-tsuki
Ventilator	senpūki
Vollpension	sanschoku-tsuki
Waschbecken	senmen-dai
Wäschewechsel	schītsu-kōkan
Wasser	mizu
kaltes ~	mizu
warmes ~	oju
~glas	koppu
~hahn	djagutchi
Wolldecke	mōhu

Zimmer	heja
~mädchen	me·ido
~telefon	denwa
Zwischenstecker	adapᵘta

Jugendherberge

Jūsu-hosᵘtelu

In Jugendherbergen herrschen meist sehr strenge Vorschriften in bezug auf Nachtruhe und Aufstehen. Die Mahlzeiten werden oft gemeinsam eingenommen.
Keine Altersbeschränkung. Preisgünstig.

Kann ich bei Ihnen Bett-   Schikihu o kalilale masᵘ ka?
wäsche leihen?

• Die Eingangstür wird um   Jolu no djū-dji ni genkan ga schimali-
22 Uhr abgeschlossen.   masᵘ.

Wortliste Jugendherberge

Benutzungsgebühr	schijō-lyō
Gemeinschaftsraum	kjōdō-beya
Geschirrspülbecken	senmen-dai
Herbergseltern	pearentsu, kanli-nin
Jugendherberge	jūsu-hosᵘtelu
Jugendherbergs|ausweis	jūsu-hosᵘtelu-kai·in-schō
~führer	jūsu-hosᵘtelu-gaido-bukku
Kinderspielplatz	jüentchi
Kocher	konlo
leihen	kalilu
Leihgebühr	kaschidaschi-ljō
Mitgliedskarte	kai·in-schō
Strom	denki
~anschluß	saschikomi
Studentenwohnheim	gakusē-ljō
Trinkwasser	nomimizu
Voranmeldung	jojaku
Waschraum	senmen-djo
Wäschetrockner	kansō-ki
Wasser	mizu

5 Gastronomie
レストラン

Essen gehen

Schokudji ni iku

Essen gehen und Einkaufen sind Lieblingsbeschäftigungen in Japan. Dementsprechend viele Lokale gibt es.

Japanische Restaurants *sind meist auf ein oder zwei Gerichte spezialisiert. Im Schaufenster steht das Sortiment in Wachsnachbildung. Man kann also zeigen, was man gerne essen möchte. Bestellen kann man, indem man auf das gewünschte Gericht deutet und* **kore o kudasai** *sagt.*
Ansonsten sagt man das Gewünschte und ... **o kudasai**, *z.B.:*
biru o kudasai (ein Bier bitte)
Supageti o kudasai (Spaghetti bitte)

Können Sie mir ...	Doko-ka
ein japanisches Restaurant	wahū res^utoran
ein Restaurant, wo man europäisch essen kann	jōschoku ga tabelalelu res^utoran
ein chinesisches Restaurant	tchūka-ljōli no res^utoran
empfehlen?	... o oschiete kudasaimasen ka?

Während der Öffnungszeiten hängen einladende Tücher am Eingang traditioneller japanischer Restaurants.

Gibt es hier in der Nähe ein Restaurant, wo man gut essen kann?	Doko-ka kono tchikaku de oischiku schokudji no dekilu resᵘtoran ga alimasᵘ ka?
Gibt es hier in der Nähe ein Restaurant, wo man günstig essen kann?	Doko-ka kono tchikaku de jasᵘku schokudji no dekilu resᵘtoran ga alimasᵘ ka?

Im Restaurant

Resᵘtoran de

🖋 *Europäisch essen kann man in den großen Hotels oder in internationalen Restaurants.*

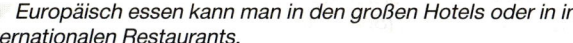

Reservieren Sie uns bitte für heute abend einen Tisch für 4 Personen.	Kon·ja jonmē de seki o jojaku schitai no desᵘ ga.
Ist dieser Tisch/Platz noch frei?	Kono tēbulu/seki wa aite imasᵘ ka?
Einen Tisch für 2/4 Personen, bitte.	Hutali/jonin jō no tēbulu o onegai schimasᵘ.
Wo sind bitte die Toiletten?	Toile wa doko desᵘ ka?
● Bitte hier entlang.	Kotchila e dozo.

レストラン	resutoran	Restaurant
食堂	shokudou	Restaurant
料亭	ryootei	Restaurant im jap. Stil
そば屋	sobaya	jap. Nudelrestaurant
喫茶店	kissaten	Café
トイレ	toire	
洗面所	senmenjo	
便所	benjo	} Toilette
化粧室	keshoushitsu	

Bestellung ▶ auch Kap. 4

Tchūmon

Herr Ober!/Fräulein!	Sumimasen!
Die Speisekarte, bitte.	Menjū o onegaischimasᵘ.

> „Herr Ober" oder „Fräulein" ist nicht üblich, vielmehr sagt man **sumimasen** („Verzeihung!", „Entschuldigung!"), wenn man etwas möchte.

Was kann ich Ihnen bringen?	Nani o omotchi itaschimaschō ka?
Was können Sie mir empfehlen?	Osᵘsᵘme-hin wa nan desᵘ ka?
Bitte kommen Sie mit, ich zeige Ihnen, was wir essen möchten.	Nani o tabetai ka, omiseschitai node isscho ni kitekudasai.
Haben Sie auch Gerichte für Kinder?	Kodomo jō no menjū ga alimasᵘ ka?
Ich nehme …	… o onegai schimasᵘ.
Ich nehme als Vorspeise/Nachtisch/Hauptgericht …	Zensai/Dezāto/me·in ni … o onegaischimasᵘ.
Ich nehme keine Vorspeise, danke.	Zensai wa kekko desᵘ.
● Wir haben leider kein/e … (mehr).	Sᵘmimasen … wa (mō) alimasen.
● Dieses Gericht servieren wir nur auf Vorbestellung.	Kono o-ljōli wa go-jojaku nomi de uketamawatte olimasᵘ.
Könnte ich statt … … … haben?	… no kawali ni … o onegai dekimasᵘ ka?
Ich vertrage kein/e … Könnten Sie das Gericht ohne … zubereiten?	… ga sukidewanai node, … naschi de ljōli schite itadakemasᵘ ka?
● Wie möchten Sie Ihr Steak haben?	Dono-jōni sutēki o ojaki itaschimaschō ka?
gut durch	uelu-dan

halbdurch	midiamu
englisch	rō

● Was wollen Sie trinken?   O-nomimono wa nani ni itaschi-maschō ka?

Bitte ein Glas …   … o ippai onegaischimas^u.

Bitte eine Flasche …   … o ippon onegaischimas^u.

Mit Eis, bitte.   kōli mo onegaischimas^u.

Bitte bringen Sie noch einen Teller/ein Glas.   Mō hitosala/kopp^u o mō hitotsu onegai schimas^u.

Bitte bringen Sie Messer und Gabel.   Naifu to fōku o onegai schimas^u.

Bitte bringen Sie noch Stäbchen.   O-haschi o onegai shimas^u.

● Haben Sie noch einen Wunsch?   Nani-ka hoka ni go-tchūmon ga gozai mas^u ka?

Bitte bringen Sie uns …   … o mottekite kudasaimas^u ka?

Könnten wir noch etwas Brot/Wasser/Reis bekommen?   Pan/O-mizu/Gohan no okawali ga dekimas^u ka?

Beanstandungen

Kudjō

Wahrscheinlich werden Sie keine Gelegenheit haben, irgend etwas zu beanstanden, da Sie in Japan äußerst zuvorkommend behandelt werden. Dies auch dann, wenn Sie sich aus Unwissenheit oder Mißgeschick falsch benehmen.

Meine Bestellung ist immer noch nicht gekommen.   Wataschi no tchūmonschita mono ga mada kite imasen.

Das habe ich nicht bestellt.   Kole wa tchūmon schite imasen.

Das Essen ist kalt/versalzen.   Kono ljōli wa tsumetai/schiokalai des^u.

Das Fleisch ist zäh.   Kono niku wa katai des^u.

Der Fisch ist nicht frisch.	Kono sakana wa schinsen dewa alimasen.
Holen Sie bitte den Chef.	Schihai-nin o jonde kudasai.

Die Rechnung

Kandjō

Rechnung: In japanischen Restaurants bekommt man mit jedem Gericht einen Koupon oder eine verdeckte Rechnung auf den Tisch. Bezahlt wird an der Kasse. Trinkgeld ist in Japan nicht üblich.

Bezahlen, bitte.	O-kandjō o onegai schimasu.
Bitte alles zusammen.	Zenbu isscho ni onegai schimasu.
Getrennte Rechnungen, bitte.	Betsubetsu ni onegai schimasu.
Ist alles inklusive?	Zenbu komi desu ka?
Entschuldigung, bitte. Rechnen Sie noch einmal nach. Da stimmt etwas nicht.	Sumimasen ga, mō itchi-do kēsan schinaoschite kudasai. Tchotto matchigatte ilumitai desu.
Geben Sie mir bitte eine Quittung.	Ljōschū-scho o onegai schimasu.

Einladung zum Essen/Essen in Gesellschaft

Schokudji e no schōtai

*Tischsitten: Ist das erste Gericht auf dem Tisch, kann man zu essen beginnen, indem man **ita dakimasu** sagt – unabhängig davon, ob ihr Tischnachbar auch ißt.*
Schlürfen beim Essen läßt in Japan nicht auf schlechte Kinderstube schließen, sondern ist ganz normal. Sie dürfen jedoch nicht Ihre Nase schnäuzen.
*Nach dem Essen verneigen Sie sich leicht und sagen **gochiso sama deshita,** dem Sinn nach „vielen Dank für das Essen".*

Darf ich Sie zum Essen einladen?	Schokudji ni go-schōtai schitai no desᵘ ga.
Auf Ihr Wohl!	Kanpai!

Trinksitten: *So mancher Abend endet bier- oder sakeselig, häufig auch mit Singen. Gläser werden stets nachgefüllt, auch wenn sie noch nicht leer sind. Man verliert leicht den Überblick über die schon genossene Menge ... Ihr Nachbar nimmt die Flasche, um Ihnen nachzuschenken; sich selbst gießt er nicht nach, das wäre sehr unhöflich. Es ist Ihre Aufgabe! Wenn Sie aufbrechen, können Sie ohne Bedenken ein volles Glas stehen lassen. Das ist eher höflich als unhöflich, da Sie damit den Gastgebern das Gefühl geben, daß die angebotene Menge auf jeden Fall ausreichend war.*

Schmeckt es Ihnen?	O-adji no ikagadesᵘ ka?
Ja, es schmeckt ausgezeichnet.	Hai, totemo oischī desᵘ.
Bitte nehmen Sie noch etwas.	Dōzo motto otoli kudasai.
Ja, gerne.	Alligatō, itadakimasᵘ.
Nein, danke.	īe, kekkō desᵘ.
Wie heißt dieses Gericht?	Kono ljōli wa nan-to īmasᵘ ka?
Können Sie mit Stäbchen essen?	O-haschi ga tsukaemasᵘ ka?
Nein, leider noch nicht.	īe, mada tsukaemasen.
Bitte zeigen Sie es mir.	Sole o misete kudasai.
Bitte versuchen Sie dieses Gericht.	Kono o-ljōli o tameschite mite kudasai.
Darf ich rauchen?	Tabako o sutte mo ī desᵘ ka?
Vielen Dank für Ihre Einladung *(zum Essen).*	Gotchisōsama deschita.
Es war ein sehr netter Abend.	Totemo tanoschī jolu deschita.

Wortliste Gastronomie ▶ auch Kap. 8, Wortliste Lebensmittel

Abendessen	jūschoku, jūgohan, bangohan
alkoholfrei	alukōlu nuki
anmachen *(Salat)*	mazeru
Aschenbecher	haizala
Bar	bā
bedienen, sich	djibun de sulu
Beilage	soemono
bestellen *(Essen, Tisch)*	tchūmon sulu
Bestellung	tchūmon
Bier	bĭru
Brot	pan
Butter	batā
Diabetiker/in	tōnjōbjō-kandja
Dressing	doresschingᵘ
durchgebraten	djūbun ni jaketa
entkorken	koruku o nuku
Essig	su
Eßstäbchen	o-haschi
fett	abulakkoi
Fisch	sakana
Fleck	schimi
frisch	schinsenna
Frühstück	tchōschoku, asagohan
Füllung	tsumemono
Gabel	fōku
Gang	kōsᵘ
gar	hi ga tōtta
gebacken	jaketa
gebraten	jaketa
gedämpft	muschita
Gedeck	schokki
gedünstet	muschita
gefüllt	tsumeta
gekocht	ljōlischita
geräuchert	kunsē no
Gericht	ljōli
geröstet	itta, itameta
Geschmack	adji
geschmort	toketa
Getränk	nomimono
Gewürz	tchōmiljō

Glas	gulasᵘ
Wasser~	koppu
Wein~	wain-gulasᵘ
Gräte	sakana no hone
Gurke	kjūli
hart	katai
Hauptspeise	me·in-disschu
hausgemacht	hōmumēdo no
heiß	atsui
hungrig sein	onaka no suita
Kalbfleisch	kouschi no niku
kalt	tsumetai
Kartoffeln	djagaimo
Kellner/in	uētā/uētoresᵘ
Ketchup	ketchappᵘ
Kinderteller	okosama jo menjū
Knoblauch	nin·niku
Knochen	hone
Koch/Köchin	kokku, ljōli-nin
kochen	ljōli o sulu
Korkenzieher	koruku-sen·nuki
Kräuter	hābu, jakumi, kōschinljō
Kümmel	kumin
Löffel	sᵘpūn
Tee~	tǐ-sᵘpūn
Lorbeer	gekkēdju
mager	abula no sukunai, tēschibōno
Mayonnaise	majonēzu
Menü	menjū
Messer	naifu
Mittagessen	tchūschoku, hilugohan
Muskatnuß	natsumegu
Nachtisch	dezāto
Nelken	tchōdji
Nudeln	men
Ober	uēta
Öl	abula, oilu
Paprika(pulver)	pǐman
Petersilie	paseli
Pfeffer	koschō
Pilze	kinoko
Portion *(eine)*	itchinin-mae
probieren	tamesᵘ

Reis	*(gekochter ~)* gohan
Reisschale	gohan-djawan
Rindfleisch	gjūniku
roh	nama no
Rost	gurilu
saftig	mizuke no ōi
Salat	salada
Salz	schio
sauer	suppai
scharf	kalai
Scheibe	sulaisu
Schonkost	daietto-schoku
Schüssel	hatchi, bōlu
Schweinefleisch	butaniku
Senf	kalaschi
Serviette	napᵘkin
Soße	sōsu
Speise	ljōli
~karte	menjū
Spezialität	mēbutsu
Strohhalm	sutolō
Suppe	sūpᵘ
Suppenteller	sūpᵘ-zala
süß	amai
Tagesgericht/-menü	higawali-menjū
Tasse	kappᵘ
Unter~	uke-zala
Teekanne	kjūsᵘ, tī-potto
Teller	sala
Trinkgeld	tchippᵘ
trocken *(Wein)*	kalakutchi no
überbacken	tenpi de jaku
vegetarisch	saischoku-schugi no
Vorspeise	zensai
Wasser	mizu
weich	jawalakai
Wein	wain
würzen	adji o tsukelu
zäh	katai
Zahnstocher	tsumajōdji
zart	jawalakai
Zitrone	lemon
Zucker	satō
Zwiebel	tamanegi

Typisch japanische Gerichte

Ein japanisches Essen besteht aus:
einer Schale Reis, einer Schüssel Miso-Shiru-Suppe (auf der
Grundlage von Sojabohnen und eiweißreichen Zutaten zubereitet),
Pickels (in Salz eingelegte Rettiche oder anderes), eine oder meh-
rere Sorten Gemüse, eine meist kleine Portion Fisch oder Fleisch,
eine Schale grünen Tee.
Getrunken wird meist Bier oder Sake (Reiswein), der sowohl kalt
als auch warm genossen wird. Wein aus Trauben ist in Japan selten. Der Weinbau hat noch keine Tradition.

Sashimi	Verschiedene Sorten von rohem Fisch
(O)Sushi	Roher oder gekochter Fisch mit Gemüsen in oder auf Reis
Tempura	In Teig gehüllte frittierte Fisch- und Gemüse-stückchen
Sukiyaki	Gemüse, Fleisch, Glasnudeln in einer Mischung aus Sojasoße, Zucker, Wasser und Reiswein gedünstet. Es wird am Tisch zubereitet.
Donburi	Einfaches Tellergericht aus Reis mit verschiede-nen Beilagen. Z.B. Hühnchen, Ei, Fleisch etc.
Okono-miyaki	„Japanische Pizza" Eine Art Omlett, das sich die Gäste bei Tisch selbst zubereiten. Gemüse und Fleisch, Schrimps und Tintenfisch werden vor dem Bak-ken in den Teig eingerührt.
Shabu-shabu	In dünne Scheiben geschnittenes Rindfleisch und Gemüse, das am Tisch kurz in einem Topf mit kochendem Wasser zubereitet wird.
Ramen	Chinesische Nudeln in Suppe
Soba	Dünne Weizennudeln
Yakisoba	Gebratene Nudeln mit Sojasoße, Gemüse und Fleisch
Udon	Dicke Weizennudeln
Onigiri	Reisröllchen mit Seetang umwickelt
Tofu	„Bohnenquark" – die älteste japanische Kü-chenspezialität

Fisch und Schalentiere

Aal	unagi	Lachs	sake
Auster	kaki	Makrele	saba
Dorsch	tala	Muschel	kai
Forelle	masᵘ	Rogen	ikula
Hering	nischin	Thunfisch	magulo
Karpfen	koi	Tintenfisch	ika
Krabbe	ebi	Wal	kudjila

Gemüse

Auberginen	nasᵘ	Meerrettich	wasabi
Bambussprosse	takenoko	Paprika	pīman
Chinakohl	hakusai	Pilz allgemein	kinoko
Erbsen	mame, gurinpisᵘ	Schwarzwurzel	gobō
		Seetang	nori
Gurke	kjūli	Sellerie	selori
Honigmelone	melon	Sojabohnen	daizu
Ingwer	schōga	Sojabohnenkeime	mojaschi
Karotten	nindjin	Spargel	asᵘparagasᵘ
Kartoffeln	djagaimo	Spinat	hōlensō
Kopfsalat	letasᵘ	Süßkartoffeln	satsumaimo
Lauch	negi	Wassermelone	suika
Lotus	hasᵘ	Weißkraut	kjabetsᵘ

Obst

Ananas	painappulu	Kaki-Frucht	kaki
Apfel	lingo	Kirsche	sakulanbo
Aprikose	anzu	Mandarine	mikan
Banane	banana	Orange	orendji
Birne	jō-naschi	Pampelmuse	gurēpᵘ furūtsu
Erdbeere	itchigo	Pfirsich	momo
Eßkastanie	kuli	Trauben	budō
Feige	itchidjiku	Zitrone	lemon

Alkoholfreie Getränke

Coca-Cola	koka-kōla	Limonade	lemonēdo
Eiskaffee	aisᵘ-kōfī	Milch	gjūnjū, miluku
Eistee	aisᵘ-tī	Mineralwasser	mineralu-sᵘi
Grapefruitsaft	gurēpu furūtsu-djūsᵘ	Orangensaft	orendji-djūsᵘ
grüner Tee	ljokutcha	Wasser	mizu

Alkoholische Getränke

Bier	bīru
Sake (Reiswein)	sake
Schnaps	schōtchū
Shochu (eine Art Schnaps)	schōtchū
Umeshu (Pflaumen, Zucker und Shochu)	umeschu
Wein (rot, weiß)	wain (aka, schiro)
Whisky	uisᵘkī

6 Kultur und Natur
文化と自然

Auf dem Verkehrsbüro

Lyokō-an·naischo de

Ich möchte einen Stadtplan haben.	Tchizu o itadakitai no desᵁ ga.
Haben Sie Prospekte von dieser Gegend?	Kono atali no panfuletto ga alimasᵁ ka?
Haben Sie einen Veranstaltungskalender für diese Woche?	Konschū no mojōschimono no puroguramu ga alimasᵁ ka?
Gibt es Stadtrundfahrten?	Schinai-kankō-basᵁ ga alimasᵁ ka?
Was kostet die Rundfahrt?	Schinai-kankō wa ikula desᵁ ka?
Wann und wo fährt der Bus ab?	Basᵁ wa nan-dji ni, doko-kala demasᵁ ka?
Wären Sie so freundlich und würden Sie für mich dort anrufen?	Sumimasen ga, wataschi no tame ni soko e denwa o kakete kudasai masen ka?

*Das Tourist Information Center bietet ein Fremdenführerprogramm "**Good-will**" Guide mit freiwilligen Fremdenführern an. Diese Personen, meist Studenten, führen Sie durch die Stadt und beantworten Ihre Fragen. Das Programm wird in Tokyo, Yokohma, Osaka, Kobe, Kyoto, Nara, Sapporo, Kagoshima, Nagoya, Hiroshima, Fukuoka, Beppu durchgeführt.*

Sehenswürdigkeiten/Museen

Midokolo/Hakubutsu-kan

Welche Sehenswürdigkeiten gibt es hier?	Koko ni wa don·na midokolo ga alimasᵁ ka?
Bitte fahren Sie mich zu den wichtigsten Sehenswürdigkeiten der Stadt.	Matchi no omona mēschō e tsulete itte kudasai.
Wieviel kostet das?	O-ikula desᵁ ka?

Wir möchten …	Wataschitatchi wa …
die Ausstellung	tenlankai
das Museum	hakubutsu-kan, bidjutsu-kan
das Schloß	o-schilo
den Tempel/Schrein	o-tela/djindja
besichtigen	o kenbutsu schitai no des^u ga.

Einer der zahlreichen Tempel Kyotos

Der **Schintoismus** ist Japans einheimische und ursprüngliche Religion, über deren Ursprung und Begründer nichts Genaues bekannt ist. Sicher ist, daß es diese Religion schon vor dem 6. Jahrhundert gab. Bis zum heutigen Tag zeichnet sich der Schintoismus durch Naturverehrung (z. B. heilige Bäume), Respekt und Verehrung der Vorfahren aus. Es gibt zwei sehr berühmte Schreine, von denen es heißt, daß sie im Zeitalter der Götter errichtet wurden: der Ise-Schrein in Ise und der Izumo-Taischa-Schrein in der Nähe von Matsue.

Im 6. Jahrhundert kam über Korea und China der **Buddhismus** ins Land. In dieser Zeit erhielt Japan erstmals eine verfassungsmäßige Regierung durch Prinz-Regent Shotoku, einem begeisterten Anhänger der buddhistischen Lehre. Zahlreiche Tempel stammen aus dieser Zeit. Der berühmteste ist der Horyuji-Tempel, von dem gesagt wird, er sei die älteste Holzkonstruktion der Welt.

Die berühmten drei Affen in der Tempelanlage von Nikko

Wann ist … geöffnet?	… wa itsu akimasᵘ ka?
Eintritt frei!	Njūdjō-muljō!
Wann beginnt die Führung?	Setsumē wa itsu hadjimalimasᵘ ka?
Gibt es auch eine Führung in Deutsch?	Doitsu-go no setsumē mo alimasᵘ ka?
Darf man hier fotografieren?	Koko de schaschin o tottemo ī desᵘ ka?
Was für ein Platz/ein Tempel ist hier?	Koko wa don·na bascho/o-tela desᵘ ka?
Ist das …?	Kole wa … desᵘ ka?
Wann wurde dieses Gebäude erbaut?	Kono tatemono wa itsu tatelalema-schita ka?
Aus welcher Epoche stammt dieses Bauwerk?	Kono kentchiku-butsu wa dono djidai no mono desᵘ ka?
Wer hat dieses Bild gemalt?	Kono e wa dale ga kaita mono desᵘ ka?
Gibt es einen Katalog zur Ausstellung?	Tendjikai no katalogu ga alimasᵘ ka?
Haben Sie das Bild als Poster/Postkarte/Dia?	Kono e no posᵘtā/ehagaki/sᵘlaido ga alimasᵘ ka?

Wortliste Sehenswürdigkeiten/Museen

Altstadt	kjū-schigai
Amphitheater	enkē-gekidjō
antik	kodai no, antchĭku no
Antike	kodai-bunka, antchĭku
Aquarell	suisai-ga
Archäologie	kōko-gaku
Architekt	kentchiku-ka
Architektur	kentchiku
Atombombenmuseum	genbaku-hakubutsukan

*Denkmal für die Atom-
bombenopfer in Hiroshima*

Ausgrabungen	hakkutsu
Ausstellung	tendji-kai, tenlan-kai
Bauwerk	kentchiku-butsu
Besichtigung	kengaku
Bibliothek	toschokan
Bild	e, schaschin
~hauer	tchōkoku-ka
Brauchtum	hūschū
Brücke	haschi

Brunnen	ido, hunsui
Buddha	schaka, hotoke-sama
Buddhastatue	butsuzō
Buddhist	bukkjō-to
Burg	schilo
Bürgermeister/in	schitchō
Büste	mune
Christ	kirisᵘto
Christentum	kirisᵘto-kjō
Collage	kolādju
Dach	jane
Decke	tendjō
Denkmal	kinen-hi, kinen-butsu
~schutz	bunkazai-hogo
Design	dezain
Edo- oder Tokugawa-Zeit *(1603-1867)*	edo-djidai, tokugawa-djidai

Edo-Zeit: 1603 verlegt der Militärherrscher Ieyasu Tokugawa seinen Regierrungssitz nach Edo, dem heutigen Tokyo. Es ist eine friedliche Zeit. In der Kunst entstehen Holzschnitte, Stein-, Porzellan- und Lackarbeiten von hoher Qualität. Das Kabuki-Theater, bunt und fröhlich, stammt ebenfalls aus dieser Zeit.

Einfluß	ēkjō
Epoche	djidai
Exponat	tchinletsu-hin
Fassade	fassādo
Fenster	mado
Festung	djōheki
Fotografie	schaschin
Fremdenführer	gaido *(Personal)*; gaido-bukku *(Buch)*
Friedhof	botchi
Führung	an·nai *(Stadt~)*, setsumē
Fürst	kōschaku
Galerie	gjalari̅, galō
Gebäude	tatemono
Geburtsstadt	schussētchi
Gedenkstätte	kinen no matchi
Geistlicher	*(ev.)* bokuschi; *(kath.)* schinpᵘ; *(buddh.)* sō
Gemälde	kaiga
~sammlung	kaiga-schūschū

Geschichte	lekischi
Giebel	kirizuma
Glasmalerei	sutendo-gulasu
Glocke	kane, belu
Glockenspiel	schikake-dokē
Gobelin	gobulan−oli
Goldschmiedekunst	tchōkin-gēdjutsu
Grab	haka
~hügel	kohun
~mal	haka-ischi
~stein	haka-ischi
Graphik	gurafikku
Heian-Zeit *(794–1192)*	Heian-djidai

Heian-Zeit: *Der Regierungssitz wird von Nara nach Kyoto verlegt. Nach chinesischem Vorbild wird die Stadt mit schachbrettartigem Grundriß angelegt. Die Einführung eines neuen japanischen Schriftsystems treibt Blüten in Literatur und Dichtkunst. Das aufgezeichnete Märchen vom Prinzen Genji ist weltweit ein früher Beginn der erzählenden Prosa. Diese Blütezeit endet mit Bürgerkriegen und der Einmündung in den Feudalismus.*

heidnisch	huschin-djinna
Hochkultur	kōdo-bunka
Hof	nakaniwa
Holz|schnitt	kiboli
Illustration	ilasutorēschon
Impressionismus	inschō-ha
Innenstadt	toschin
Jahrhundert	sēki
Kaiser/in	ten·nō, kōtē/kōgō, djotē
Kamakura-Zeit *(1192–1333)*	kamakula-djidai

Kamakura-Zeit: *1192 übernimmt eine Militärregierung in Kamakura die Macht. Er ist die erste Militärregierung einer 700 Jahre währenden Phase von Militärregierungen.*
In dieser Zeit werden die Lehren des Buddhismus formuliert. Die 4 Hauptsekten waren Jodo-Shinshu, Shingon, Zen und Nichiren. Heute spielen Jodo und Nichiren noch eine Rolle. Der Zen-Buddhismus war die Religion des Ritterstandes.
Maxime: das Leben ist einfach und hart.

Kapelle	tchapelu
Katholik	katolikku-schindja
Keramik	tōki
Kirche	kjōkai
Klassizismus	koten-schugi
Kloster	schūdō in
König/in	ō/ōhi
Kopie	kopī
Kubismus	littai-ha
Kultstätte	lēhai djo
Kunst	gēdjutsu
~gewerbe	kōgē
Lampion	tchōtchin
Landschaftsmalerei	hūkē-ga
Laterne	gaitō, tsōtchin
Lithographie	sekihanga, litogulafu
Maler/in	gaka
Malerei	kaiga
Markt	itchiba
Marmor	dailiseki
Material	genljō
Mauer	kabe, djōheki
Meiji-Zeit *(1868–1911)*	mēdji-djidai

Meiji-Zeit: 1868 Sitz der kaiserlichen Meiji-Regierung in To-kyo. Es ist das Zeitalter der industriellen Revolution. Diese Pha-se endet mit der Umwandlung Japans in ein demokratisches Land. Japan erhält am 3. Mai 1947 seine Verfassung.

Modell	modelu
modern	modan·na
Mosaik	mozaiku
Muromachi- und Azuchi-Momoyama-Zeit *(1336–1598)*	Mulomatchi-djidai, Azutchi-Momoja-ma-djidai

Muromachi- und Azuchi-Momoyama-Zeit: Die neue Mili-tärregierung hat ihren Sitz in Muromachi, Kyoto. Vom Reichtum der Militärherrscher zeugen heute noch der goldene und silber-ne Pavillion, deren damalige Villen. In der Zen-Kunst stammt der Steingarten des Ryoanji-Tempels aus dieser Zeit. Obwohl die Azu-chi-Momoyama-Zeit ein Jahrhundert Bürgerkrieg bedeutet, blüht das künstlerisch-kreative Leben. Noh-Theater, Teezeremonie, Ike-bana und Gartenarchitektur stammen aus dieser Zeit.

Zen-Garten des Ryoanji-Tempels, Kyoto

Museum   hakubutsu-kan, bidjitsu-kan
Nara-Zeit *(710–784)*   Nala-djidai

***Nara-Zeit**: Der Regierungssitz des Kaisers ist in Nara. Es ist die Blütezeit des Buddhismus, aus der viele Tempel und durch den Buddhismus beeinflußte Kunstgegenstände stammen. Die größte Buddha-Statue Japans, die Sie im Todaiji-Tempel in Nara sehen können, ist in dieser Zeit entstanden.*

Oper	opera
Original	oridjinalu, genbutsu, gensaku
Pagode	pagoda
Palast	kjūden
Pavillon	pabilion
Pilger	djunlē-scha
~fahrt	djunlē no tabi
Plakat	posᵘtā
Platz	bascho, seki, hiloba
Porzellan	tōki
Protestant	pᵘrotesᵘtanto, schinkjō-to
Rathaus	schijakuscho
Realismus	gendjitsu-schugi
rekonstruieren	hukugen sulu
Religion	schūkjō
Restaurierung	schūhuku
Ruine	haikjo
Rundfahrt	schūjū, kankō, jūlan
Schintoismus	schintō
Schloß	schilo
Schnitzerei	tchōkoku
Shoowa-Zeit	schōwa-djidai
(1926–heute)	

Geburt des modernen Japan: *Im Jahre 1853 landet Commodore Perry von der amerikanischen Marine mit seiner Flotte in der Nähe von Tokyo. Er zwingt Japan, mit den USA Handel zu treiben. Die Edo-Zeit (s. S. 110) endet mit diesem erzwungenen Zusammentreffen der östlichen und westlichen Kultur.*

Schrein	djindja
Schule	gakkō
Sehenswürdigkeiten	midokolo, mēscho
Skulptur	tchōkoku
Stadtrundfahrt	schinai-kankō
Statue	litsuzō, tchōzō
Steinlaterne	tōlō
Stil	jōschiki
Strohseil (beim Schrein)	nawa
Studienreise	kenschū-ljokō
Surrealismus	tchō-gendjitsu-schugi
Symbolismus	schōtchō-schugi
Taishoo-Zeit *(1912–1925)*	taischō-djidai

Die Teezeremonie – eine in Japan sehr beliebte Kulthandlung.
In Schulen werden die Arten des Zelebrierens gelehrt.

Teezeremonie	sadō
Tempel	o-tela
Theater	geki, geki-djō, schibai
Töpferei	tōgē
Tor	mon
Turm	tō, jagula
Tusche	sumi
Überreste	iseki
Vase	kabin
Wandmalerei	heki-ga
Werk	sakuhin
wiederaufbauen	saiken sulu
Zeichnung	sᵘkettchi
Zen-Buddhismus	zen-shū

Ausflüge

Ensoku

Kann man von hier aus … sehen?	Koko kala … ga miemasᵘ ka?
In welcher Richtung liegt …?	Dono hōkō ni … ga alimasᵘ ka?

Was besichtigen wir alles?	Koko de nani o kenbutsu sulu no des^u ka?
Besichtigen wir auch …?	… mo kengaku schimas^u ka?
Wo ist der Tempel/ Schrein?	O-tela/Djindja wa doko ni alimas^u ka?
Wieviel freie Zeit haben wir in …?	… de wa dono gulai djijū-djikan ga alimas^u ka?
Wann fahren wir zurück?	Itsu modotte kimas^u ka?
Wann kommen wir zurück?	Itsu modotte kimas^u ka?

Wortliste Ausflüge

Ausflug	ensoku, kōlaku
Aussichtspunkt	tenbō-dai
Bauernhof	nōka

Typischer Bauernhof auf Honshu. Hier leben und arbeiten japanische Reisbauern seit Generationen.

Bergdorf	sanson
Botanischer Garten	schokubutsu-en
Einkaufsstraße	schoppingu-gai

Fischerhafen	gjokō
Freizeitpark	jüentchi
Gebirge	sanmjaku
Geschäftsviertel	schōten-gai
Höhle	dōkutsu
Insel	schima
Inselrundfahrt	schima-meguli
Japanischer Garten	nihon-tēen

*Das Wachsen und Gedei-
hen der Bäume wird nicht
dem Zufall überlassen.*

Kirschblüte	sakula no hana
Landschaft	hūkē
malerisch	kaiga tekina
Markt	itchiba
Naturschutzgebiet	schizen-hogo-tchĭki
Park	kōen
Paß	komitchi
Pavillon	pabilion, kjūkē-djo
Platz	bascho, hiloba, seki
Quelle, heiße	onsen
Rundblick	panorȧma
Schlucht	kēkoku
See	mizūmi
Tagesausflug	higaeli-ljokō

Tal	tani
Thermalquelle	onsen
Umgebung	schūi, schūhen
Vogelschutzgebiet	tchōlui-hogo-tchĭki
Vorort	kōgai, kinkō
Vulkan	kazan
Wald	moli
~brand	jama-kadji
Wasserfall	taki
Zoo	dōbutsu-en

Veranstaltungen/Unterhaltung

Mojōschimono/Golaku

Theater/Konzert/Kino	Schibai/Konsāto/Ēga
Welches Stück wird heute abend im Theater gespielt?	Kon ja don·na o-schibai ga djōen salemasᵘ ka?
Was läuft morgen abend im Kino?	Aschita no ban ēga-kan de nani ga djōē salemasᵘ ka?
Können Sie mir ein gutes Theaterstück/einen guten Film empfehlen?	Nanika ĭ o-schibai/ēga o oschiete kudasaimasen ka?
Wann beginnt die Vorstellung?	Nandji ni mojōschimono ga hadjimalimasᵘ ka?
Wo bekommt man Karten?	Tchiketto wa doko de kaemasᵘ ka?

切符売場	kippu-uriba	Kasse
プレイガイド	pureigaido	Vorverkaufskasse
売り切れ	urikire	ausverkauft
映画館	eiga-kan	Kino
非常口	hijouguchi	Notausgang
禁煙	kinen	Rauchverbot

Bitte zwei Karten für heute abend.	Konban no tchiketto o ni-mai onegai schimasᵘ.
Bitte zwei Plätze zu … Yen.	… en no seki o ni-mai kudasai.
Zwei Erwachsene, ein Kind.	Otona ni-mai ni, kodomo itch-mai.
Diese Vorstellung ist ausverkauft.	Kono mojōschimono wa ulikile maschita.
Kann ich bitte ein Programm haben?	Puroguramu o molaemasen ka?
Wann ist die Vorstellung zu Ende?	Mojōschimono wa nandji ni owali masᵘ ka?
Wo ist die Garderobe?	Kulōku wa doko desᵘ ka?

Wortliste Theater/Konzert/Kino

Akt	maku
Aufführung	djōen *(Theater)*, djōē *(Film)*, ensō *(Musik)*
Ballett	balē
Begleitung	dōhan
Bühne	butai
Bunraku	bunlaku
Chor	gasschōdan, kōrasᵘ
Dirigent	schiki-scha
Drama	dorama
Eintrittskarte	njūdjō-ken
Festival	fesᵘtibalu, gēdjutsu-sai
Festspiele	fesᵘtibalu, kinenkōen
Film	ēga
~schauspieler/in	ēga-haijū *(m)*/ēga-djōjū *(f)*
Garderobe	kulōku
Inszenierung	enschutsu
Kabarett	jose
Kabuki	kabuki
Kino	ēga-kan
Komödie	komedī, kigeki
Komponist/in	sakkjoku-ka

Traditionelle japanische Musikinstrumente

Shamisen: *Dreisaitiges, einer Balalaika vergleichbares Musikinstrument. Der Klang dieses Instruments ist „typisch japanisch".*

Koto: *Ein 13saitiges Musikinstrument, das gezupft wird. Vor allem Frauen spielten und spielen dieses Instrument zur Unterhaltung – heute meist für Solostücke.*

Shakuhachi: *Eine vertikal gespielte Bambusflöte. Der Sinn des Spielens lag weniger in der Musik als solcher, sondern sollte viel mehr der Sammlung des Geistes dienen, um von der flüchtigen Gegenwart einen Blick in nicht diesseitige Mysterien zu werfen. Der Ton erinnert an Wind und Bambus.*

Taiko: *Japanische Trommel. Japaner lieben Feste – und Trommeln gehören dazu. Die Trommler haben die Rhythmen als Silben im Kopf, z. B.: ten-te-ka, ten-te-ka to-to ten-ten. Auch wenn Sie nur kurz in Japan sind, werden Sie sicher die Gelegenheit haben, diese Trommler in einem Schrein oder auf der Straße zu hören.*

Konzert	konsāto, ongaku-kai
Jazz~	djazu ~
Kammer~	schitsunai ~
Kirchen~	kjōkai ~
Pop~	popp^u ~
Sinfonie~	sinfonī ~
Koto	koto
Loge	bokkusu, schikili-seki
Musical	mjūdjikalu
Nachmittagsvorstellung	gogo no mojōschimono
Oper	opera
Operette	operetta
Opernglas	opera-gulas^u
Orchester	ōkes^{u}tora, kōkjōgaku-dan
Originalfassung	genpon, oridjinalu-tekis^{u}to
Pause	kjūkē
Premiere	schoen
Programm	p^{u}roguramu
Rang	kaidjō-seki
erster ~	nikai no seki
zweiter ~	sangai no seki
Regie	enschutsu
Regisseur/in	enschutsu-ka
Rolle	jaku
Haupt~	schu-jaku

Noh: Das Noh-Theater ist mit seiner 700jährigen Tradition das älteste. Ursprünglich war es ein lyrisches Drama, das bei schintoistischen Festen zwischen religiösen Handlungen dargeboten wurde. Die Bühne gleicht auch heute einem schintoistischen Schrein. Der Text wird rhythmisch zu klassischer japanischer Musik vorgetragen. Anstatt Schminke tragen die Schauspieler Masken, die bestimmte Charaktere symbolisieren. Die Kostüme entsprechen der Kleidung des 15. Jahrhunderts.

Kabuki: Vielleicht weil es fröhlicher ist, ist das Kabuki-Theater populärer als das Noh. Es ist eine Verbindung von rhythmisch vorgetragenen Versen und Tänzen zu Shamisen-Musik. Kostüme und Bühnenbild sind farbenfroh. Erstaunlich für uns: die hübschen Frauen sind Männer. Im Kabuki werden alle Frauenrollen von männlichen Schauspielern gespielt. Die großen Kabuki-Bühnen legen ihren Programmheften eine englischsprachige Kurzdarstellung der Stücke bei.

Bunraku: Das Bunraku-Theater ist ein Puppentheater. Die wichtigen Puppen werden von 3 Personen manipuliert, was erstaunliche, fast lebendig wirkende Bewegungen hervorbringt. Inhaltlich werden romantische Balladen zu Shamisen-Musik vorgetragen.

Sänger/in	kaschu, sēgaku-ka
Schamisen	schamisen
Schakuhachi	schakuhatchi
Schauspiel	schibai, geki
Schauspieler/in	haijū *(m)*, djojū *(f)*

Solist/in	solisᵘto
Spielplan	djōen-pᵘroguramu
Tänzer/in	dansā
Theaterstück	schibai, gikjoku
Tragödie	higeki
Untertitel	sabu-taitolu, djimaku
Veranstaltungskalender	mojōschimono-pᵘroguramu
Vorstellung	djōen, djōē, ensō, mojōschimono
Vorverkauf	maeuli
Zirkus	sākasᵘ

Bar/Diskothek/Nachtclub

Bā/Disᵘko/Naito-kulabu

Was kann man hier abends unternehmen?	Jolu koko de nani ga dekimasᵘ ka?
Gibt es hier eine gemütliche Kneipe?	Koko ni ī nomija ga alimasᵘ ka?
Gibt es hier eine Diskothek/ein Tanzcafe?	Kono tchikaku ni disᵘko ga alimasᵘ ka?
Wollen wir tanzen gehen?	Dansᵘ ni ikimaschō ka?
Wollen wir (noch einmal) tanzen?	(Mō itchido) odolimaschō ka?
Wollen wir noch einen Bummel machen?	Sᵘkoschi alukimaschō ka?

Wortliste Bar/Diskothek/Nachtclub

ausgehen	soto e iku
Band	bando
Bar	bā
Discjockey	disukudjokkī
Diskothek	disᵘko
Live-Musik	laibu-mjūsikku
Nachtclub	naito-kulabu
Show	schō
Spielhalle	gēmu-sentā
tanzen	odolu
Tanzmusik	dansᵘ-mjūsikku

7 **Am Strand/Sport**
海岸で / スポーツ

Im Schwimmbad/Am Strand

Pūlu de/Kaigan de

Gibt es hier ein Freibad/Hallenbad/eine Sauna?	Koko ni jagai-pūlu/schitsunai-pūlu/sauna ga alimasᵘ ka?
Hineinspringen verboten!	Tobikomi-kinschi!
● Baden verboten!	Suiē kinschi! 水泳禁止
Gibt es hier einen Badestrand?	Kono atali ni kaisui-jokudjō ga alimasᵘ ka?
Ist der Strand sandig/steinig?	Kaigan wa sunahama/Ischi ga ōi desᵘ ka?
Gibt es hier Quallen?	Koko ni kulage ga imasᵘ ka?
Wie weit darf man hinausschwimmen?	Doko made ojoidemo daidjōbu desᵘ ka?
Ist die Strömung stark?	Nagale ga hajaidesᵘ ka?
Ist es für Kinder gefährlich?	Koko wa kodomo ni wa kiken desᵘ ka?
Wann ist Ebbe/Flut?	Mitchischio/Hikischio wa itsu desᵘ ka?
Ich möchte ein Boot mieten.	Bōto o kalitai no desᵘ ga.
Was kostet es pro Stunde/Tag?	Itchi-djikan/Itchi-nitchi o-ikula desᵘ ka?

*Das Baden in den **heißen Quellen** (Onsen) ist bei Japanern sehr populär und beliebt. Die ca. 13 000 Quellen finden sich überall in Japan. Dank der den heißen Quellen zugesprochenen Heilkraft sind die Badeorte ein beliebtes Erholungsziel und haben auch als Kurbäder Bedeutung. Als bekanntester Badeort gilt Beppu auf Japans südlichster Halbinsel Kyushu.*

Sport

Supōtsu

Welche Sportveranstaltungen gibt es hier?	Koko de don·na supōtsu-kjōgi ga alimasu ka?
Welche Sportmöglichkeiten gibt es hier?	Koko de don·na supōtsu ga dekimasu ka?
Gibt es hier einen Golfplatz/einen Tennisplatz?	Koko ni golufu-djō/tenisu-djō ga alimasu ka?

*Das , was bei uns der Fußball ist, ist in Japan **Baseball**: ein Nationalgeschehen. Der moderne, gut betuchte Japaner spielt **Golf,** auch wenn es sich aus Platzmangel nur in einem Riesenkäfig an einer Stadtautobahn und ganz ohne grünen Rasen abspielt. Japaner lieben den Sport, sie haben ihm sogar einen Tag gewidmet, den 10. Oktober.*

*Neben allen westlichen werden auch die traditionellen Sportarten wie **Judo, Yoga, Karate, Aikido** sehr gepflegt.*
***Kendo**, Stockfechten, ist ein Pflichtfach an vielen Schulen. Diese Kampfsportart stammt aus Japans Samuraizeit. Heute wird eine weniger kämpferische als vielmehr sportliche Form betrieben. Kendo wird mit Bambusschwertern ausgefochten; die Kämpfer tragen Schutzkleidung.*

Wo kann man hier angeln?	Doko de tsuli ga dekimasᵘ ka?
Ich möchte mir den Sumokampf/das Baseballspiel ansehen.	Sumō/jakjū ga mitai no desᵘ ga.
Wann/Wo findet es statt?	Itsu/Doko de milalemasᵘ ka?
Was kostet der Eintritt?	Njūdjō-ken wa o-ikula desᵘ ka?
Gibt es in den Bergen gute Skipisten?	Ῐ sᵘkῑ-djō ga alimasᵘ ka?
Ich möchte eine Bergtour machen.	Tozan o schitai no desᵘ ga.
Können Sie mir eine interessante Route empfehlen?	Omoschiloi rūto o oschiete kudasaimasen ka?
Wo kann ich … ausleihen?	Doko de … ga kalilalemasᵘ ka?
Welchen Sport treiben Sie?	Don·na supōtsu o schimasᵘ ka?
Ich spiele …	… o schimasᵘ.
Ich bin ein Fan von …	Watschi wa … no fan desᵘ.

Wortliste Strand/Sport

Aerobic	earobikku
Anfänger/in	schoschin-scha
Angel	tsuli
angeln	tsuli o sulu
Bad	hulo, suijoku
Bade|ort	*(heiße Quelle)* onsen-tchi; *(See)* kai-suijoku-djō
~tuch	taolu, basu-taolu
Badminton	badominton
~schläger	raketto
Ball	bōlu
Baseball	jakjū
Basketball	basᵘ ketto-bōlu

Bergsteigen	tozan
Bootsverleih	kaschi-bōto
Bowling	bōlingu
Boxkampf	bokuschingu
Doppel	dabulu
Drachenfliegen	takoage
Düne	sakjū
Dusche	schawā
Eintrittskarte	njūdjō-ljō
Einzel	kobetsu
Eis|bahn	sᵘkēto-rinku
~hockey	aisᵘ-hokkē
~kunstlauf	figjuā-sukēto
~lauf	sukēto
Ergebnis	kekka
Fallschirmspringen	lakkasan
Fortgeschrittener	djōkjū-scha
Freibad	pūlu
Fußball *(Spiel)*	sakkā
~mannschaft	sakkā-tchĩmu
~platz	sakkā-djō
~spiel	sakkā-gēmu
gewinnen	katsu
Golf	golufu
~platz	golufu-djō
~schläger	kulabu
Gymnastik	taisō
Halbzeit	hāfu-taimu
Handball	hando-bōlu
Hochseefischen	enjō-gjogjō
Hockey	hokkē
~schläger	sᵘtikku
Jazztanz	djazudansᵘ
joggen	djogingu o sulu
Jogging	djogingu
Judo	djūdō
Kanu	kanū
Karate	kalate
Kasse	kaikē
kegeln	bōlingu
Kiesel	koischi
Konditionstraining	kondischon-torēningua
Kricket	kurikketto

Kurs	kōsᵘ
Leichtathletik	likudjō
Luftmatraze	eā-matto
Mannschaft	tchĩmu
Meisterschaft	senschuken
Minigolf	mini-golufu
Motor|boot	mōtā-bōto
~sport	mōtā-rēsᵘ
Netz	ami, kailo
Niederlage	haischa
Paddelboot	padolu-bōto
Paraglider	paragulaidā
Pfeilwerfen	jali-nage
Pferd	uma
Pferderennen	kēba
Polo	polo
Programm	pᵘroguramu
radfahren	djitenscha ni nolu
Rad|rennen	kēlin
~sport	djitenscha-kjōgi, saikulingu
Rafting	rafutingu
Regatta	regatta
reiten	djōba
Reitsport	djōba-sᵘpōtsu
Rennen	kjōsō, kēba *(Pferd)*; kēlin *(Rad)*; rēsu *(Auto)*
Ringkampf	resᵘlingu
Rollschuhe	rōlāsukēto
Ruderboot	bōto
rudern	kogu
Rugby	ragubĩ
Rutschbahn	sᵘbelidai
Sand	suna
Sauna	sauna
Schiedsrichter	schinpan
Schlauchboot	kjūmē-bōto
Schlitten	soli
Schlittschuhe	sᵘkēto-gutsᵘ
Schnorchel	sunōkelu
Schwimmbad	pūlu
schwimmen	suiē sulu
Schwimmer/in	suiē-senschu
Schwimm|flossen	fin
~ring	ukiwa

Segelboot	jotto
segeln	sēlingu
Seilbahn	kēbulu-kā
Sessellift	lifuto
Skateboard	sᵘkēto-bōdo
Ski	sᵘkī̄
~ alpin	alupen-sᵘki
~bindung	bindingu
~kurs	sᵘkī̄-gakkō, kōsᵘ
~laufen	sᵘkī̄
~lehrer	sᵘkī̄-schidō-in
~piste	sᵘkī̄-djō
~stöcke	sᵘkī̄-sᵘtokku
Solarium	salarium
Sonnen|brand	hijake
~schirm	higasa
Spiel	gēmu
Sportler/in	sᵘpōtsu-senschu
Sportplatz	undō-djō
Sprungbrett	humikili-dai
Squash	sᵘkosschu
~schläger	raketto
Strandbad	kaisui-joku
Sumo	sumō

*Das **Sumoringen** ist der japanische Nationalsport, der mit keinem unserer Sportarten vergleichbar ist, da das Sumoringen tief mit der japanischen Kultur verbunden ist. Sumo gibt es schon 1000 Jahre. Laut Mythos ein Zeitvertreib, den die Shinto-Götter höchstpersönlich erfunden und den Menschen verordnet haben. Ursprünglich fanden diese Ringkämpfe in Shinto-Schreinen statt, die ersten Turniere organisierten Priester und Obrigkeit gemeinsam. Beim Sumoringkampf spielen Form und Zeremonie wie in den meisten japanischen Künsten eine maßgebliche Rolle. Westliche Beobachter wundern sich manchmal, warum die Show nicht beginnt, aber mit den Füßen aufstampfen, in die Hände klatschen, Salz in den Ring streuen, den Gegner anstarren usw. gehören dazu. Das Ritual dauert vier Minuten, der Kampf selbst eine Minute. Die Sumoringer, die 200 kg und mehr wiegen, sind jedoch nicht nur einfach fett, sondern Athleten. Das Fett erhöht die Stoßkraft. Ziel des Kampfes ist es, den Gegner zu zwingen, den Boden mit irgendeinem Körperteil – außer den Füßen – zu berühren, oder ihn aus dem Ring zu drängen. Erlaubt ist alles außer Boxen, Fußtritten, Haareziehen, Würgen und derlei Grobheiten.*

Surfbrett	sāfin-bōdo
surfen	sāfin
Tagespaß	itchinitchi-ken
Taiko	taiko
Talstation	humoto-eki
tauchen	mogulu
Taucher|anzug	sensui-sūtsu
~ausrüstung	sensui-dōgu
~brille	sensui-megane
Tennis	tenisᵘ
~schläger	raketto
Tischtennis	takkjū
~schläger	raketto
Tor	gōlu
~wart	gōlu-kīpā
Turnen	taisō
Umkleidekabine	kōischitsu
unentschieden	hikiwake
verlieren	makelu
Volleyball	balēbōlu
wandern	haikingu
Wanderweg	haikingu-kōsu
Wasserball	suikjū
Wellenreiten	naminoli, sāfin
Wettkampf	kjōgi, schiai
Wochenpaß	uīkudē-pasᵘ, hēdjitsu-ken
Yoga	joga

8 **Einkaufen/Geschäfte**
買い物 / 店

Fragen/Preise

Schitsumon/Nedan

Öffnungszeiten	Eigjō-djikan
offen/geschlossen	Kaiten/hēten 営業中 / 休業中

Einkaufen ist eine Lieblingsbeschäftigung der Japaner. Die zahlreichen kleinen Geschäfte haben 7 Tage in der Woche rund um die Uhr offen. Die großen Warenhäuser haben abends Ladenschlußzeiten, sonntags haben sie aber geöffnet.

Guten Tag! *(im Laden)*	Ilasschaimase!
Wo kann man … kaufen?	… wa doko de kaemasu ka?
Können Sie mir ein …-Geschäft empfehlen?	… no omise o schōkai schite kudasai masen ka?
• Suchen Sie etwas bestimmtes?	Nani o osagaschi desu ka?
Danke, ich sehe mich nur um.	Tchotto mite ilu dake desu.
Ich möchte …	… ga hoschī desu.
Haben Sie …?	… ga alimasu ka?
Geben/Zeigen Sie mir bitte …	… o kudasai./… o misete kudasai.
Bitte … ein Paar … ein Stück …	… o hito-kumi kudasai. … o hitotsu kudasai.
Haben Sie auch etwas Besseres/Billigeres?	Mōtchotto ī/jasui mono ga alimasu ka?
Das gefällt mir. Ich nehme es.	Kole ga kini ilimaschita. Kole o kudasai.
Wieviel kostet es?	Kole wa ikula desu ka.
Kann ich mit Reiseschecks bezahlen?	Tolabelāzu-tchekku de halaemasu ka?
Kann ich mit Kreditkarte bezahlen?	Kuredjitto-kādo de halaemasu ka?
Ich möchte dies umtauschen.	Kole o kōkan schitai no desu ga.

Wortliste Geschäfte

Antiquariat	huluhon-ja
Antiquitätengeschäft	kottō-ja
Apotheke	kusᵘli-ja, jakkjoku
Bäckerei	pan-ja, bēkari̇̀
Blumengeschäft	hana-ja
Boutique	butikku
Buchhandlung	hon-ja
Drogerie	kusᵘli-ja
Einkaufszentrum	schoppingu-sentā
Eisenwarengeschäft	kanamono-ja
Elektrohandlung	denki-ja
Fischgeschäft	sakana-ja
Fotogeschäft	kamera-ja
Friseur	bijō-schi, tokoja
Gemüsehändler	jaoja
Haushaltswarengeschäft	nitchijō-zakkahin-ten
Juwelier	kikinzoku-schō, hōseki-schō
Kaufhaus	hjakka-ten, depāto
Konditorei	okaschi-ja, kēki-ja
Kosmetiksalon	keschōhin-ten
Kunst|gewerbeladen	bidjutsu-kōgēhin-ten
~händler	gaschō

✎ Andenken/Mitbringsel

Perlen	*schindju*
Holzpuppen	*kibori ningjō*
Puppen	*ningjō*
Lackartikel	*kjōdo-mingēhin*
Bambusartikel	*take-dzaiku*
Töpferwaren	*tōgē*
Porzellan	*tōki*
Japanische Rollbilder	*kake djuku*
Holzdrucke	*hanga*
Tuschmalerei	*sumie*
Fächer	*sensu*
Seide	*kinu*
Origami	*origami*

Der Weg zu einem Tempel führt Sie mitunter durch eine kilometer-
lange Handwerkerstraße, wo viele dieser Dinge verkauft werden.

Lebensmittelgeschäft	schokuljōhin-ten
Lederwarengeschäft	kawa-sēhin-ten
Markt	itchi
Metzgerei	niku-ja
Möbelgeschäft	kagu-ja
Musikgeschäft	gakki-ten
Obsthandlung	kudamono-ja
Optiker	megane-ja
Parfümerie	keschōhin-ten
Pelzgeschäft	kegawa-schō
Porzellangeschäft	tōdjiki-ten
Reinigung, chemische	kulīningu, dorai-kulīningu
Reiseandenken	omijage
Reisebüro	ljokō-gaischa
Schallplattengeschäft	rekōdo-ja
Schneider/in	schitate-ja, jōsai-schi
Schneiderei	jōsai-ten
Schreibwarengeschäft	bunbōgu-ten, bunbōgu-ja
Schuhgeschäft	kutsu-ja
Schuhmacher	kutsu-schokunin
Selbstbedienungsladen	selufu-sābisᵘ no mise
Spielwarengeschäft	omotcha-ja
Spirituosengeschäft	saka-ja
Sportartikelgeschäft	undōgu-ten, sᵘpōtsu-jōhin-ten
Supermarkt	sūpā-māketto
Süßwarengeschäft	okaschi-ja
Tabakladen	tabako-ja
Uhrmacher	tokē-ja
Wäscherei	kulīningu-ja
Waschsalon	koin-landolī
Weinhandlung	saka-ja, jōschu-ten
Zeitungskiosk	schinbun-ja

Lebensmittel

Schokuhin

● Was darf es sein?   nani ni itaschimaschō?

Geben Sie mir …
   ein Kilo …   … o itchi-kilo
   100 Gramm …   … o hjaku-guramu
   10 Scheiben …   … o djū-mai

ein Stück von …	… o ikko
eine Packung …	… o hito-pakku
ein Glas …	… o ippai
eine Dose …	… o hito-kan
eine Flasche …	… o ippon
eine Einkaufstüte. bitte.	kaimono bukulo o hitotsu kudasai.

● Darf es sonst noch etwas sein?   Hokani nani-ka gozaimasᵘ ka?

Danke, das ist alles.   Sole de, zenbu desᵘ.

Wie in England gibt es nur Weißbrot.
In den Supermärkten gibt es immer fertig frittierte Gemüse-, Hähnchen- und Fischstücke, genannt Tempura. Imbißbuden gibt es weniger, dafür unzählige Getränkeautomaten. In kleineren Lokalen kann man sehr preiswert Udon oder Soba (Nudeln in Suppe) essen.

Wortliste Lebensmittel

Aal	unagi
Ananas	painappulu
Äpfel	lingo
Apfelsinen	mikan
Aprikosen	anzu
Auberginen	nasu
Austern	kaki
Avocado	abogado
Babynahrung	bebĭ-fūdo
Bananen	banana
Barsch	suzuki
Basilikum	Basiliko
Bier	bĭru
Birnen	naschi
Blumenkohl	kalihulāwā
Bohnen	mame
Brot	pan
belegte ~e	sandoitschi
Brötchen	pan
Butter	batā
Champignons	masschurūmu
Chicoree	tchikori

Chips	tchip
Eier	tamago
Eis	aisukurīmu
Erbsen	mame, gurinpīsu
Erdbeeren	itchigo
Essig	su
Fisch	sakana

Fleisch	niku
frisch	schinsen·na
Garnelen	ebi
Gemüse	jasai
Gurke	kjūli
Hackfleisch	hiki-niku
Hähnchen	toli-niku, niwatoli
Hering	nischin
Honig	hatchimitsu
Joghurt	jōguruto
Kaffee	kōhī
Kalbfleisch	kōschi no niku
Kaninchen	ana-usagi
Karotten	nindjin
Kartoffeln	djagaimo
Käse	tchizu
Kastanien	kuli
Kekse	kukkī, bisuketto

Kindernahrung	jōdji-schoku
Kirschen	sakulanbo, tcherī
Knoblauch	nin·niku
Kohl	kjabetsu
Kohlrabi	kōlurabi, kabu
Kokosnuß	kokonattsu
Konserven	kanzume
Kopfsalat	saladana
Kotelett	katsuletsu
Krabben	ebi
Kuchen	kēki
Kürbis	kabotcha
Lammfleisch	lamu-niku
Languste	ise-ebi
Lauch	negi
Limonade	lemonēdo
Mais	tōmolokoschi, kōn
Mandarine	mikan
Mandeln	āmondo
Margarine	māgarin
Marmelade	djamu
Mayonnaise	majonēzu
Mehl	komugiko
Melone	melon/suika
Milch	gjūnjū, miluku
Mineralwasser	mineralu-sui
Muscheln	kai
Nudeln	men, nūdolu
Spaghetti	supagettī
Nüsse	nattsu
Obst	kudamono
Öl	oilu, abula
Oliven	olību
~öl	olību-oilu
Orangensaft	orendji-djūsu
Paprika	pīman
Petersilie	paseli
Pfeffer	koschō
Pfirsiche	momo
Pflaumen	ume, sumomo
Pilze	kinoko
Rauchfleisch	kunsē-niku
Reis	gohan *(gekocht)*, kome

Rindfleisch	gjū-niku
Rosinen	hoschi-budō
Sahne	nama-kurīmu
Salami	salami
Salat	salada
Salz	schio
Schinken	hamu
Schokolade	tchokolēto
Schweinefleisch	buta-niko
Seeteufel	ankō
Seezunge	schitabilame
Senf	kalaschi
Spargel	as^{u}paragas^u
Spinat	hōlensō
Suppe	sūp^u
Süßigkeiten	o-kaschi
Tee	o-tcha
Thunfisch	magulo
Tintenfisch	ika
Toast	tōsuto
Tomaten	tomato
Wein	wain
Rosé~	roze
Rot~	aka-wain
Weiß~	schilo-wain
Weintrauben	budō
Wurst	sōsēdji
Zitronen	lemon
Zucchini	zukkīni
Zucker	satō
Zwiebeln	tamanegi

Drogerieartikel

Jakuhin, Zakkahin

Wortliste Drogerieartikel

Augenbrauenstift	majuzumi
Babyfläschchen	honjūbin
Babynahrung	bēbi-fūdo
Bettflasche	jutanpo
Bürste	buraschi
Creme	kurĭmu
~ für trockene/normale/fettige Haut	kansō/hutsū/abulaschō no hada jō
Hand~	hando-krĭmu
Damenbinden	sēli-jōhin, napukin
Deo(dorant)	deodoranto
Duschgel	schawā jō ekitai-sekken
Erfrischungstücher	otehuki
Eyeliner	ailainā
Fleckenwasser	schiminuki-eki
Haar|bürste	heā-buraschi
~festiger	setto-lōschon
~klammern	heā-pin
~spray	heā-s^{u}p^{u}rē
~waschmittel	schanpū
~~ für fettiges/normales/trockenes Haar	abulaschō/hutsū/kansō no
~~ gegen Schuppen	huke bōschi jō
Kamm	kuschi
Kleiderbürste	jōhuku jō buraschi
Kölnisch Wasser	ōde kolon
Körpermilch	bodĭ-kurĭmu
Lidschatten	ai-schadō
Lippenstift	kutchibeni
Lockenwickler	heā-kālā
Nagel|feile	tsume-jasuli
~lack	manikjua
~lackentferner	djokō-eki
~schere	tsumekili
Papiertaschentücher	tchiligami, tisschu
Parfüm	kōsui
Pflaster	bando-e·ido

Pinzette	pinsetto
Präservativ	hiningu, kondōmu
Puder	paudā
Gesichts~	oschiloi
Körper~	bodī-paudā
Rasier|apparat	kamisoli, denki-kamisoli *(el.)*
~klinge	kamisoli no ha
~pinsel	higesoli jō hake
~seife	higesoli jō sekken
~wasser	higesoli jō keschōsui
Reinigungsmilch	sengan jō njūeki
Reisenecessaire	ljokō jō senmen-jōgu
Saugflasche	honjū-bin
Schaumfestiger	mūsu
Schere	hasami
Schnuller	oschabuli
Schwamm	s^upondji

Seife	sekken
Sicherheitsnadeln	anzen-pin
Sonnen|creme	san-kurīmu
~öl	san-oilu
Spiegel	kagami
Spül|bürste	tawaschi
~mittel	senzai (shokki alai jō)
~tuch	hukin
Stoffwindeln	oschime
Tampons	tanpon
Toilettenpapier	toiletto-pēpā
Wasch|lappen	tenugui
~mittel	senzai (sentaku-jō)
Watte	wata
~stäbchen	menbō
Wimperntusche	mas^ukala
Windeln	omutsu, oschime
Windelhöschen	oschime-kabā
Zahn|bürste	haburaschi
~pasta	nelihamigaki

Tabakwaren

Tabako

Haben Sie deutsche/amerikanische Zigaretten?	Doitsu/amerika no tabako ga alimasᵘ ka?
Zehn Zigarren/Zigarillos, bitte.	Hamaki/tchigarilo o djuppon kudasai.
Eine Schachtel „Mild Seven", bitte.	"Mailudo sebun" o hito-hako kudasai.
Ein Feuerzeug, bitte.	Laitā o ikko kudasai.

Kleidung/Lederwaren/Reinigung ▶ auch Kap.1 – Farben

Jōhuku/Kawasēhin/Kulīningu

Können Sie mir … zeigen?	… o misete kudasai?
● Denken Sie an eine bestimmte Farbe?	Don·na ilo o osagaschi desᵘ ka?
Ich möchte etwas Passendes hierzu.	Kole ni atta no ga hoschī no desᵘ ga.
Darf ich es anprobieren?	Schitchaku schitemo ī desᵘ ka?
● Welche (Konfektions-)Größe haben Sie?	Ōkisa wa o-ikutsu desᵘ ka?
Das ist mir zu …	Kole wa tchotto …
eng/weit.	kitsu/ōki sugimasᵘ.
kurz/lang.	midjika/naga sugimasᵘ.
klein/groß.	tchīsa/ōki sugimasᵘ.
Das paßt gut. Ich nehme es.	Kole ga tchōdo aimasᵘ. Kole ni schimasᵘ.
Das ist nicht ganz, was ich möchte.	Kole wa wataschi ga hoschī mono to tchotto tchigai masᵘ.
Ich möchte ein Paar …	
Schlappen	Sᵘlippa
Kinderschuhe	Kodomo no kutsu
Sandalen	Sandalu
Stiefel	Būtsu
	… ga issoku hoschī no desᵘ ga.

Ich habe Schuhgröße …	Wataschi no kutsu no ōkisa wa … desu.
Sie drücken mich.	Kitsui desu.
Sie sind zu klein/groß.	Tchīsa/Ōki sugimasu.
Bitte noch eine Dose Schuhcreme/ein Paar Schnürsenkel.	Kutsu-kurīmu/kutsu-himo o kudasai.
Ich möchte diese Schuhe neu besohlen lassen.	Kono kutsuzoko o halikaete hoschī no desu ga.
Können Sie bitte die Absätze neu machen?	Kakato o naoschite kudasaimasen ka?
Ich möchte diese Sachen zur Reinigung geben.	Kono jōhuku o kulīningu ni daschitai no desu ga.
Wann ist es fertig?	Itsu deki agalimasu ka?

Traditionelle japanische Kleidung

geta: japanische Holzschlappen mit zwei Absätzen
zori: Schlappen aus leichterem Material ohne Absätze
kimono obi: farbiger Gürtel zum Kimono
yukata: leichter japanischer Baumwollkimono. Meist im Sommer getragen und wenn man ins japanische Bad (Furo) geht.
tabi: weiße Zehensocken

Wortliste Kleidung/Lederwaren/Reinigung

Abendkleid	jakai-huku
Anorak	anorakku
Anzug	sūtsu
Ärmel	sode
Bade|anzug	mizu-gi
~hose	suiē-pantsu
~mütze	suiē-bō
Baumwolle	men, kotton
Bikini	bikini
Blazer	bulezā
Bluse	bulausu
bügelfrei	nō airon no
bügeln	airon o kakelu
Büstenhalter	buladjā
chemisch reinigen	dorai-kulīningu sulu

Druckknopf	botan
Farbe	ilo
Fliege	tchōnekutai
Frottee	taoru-dji
Futter	ula-dji
gestreift	schima
Gummistiefel	gomu-nagagutsu
Gürtel	beluto
Halstuch	sukāhu, elimaki
Hand|schuhe	tebukulo
~tasche	hando-bakku
Hausschuhe	s^ulippa
Hemd	waischats^u, schatsu
Hose	zubon
kurze ~	han-zubon
Hut	bōschi
Jacke	uwagi
Jeans	djīnzu
Jogging|anzug	djogging^u-sūtsu
kariert	tchekku no
Kimono	kimono
Kinderschuhe	kodomo no kutsu
Kleid	jōhuku, wanpīs^u
Kniestrümpfe	haisokkus^u
Knopf	botan
Koffer	kaban
Kostüm	kos^utchūmu, sūtsu
Kragen	eli
Krawatte	nekutai
Kunstfaser	kagaku-sen·i
Leder|hose	kawa-zubon
~jacke	lezā-djaketto
~mantel	lezā-kōto
Leinen	lin·neru, asa
Mantel	kōto
Minirock	mini-s^ukāto
Morgenrock	gaun
Mütze	bōschi
Nachthemd	nemaki
Overall	ōbāōlu
Pelzjacke/-mantel	kegawa no uwagi/kōto
pflegeleicht	te·ile no jasaschī
Pullover	sētā

Pyjama	padjama
Regenmantel	re·in-kōto, amagappa
Reisetasche	ljokō jō kaban
Reißverschluß	fasᵘnā, tchakku
Rock	sᵘkāto
Rucksack	rjukku-sakku
Sakko	sebilo
Sandalen	sandalu
Schal	mahulā
Schirm	kasa
Schuh|e	kutsu
~bürste	kutsu-buraschi
~creme	kutsu-kurīmu
~größe	kutsu no ōkisa
Seide	kinu, siluku
Shorts	schōtsu
Skihose	sᵘkī-zubon
Slip	sᵘlippu, pantī
Socken	kutsuschita
Sohle	soko, kutsuzoko
Sommerkleid	natsu-huku
Stiefel	būtsu
Ski~	sᵘkī-gutsu
Strandschuhe	gomuzōli
Strickjacke	kādigan
Strümpfe	kutuschita, sᵘtokkingu
Strumpfhose	panti-sutokkingu
Tasche	kaban
Taschentuch	hankatchi
Trainingsanzug	tolēnā-sūtsu
T-Shirt	tī-schatsu
Turnschuhe	undō-gutsu
Umhängetasche	scholudā-bakku
Unter|hemd	schitagi
~hose	pantsu
~rock	petchikōto
~wäsche	schitagi
Volkstracht	minzoku-ischō
waschmaschinenfest	sentaku ni tsujoi
Weste	tchokki
Wildleder|jacke	bakku-sᵘkin no uwagi
~mantel	bakku-sᵘkin no kōto
Wolle	ūlu, ke

Bücher/Schreibwaren

Hon/Bunbōgu

Ich hätte gern …
   einen Stadtplan in la-   Rōmadji de kaite alu tchizu
   teinischer Schrift.
   ein Wörterbuch   Doku-wa-djiten
   deutsch-japanisch.
   ein Wörterbuch eng-   Ē-wa-djiten
   lisch-japanisch.

                     … ga hoschī no desᵘ ga.

Haben Sie deutsche/eng-   Doitsu-go/ē-go no schinbun/zasschi
lische Zeitungen/Zeit-   ga alimasᵘ ka?
schriften?

Wo kann man deutsche   Doitsu-go no schinbun wa doko de
Zeitungen kaufen?   kaemasᵘ ka?

Haben Sie auch ein Wör- Rōmadji de kakaleta wa-doku-djiten
terbuch japanisch-   ga alimasᵘ ka?
deutsch in lateinischer
Schrift?

Ich hätte gerne ein einfa- Nihon-go ga benkjō dekilu kan-
ches Japanisch-Lehr-   tan·nahon ga hoschī no desᵘ ga.
buch.

Haben Sie einen Reise-   Doitsu-go/ē-go no gaido-bukku ga
führer in deutscher/eng- alimasᵘ ka?
lischer Sprache?

Wortliste Bücher/Schreibwaren

Deutsch	Japanisch
Ansichtskarte	e-hagaki
Autokarte	djidōscha jo dōlo-tchizu
Bleistift	enpitsu
~spitzer	enpitsu-kezuli
Brief|marke	kitte
~papier	binsen
~umschlag	hūtō
Büroklammern	kulippᵘ
Farbstift	ilo-enpitsu
Filzstift	hueluto-pen
Füllfederhalter	man·nenhitsu

Geschenkpapier	hōsōschi
Illustrierte	zasschi
Klebstoff	settchaku-zai
Kochbuch	ljōli no hon
Kugelschreiber	bōlu-pen
Landkarte	tchizu
Lehrbuch	kjōkascho
Luftpost-Briefpapier	kōkūbin jō binsen
Malbuch	nuli·e-tchō
Notiz|block	memo-jōschi
~buch	memo-tchō
Papier	kami
Radiergummi	keschigomu
Reiseführer	gaido-bukku
Spielkarten	tolanpu
Stadtplan	schigai-tchizu
Straßenkarte	dōlo-tchizu
Taschenbuch	pokettoban no hon
Tesafilm®	selohan-tēpu
Wörterbuch	djischo
Zeichenblock	gajōschi
Zeitschrift	zasschi
Zeitung	schinbun

Haushaltswaren

Katē-jōhin

Wortliste Haushaltswaren

Abfallbeutel	gomi-bukulo
Alufolie	alumi-hoilu
Besen	hōki
Dosenöffner	kan-kili
Eßbesteck	fōku, supūn, naifu
Flaschenöffner	sen-nuki
Frischhaltefolie	lappu
Glas	koppu
Handfeger	te-bōki
Kaffeefilter	kōhī jō filutā
Kehrblech	tchilitoli
Kerzen	lōsoku
Kochtopf	nabe

Korkenzieher	kor^uku-sen-nuki
Papierservietten	nap^ukin
Plastikbeutel	p^ulas^utchiku-bukulo
Sonnenschirm	higasa
Taschenmesser	pokketto-naifu
Thermosflasche	suitō
Wäscheklammern	sentaku-basami

Elektro- und Fotoartikel

Denki to schaschin jōhin

Ich möchte …

einen Film für diesen Fotoapparat.	Kono kamera jō no fuilumu
einen Farbfilm.	Kalā fuilumu
einen Schwarzweiß-Film.	Schilo-kulo no fuilumu
einen Diafilm.	Sulaido jō no fuilumu
einen Film mit 36/24/12 Aufnahmen.	Sandjū-loku/nidjū-jon/djū-ni mai doli no fuilumu
einen Videofilm.	Bideo jō no fuilumu

… o kudasai.

Auf dem Weg zum Sensoji-Tempel, Tokyo

Könnten Sie mir bitte den Film einlegen?

Ataraschī fuilumu o ilete kudasai masen ka?

Würden Sie mir bitte diesen Film entwickeln?

Kono fuilumu o genzō schite kudasai masen ka?

● Welches Format bitte?

Ōkisa wa dole ni schimasᵘ ka?

Sieben mal zehn/neun mal neun.

Nana kakelu djū/kjū kakelu kyū.

● Wünschen Sie Hochglanz oder matt?

Kōtaku desᵘ ka, soletomo kinume desᵘ ka?

Wann sind die Bilder fertig?

Schaschin wa itsu dekiagalimasᵘ ka?

   morgen
   heute nachmittag

   aschita
   kjō no gogo

Der Sucher/Der Auslöser funktioniert nicht.

Faindā/Schattā no tchōschi ga walui desᵘ.

Das ist kaputt. Können Sie es bitte reparieren?

Kole ga kowaleta node, schūli o onegai dekimasᵘ ka?

Können Sie mir bitte die neuesten Modelle von Fotoapparaten/Filmkameras zeigen?

Itchi ban ataraschī kamera/Bideo o misetekudasai masen ka?

Wortliste Elektro- und Fotoartikel

Adapter	adaptā
Auslöser	schattā
Batterie	dentchi
Belichtungsmesser	loschutsu-kē
Blende	schiboli
Blitzgerät	hulasschu
CD/Compactdisc	schī-dī
Fön	heā-dolaijā
Glühbirne	denkjū
Kassette	kasetto
~rekorder	kasetto-rekōdā
Kopfhörer	heddo-hōn
Lautsprecher	sᵘpīkā
Linse	lenzu
Netzgerät	eliminētā

Objektiv	lenzu
Paßbild	pasᵘpōto jō schaschin
Schwarzweiß-Film	schilo-kulo no fuilumu
Selbstauslöser	selufu-taimā
Stativ	sankjaku
Stecker	puragu
Sucher	faindā
Taschen|lampe	kaitchū-dentō
~rechner	dentaku
Teleobjektiv	bōen-lenzu
Verschluß	schattā
Video	bideo
~kamera	bideo-kamera
~kassette	bideo no kasetto
~rekorder	bideo-rekōdā
Walkman	uōkuman

Beim Optiker

Megane-ja de

Würden Sie mir bitte das Gestell reparieren?	Kono megane no hutchi o naoschite kudasai masen ka?
Meine Brille sitzt nicht mehr gut. Würden Sie sie bitte zurechtbiegen?	Megane no suwali ga walui no desᵘ ga. Tchōsē schite kudasai masen ka?
Mir ist ein Glas meiner Brille zerbrochen.	Megane no lenzu ga kowalemaschita.
Ich bin kurzsichtig/weitsichtig.	Wataschi wa kinschi/enschi desᵘ.
● Wie ist Ihre Sehstärke?	Schiljoku wa dono kulai desᵘ ka?
Wann kann ich die Brille abholen?	Itsu megane o tolini kitala ĭ desᵘ ka?
Ich brauche Aufbewahrungslösung/Reinigungslösung für harte/weiche Kontaktlinsen.	Hādo/Sofuto jō kontakuto lenzu no hozon-eki/sendjō-eki ga hoschĭ no desᵘ ga.
Ich suche eine Sonnenbrille/ein Fernglas.	San-gulasu/Bōenkjō o sagaschite imasᵘ.

Beim Uhrmacher/Juwelier

Tokē-ja/Hōseki-ten de

Meine Uhr geht nicht mehr. Können Sie mal nachsehen?	Kono tokē ga ugokimasen. Tchotto mite kudasai masen ka?
Können Sie dies bitte reparieren?	Kole o schūli schite kudasai masen ka?
Ich möchte ein hübsches Andenken/Geschenk.	Sutekina omijage/Purezento ga hoschī no desu ga.
●Wieviel wollen Sie ausgeben?	Dono kulai no go-josan desu ka?
Ich möchte etwas nicht zu Teures.	Amali takakunai no ga hoschī no desu ga.
Haben Sie Zuchtperlen?	Jōschoku-schindju ga alimasu ka?

Wortliste Uhrmacher/Juwelier

Anhänger	pendanto
Armband	buresu letto
~uhr	udedokē
Brosche	burōtchi
echt	honmono no
Gold	kin, gōludo
Vergoldung	kin-mekki
Kette	kusali
Koralle	sango
Kristall	kurisutalu
Ohrringe	mimi-kazali, ijalingu
Perle	schindju
Ring	jubiwa
Schmuck	kazali akusesarī
Silber	gin
Versilberung	gin-mekki

Beim Friseur

Bijōin de/Tokoja de

Kann ich mich für morgen anmelden?	Jojaku o aschita de onegai dekimasᵘ ka?
• Wie hätten Sie gern Ihr Haar?	Don·na kamigata ni schitai desᵘ ka?
Waschen und fönen, bitte.	Kami o alatte, bulō schite kudasai.
Schneiden mit/ohne Waschen, bitte.	Kami o alatte/alawazu ni kitte kudasai.
Eine Kurpackung, bitte.	heā-pakku o onegai schimasᵘ.

Ich möchte …
  eine Dauerwelle.
  mir die Haare färben/ tönen lassen.
	Pāma o onegai schimasᵘ.
	Kami o somete kudasai.

Lassen Sie es bitte lang.	Nagasa wa sonomama ni schite oite kudasai.
Nur die Spitzen.	Kami-saki dake.
Nicht zu kurz/Ganz kurz/Etwas kürzer, bitte.	Amali midjikaku schinaide/Kanali midjikaku schite/Sᵘkoschi midjikaku schite kudasai.
Bitte hinten/vorn/oben/ an den Seiten (noch) etwas wegnehmen.	Uschilo/mae/ue/joko o (mo) sᵘkoschi kitte kudasai.
Die Ohren sollen frei sein/bedeckt bleiben.	Mimi wa misete/misenaide kudasai.
Den Scheitel links/ rechts, mittig, bitte.	Wakeme wa hidali/migi/man·naka de onegai schimasᵘ.
Einen Messerschnitt, bitte.	Soide kudasai.
Bitte etwas toupieren.	Sakage o tatete, kami o hukulamaste kudasai.
Bitte kein/nur wenig Haarspray.	Heā-sᵘpulē wa schinaide/sᵘkoschi dake schite kudasai.
Rasieren, bitte.	Hige o sotte kudasai.

Stutzen Sie mir bitte den Bart.	Hige o totonoete kudasai.
Können Sie mir Maniküre machen?	Manikjua o onegai dekimas^u ka?
Vielen Dank. So ist es gut.	Aligatō gozaimas^u. Sole de ī des^u.

Wortliste Friseur

Augenbrauen	majuge
Bart	hige
blond	kinpatsu no, bulondo no
Dauerwelle	pāma
färben	senschoku sulu
fönen	doraijā o kakelu, bulō sulu
frisieren	kami o setto sulu
Frisur	kamigata
Haar	kami
fettiges ~	abulakkoi-kami
trockenes ~	kansōschita-kami
Haar|ausfall	nukege
~kur	heā-pakku
~schnitt	kamigata
~spray	heā-s^{u}p^{u}rē
~teil	heā-pīs^u
kämmen	kami o tokas^u
Koteletten	momiage
legen	uēbu o tsukelu
Locken	kālu
~wickler	kālā
Perücke	katsula
Pony	ponītēlu, kilisagegami
sich rasieren lassen	hige o sotte molau
Scheitel	kamino wakeme
Schnurrbart	kutchi-hige
Schuppen	huke
Shampoo	schanpū
Stufenschnitt	dan-katto
stutzen	kilu
tönen	kami o somelu

9 **Allgemeine Dienste**
一般業務

Geldangelegenheiten

Kin·jū·kankē

Wo ist die nächste Bank, in der deutsches Geld gewechselt wird?	Kono tchikaku no ginkō de doitsu no okane o ljogae dekilu tokolo wa doko desu ka?
Wann öffnet/schließt die Bank?	Ginkō wa itsu akimasu ka/schimalimasu ka?
Ich möchte … DM (Schilling, Schweizer Franken) in Yen wechseln.	… doitsu-maruku (schilingu, suisu-fulan) o en ni ljōgae schitai no desu ga.
Wie ist heute der Wechselkurs?	Kjō no kawase-sōba/rēto wa ikula desu ka?
Wieviel Yen bekomme ich für 100 DM?	Hjaku-maruku wa en de ikula ni nalimasu ka?

Fremde Währungen und auch Reiseschecks kann man nur bei Banken mit dem Schild „Authorized Foreign Exchange Bank" einlösen. Diese Banken gibt es in den großen Städten recht zahlreich, auf dem Land jedoch seltener. Wer nicht immer viel Bargeld mit sich herumtragen möchte, kann ein Konto bei der Post eröffnen.

In Japan kann man nicht wie in anderen asiatischen Ländern mit Dollar bezahlen. Es gilt nur der Yen.

Der Wechselkurs alleine sagt jedoch wenig über die tatsächliche Kaufkraft des Yen aus. Die Waren des täglichen Bedarfs sind oft doppelt so teuer als bei uns.

Ich möchte diesen Reisescheck einlösen.	Kono torabelāzu-tchekku o genkin ni schitai no desu ga.
Auf welchen Betrag kann ich den Scheck maximal ausstellen?	Saikō ikula made tchekku o kaelalemasu ka?
• Ihre Kreditkarte, bitte.	Kuredjitto-kādo o onegaischimasu.
Kann ich das Bargeld sofort mitnehmen oder dauert das etwas?	Sugu ni genkin o itadakemasu ka, soletomo djikan ga kakalimasu ka?
Wie lange wird es dauern?	Dono kulai djikan ga kakalimasu ka?

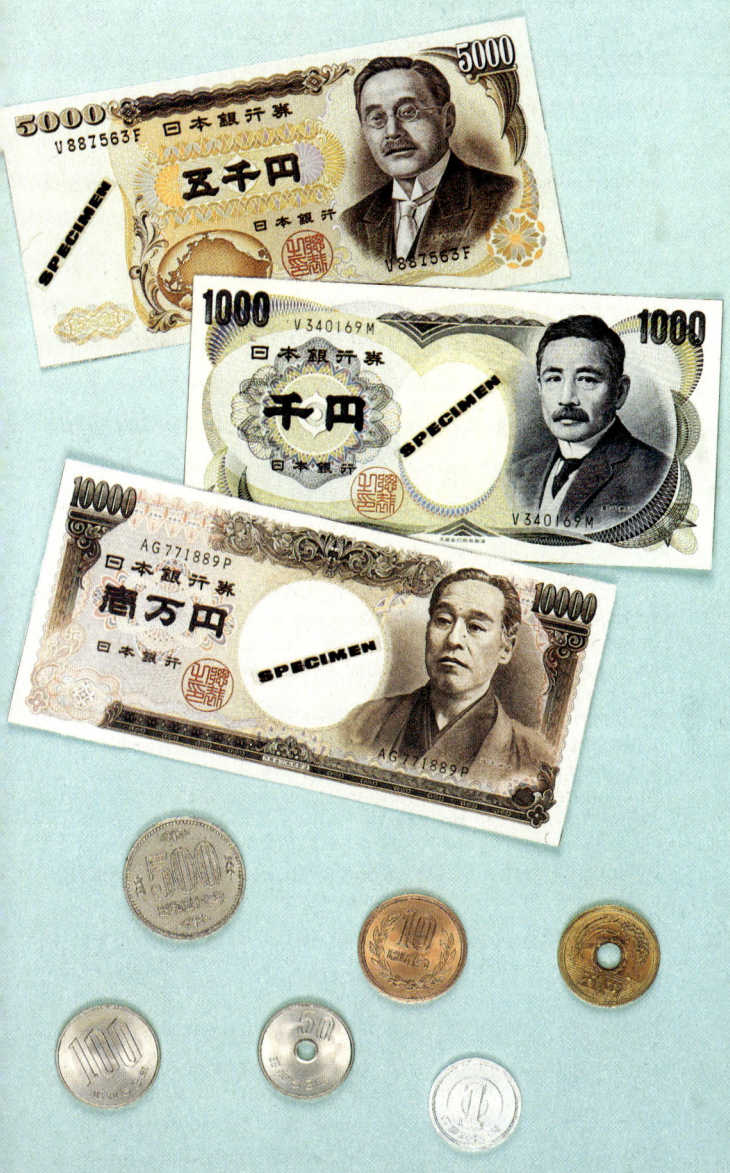

● Darf ich bitte Ihren Paß/ Ausweis sehen? — Anata no pasᵘpōto/mibun-schōmē-scho o misete itadakemasᵘ ka?

● Würden Sie bitte hier unterschreiben? — Koko ni sain o schite kudasai masen ka?

Ist Geld für mich überwiesen worden? — Wataschi ate ni okane ga sōkin salete imsᵘ ka?

Geldtransfer, Überweisungen
Es gibt zwei Möglichkeiten:
1. Wenn es nicht sehr eilt, läßt man sich eine auf Yen ausgestellte Zahlungsanweisung schicken (postlagernd und mit Eilzustellung: „poste restante"; „special delivery").
2. Man kann sein Geld direkt an eine Bank schicken lassen. Entweder brieflicher Transfer oder telegraphische Überweisung.

銀行	ginkou	Bank
両替	ryougae	Geldwechsel

Ich möchte mein Geld von meinem Konto/Postsparbuch abheben. — Wataschi no okane o kōza/jokin-tsūtchō kala oloschitai no desᵘ ga.

● Gehen Sie bitte zur Rezeption Nr. … — … ban no madogutchi e itte kudasai.

● Wie wollen Sie das Geld haben? — Okane no schului wa dono-jōni itaschimaschō ka?

Bitte nur Scheine. — Osatsu dake ni schite kudasai.

Auch etwas Kleingeld. — Kozeni mo sᵘkoschi ilete kudasai.

Ich habe meine Reiseschecks verloren. Was muß ich tun? — Wataschi no torabelāzu-tchekku o nakuschimaschita. Dō schitala ĭ deschō ka?

Wortliste Geldangelegenheiten

abheben	okane o hikidasᵘ, olosᵘ
auszahlen	schihalau
Bank	ginkō
~konto	kōza
~leitzahl	ginkō-bangō
bar	genkin no
Bargeld	genkin
Betrag	sōgaku, kingaku

Devisen	gaikoku-kawase
D-Mark	doitsu-maruku
einzahlen	halaikomu
Formular	kinjū-jōschi
Geheimzahl	anschō-bangō
Geld	okane
~automat	kjasschu-kōnā
~anweisung *(Post)*	kawase
~schein	schihē, osatsu
~wechsel	ljōgae
Kasse	kaikē, redji
Kleingeld	kozeni
Konto	kōza
Kreditkarte	kuredjitto-kādo
Kurs	kawase-sōba, rēto
Münze	kōka, kahē
Post|anweisung	jūbin-gawase
~sparbuch	jūbin-jokin-tsūtchō
~sparkasse	jūbin-tchokin
Provision	tesūljō
Quittung	uketoli, ljōschūscho
Reisescheck	ljokō-kogitte, torabelāzu-tchekku
Schalter	madogutchi
Scheck	kogitte, tchekku
einen ~ ausstellen	kogitte o kilu/hulidasu
einen ~ einlösen	kogitte o genkin ni kaelu
~buch	kogitte-tchō
~gebühr	kogitte-tesūljō
Schilling	schilingu
Schweizer Franken	suisu-furan
Spar|buch	jokin-tsūtchō
~kasse	ginkō
~konto	jokin-kōza
Überweisung	hulikae-sōkin
telegrafische ~	denschin-gawase
umtauschen	ljōgae sulu
Unterschrift	schomē, sain
Währung	tsūka
Wechsel|kurs	sōba, rēto
~stube	ljōgae-djo
zahlen	schihalau
Zahlkarte	hulikae-halaikomijōschi
Zahlung	schihalai
Zahlungsanweisung	schihalai-saschizuscho, kawase

Auf der Post

Jūbinkjoku de 郵便局 〒

Wo ist das Postamt/der Briefkasten?	Jūbin-kjoku/Posᵘto wa doko desᵘ ka?

Werfen Sie Ihre Post in die roten Briefkästen, die Sie überall auf der Straße finden.

Was kostet ein Brief/eine Postkarte …	Tegami wa/Hagaki wa …
nach Deutschland?	doitsu made
nach Österreich?	ōsᵘtoria made
in die Schweiz?	suisᵘ made
	ikula desᵘ ka?
Drei Briefmarken zu … Yen, bitte.	… en no kitte o san-mai kudasai.
Diesen Brief bitte per …	Kono tegami o …
Express.	sokutatsu
Einschreiben.	kakidome
Luftpost.	kōkū-bin
mit dem Schiff.	hunabin
	de onegai schimasᵘ.

Wie lange braucht ein Brief nach Deutschland?	Tegami wa doitsu made dono kulai kakalimasᵘ ka?

Wie lange braucht ein Brief nach Deutschland?
Tegami wa doitsu made dono kulai kakalimasᵘ ka?

Kann ich bei Ihnen auch Sondermarken bekommen?
Koko de kinen-kitte mo kaemasᵘ ka?

Wir haben leider keine mehr. Gehen Sie bitte zum Hauptpostamt in …
Zan·nen desᵘ ga, mō alimasen. … no honkjoku e itte kudasai.

Wann kommen neue Sondermarken heraus?
Atalaschī kinen-kitte wa itsu demasᵘ ka?

Diesen Satz, bitte.
Kono setto o onegai schimasᵘ.

Je eine Marke, bitte.
Itchi-mai zutsu onegai schimasᵘ.

Postlagernd
Kjoku-dome de

Ist Post für mich da? Mein Name ist …
Wataschi ate ni jūbin ga kite imasᵘ ka? Wataschi no namae wa … desᵘ.

Nein, es ist nichts da.
īe, kite imasen.

Ja, es ist etwas da.
Hai, kite imasᵘ.

Ihren Ausweis, bitte.
Mibun-schōmē-schō o onegai schimasᵘ.

Telegramme/Telefax
Denpō/Fakkusᵘ

Ich möchte ein Telegramm aufgeben.
Denpō o utchitai no desᵘ ga.

Können Sie mir bitte beim Ausfüllen helfen?
Kinjū o suluno o tetsudatte itadakemasᵘ ka?

Was kostet ein Buchstabe?
hito-modji ikula desᵘ ka?

Die Grundgebühr beträgt … zuzüglich … pro Wort.
Kihon-ljōkin wa … de, hito-modji ni tsuki … desᵘ.

Kommt das Telegramm heute noch in … an?
Denpō wa kjōdjū ni … ni tsukimasᵘ ka?

Kann ich von hier ein Telefax nach … schicken?
Fakkusᵘ o koko kala okulemasᵘ ka?

Wortliste Post   ▶ auch Wortliste Geldangelegenheiten

absenden	okulu
Absender	okulinuschi, hassōnin
Adresse	djūscho
aufgeben *(Telegramm)*	denpō o utsu
ausfüllen	kinjū sulu
Bestimmungsort	ikisaki, mokuteki-tchi
Brief	tegami
~kasten	posᵘto
~marke	kitte
~markenautomat	kitte-djidō-hanbaiki
~träger/in	jūbin-ja, jūbin-haitatsu-nin
~umschlag	hūtō
Drucksache	insatsu-butsu
Eilbrief	sokutatsu
Einschreibebrief	kakitome
Empfänger	uketoli-nin
Empfangsbestätigung	uketoli-kakunin-scho
Formular	kinjū-jōschi
frankieren	kitte o halu
Gebühr	ljōkin
Gewicht	omosa
Hauptpostamt	honkjoku
Luftpost, mit	kōkūbin de
Nachnahme, per	tchakubalai, daikin-hikikae
nachsenden	tensō sulu
Päckchen	kozutsumi
Paket	kozutsumi
Porto	sōljō
Post|amt	jūbin-kjoku
~karte	jūbin-hagaki
~lagernd	kjoku-dome
~leitzahl	jūbin-bangō
Schalter	madogutchi
~stunden	madogutchi-gjōmudjikan
Sondermarke	kinen-kitte
Telefax	fakkusᵘ
Telegramm	denpō
Telex	telekkusᵘ
Vordruck	kinjū-jōschi
Wertangabe	kakaku-hjōki
Zollerklärung	tsūkan-schinkoku

Telefonieren

Denwa o kakelu

Dürfte ich wohl Ihr Telefon benutzen?
Denwa o tsukattemo ī desu ka?

Wo ist die nächste Telefonzelle?
Itchiban tchikai denwa-bokkusu wa doko desu ka?

Können Sie mir bitte wechseln? Ich brauche 10-Yen- und 100-Yen-Münzen.
Okane o kuzushite kudasaimasen ka? Djū-en dama to hjaku-en dama ga hoschī no desu ga.

Haben Sie ein Telefonbuch?
Denwa-tchō ga alimasu ka?

Wie ist die Vorwahl von …?
… no schigai-kjokuban wa nan-ban desu ka?

(Auskunft) bitte, geben Sie mir die Nummer von …
(Denwo-kjoku) … no denwa-bangō o onegai schimasu.

Bitte ein Ferngespräch nach …
… e no tchōkjoli-tsūwa o onegaischimasu.

Ich möchte ein R-Gespräch anmelden.
Kolekuto-kōlu o onegai schimasu.

Können Sie mich bitte mit … verbinden?
… ni tsunaide itadakemasu ka?

● Gehen Sie in Kabine Nr. …
…-ban bokkusu e dōzo.

Die Leitung ist besetzt.
Hanaschi-tchū desu.

Es meldet sich niemand.
Dalemo demasen.

● Bleiben Sie bitte am Apparat.
Denwa o kilazuni sonomama omatchi kudasai.

Hallo, mit wem spreche ich?
Moschi-Moschi, sotchila wa donatasama desu ka?

Hier spricht …
Kotchila wa … desu.

Kann ich bitte Herrn/Frau/Fräulein … sprechen?
… san o onegai dekimasu ka?

Öffentliche Telefone					
	Grün	Grün	Grün*	Grün*	Rosa
Ortsgespräche	Ja	Ja	Ja	Ja	Ja
Überseegespräche	Nein	Ja	Ja	Ja	Nein
Ferngespräche	Ja	Ja	Ja	Ja	Ja
Information-Service (English) Mon.-Frei. 9.00-17.00, Sam. 9.00-12.00 Wählen Sie 3277-1010	¥10/3 Min.	¥10/3 Min.	¥10/3 Min.	¥10/3 Min.	¥10/3 Min.
**Münzen	¥100/¥10	¥100/¥10	Nein	Nein	¥100/¥10
Telefon Karte	Ja	Ja	Ja	Ja	Nein

* Grüne öffentliche Telefone mit Goldfarbenenschild.   ** Für Übersee-Gespräche, Verwenden Sie bitte ¥100 Yen Münzen oder Karte.

Japanische Telefonnummern bestehen aus 9 oder 10 Ziffern, meist in 3 Gruppen. Die erste Gruppe ist die Vorwahl für Ferngespräche. Hier einige Vorwahlnummern:

Hiroshima	*082*	*Nara*	*0742*
Kamakura	*0467*	*Nikko*	*0288*
Kobe	*078*	*Osaka*	*06*
Kyoto	*075*	*Sapporo*	*011*
Nagoya	*052*	*Tokyo*	*03*
Naha	*0988*	*Yokohama*	*045*

Japanische Telefonteilnehmer melden sich mit **moschi-moschi** *und nennen dann ihren Namen.*

Benutzung

Hörer abnehmen
Geld einwerfen (10- oder 100-Yen-Münzen)
Nummer wählen (schnelle Pieptöne bedeuten besetzt)

Zeitverschiebung

Gegenüber der mitteleuropäischen Zeit werden die Uhren während der Winterzeit 8 Stunden, während der Sommerzeit 7 Stunden vorgestellt. Ganz Japan mit sämtlichen Inseln gehört einer Zeitzone an.

Überseegespräche

Im Hotel kann man sich Überseegespräche vermitteln lassen oder unter der Nummer 0051 selbst anmelden. Nachdem man das gewünschte Land plus Telefonnummer genannt hat, wird man schnell verbunden. Von einigen Telefonapparaten (s. Übersicht oben) lassen sich auch Überseegespräche im Selbstwählverkehr führen.

Vorwahlnummern:	*Deutschland*	*00149*
	Österreich	*00143*
	Schweiz	*00141*

Vermittlung für Überseegespräche	*0051*
Auslandsauskunft	*03-270-5111*
Notruf für Polizei	*110*
Notruf im Falle eines Unfalls	*119*

● Am Apparat.	Hai, wataschi des^u.
● Ich verbinde.	Otsunagi schimas^u.
● Tut mir leid, Herr/Frau … ist nicht da.	…-san wa mōschiwake alimasen ga, ima huzei des^u.
Wann wird Herr/Frau … zurück sein?	Itsu okaeli deschō ka?
● Kann Herr/Frau … Sie zurückrufen?	Olikaeschi o-denwa sasemaschō ka?
Ja, meine Nummer ist …	Hai onegai schimas^u, wataschi no denwa-bangō wa … des^u.
● Möchten Sie eine Nachricht hinterlassen?	Nanika o-tsutae schimaschō ka?
Würden Sie ihm/ihr bitte sagen, ich hätte angerufen?	Wataschi ga denwa o kaketa koto o kale/kanodjo ni tsutaete kudasai masen ka?
Könnten Sie ihm/ihr etwas ausrichten?	Dengon o onegai dekimas^u ka?
Ich rufe später nochmal an.	Mō itchi-do denwa o schimas^u.
● Falsch verbunden.	Matchi gae des^u.
● Kein Anschluß unter dieser Nummer.	Kono denwa-bangō wa genzai tsukawalete olimasen.
Ich habe mich verwählt.	Denwa-bangō o matchigae maschita.

Wortliste Telefonieren

abnehmen	denwa o tolu
Anruf	denwa
~beantworter	lus^{u}ban-denwa
anrufen	denwa o sulu, denwa o kakelu
Auskunft	infomēschon
Auslandsgespräch	kaigai-tsūwa
besetzt	hanaschi-tchū
Branchenverzeichnis	schokugjō betsu-denwatchō
durchwählen	tchokutsū, dairekuto-kōlu
Fern|gespräch	tchōkjoli-denwa, schigai-denwa
~sprechamt	denwakjoku, denwagaischa
Freizeichen	jobidaschi-on

Gebühr	ljōkin
Gebühreneinheit	tsūwa-kihon-ljōkin
Gespräch	hanaschi
Hörer	djuwaki
Münzfernsprecher	kōschū-denwa
Ortsgespräch	schinai-tsūwa
R-Gespräch	kolekutokōlu
Rufnummer	denwa-bangō
Störungsstelle	koschō-gakali
Telefon	denwa
~buch	denwa-tchō
~gespräch	denwa, tsūwa
~karte	telefon-kādo
~nummer	denwa-bangō
~zelle	denwa-bokkusu
Verbindung	setsuzoku
Vermittlung	denwa-kōkan
Vorwahlnummer	schinai-bangō
wählen	daijalu o mawasu

Auf der Polizei

Kēsatsu de

▶ auch Kap. 3, Auto/Motorrad/Fahrrad – Verkehrsunfall

Wo ist bitte das nächste Polizeirevier?	Itchiban tchikai kēsatsu-scho wa do-ko desu ka?
Ich möchte einen Diebstahl/Verlust/Unfall anzeigen.	Tōnan/Funschutsu/Djiko no todoke-de o schitai no desu ga.

Japan ist ein sehr sicheres Land. Gestohlen wird so gut wie nichts. Hat man etwas verloren, soll man die Hoffnung nicht aufgeben. Fundsachen werden in der Regel abgegeben.

Mir ist …	Wataschi no …
die Handtasche	hando-baggu
die Brieftasche	scholui-ile
mein Fotoapparat	kamera
mein Auto	kuluma
gestohlen worden.	ga nusumalemaschita.
Mein Auto ist aufgebrochen worden.	Wataschi no kuluma ga kowasale maschita.

Aus meinem Auto ist … gestohlen worden.	Wataschi no kuluma kala … ga nusu-male maschita.
Ich habe … verloren.	Wataschi wa … o nakuschimaschita.
An wen soll ich mich wenden?	Dale ni kĩtala/tazunetala ĩ desu ka?
Mein Sohn/Meine Tochter ist seit … verschwunden.	Wataschi no musuko/musume ga … kala inaku nalimaschita.
Können Sie mir bitte helfen?	tasukete kudasai masen ka?
● Wann genau ist das passiert?	Sēkakuni wa sole wa itsu no koto desu ka?
● Wir werden der Sache nachgehen.	Tchōsa ni kakalimasu.
Ich habe damit nichts zu tun.	Wataschi wa sole to wa kankē alimasen.
● Ihren Namen und Ihre Anschrift, bitte.	Anata no namae to djūscho o onegai schimasu.
● Wenden Sie sich bitte an das deutsche/österreichische/Schweizer Konsulat.	Doitsu/Ōsutoria/Suisu no ljodjikan ni lenlaku o totte kudasai.
Können Sie mir sagen, wie ich … finden kann?	Dōschitala … ga mitsukaluka oschiete kudasai.
Können Sie mir sagen, wie ich diese Adresse finden kann?	Kono djūscho no tokolo e ikitai node, dono-jōni ittala ĩ ka, oschiete kudasai masen ka?

Wortliste Polizei

anzeigen	todokedelu
aufbrechen	kodjiakelu
Auto|radio	kā-radjio
~schlüssel	kuluma no kagi
belästigen	meiwaku o kakelu
beschlagnahmen	saschiosaelu, ōschū sulu
Brieftasche	satsuile, scholui ile
Dieb	dolobō
~stahl	tōnan
Gefängnis	kēmuscho

Geld	okane
~börse	saihu
Gericht	saiban-scho
Kfz-Schein	djidōscha-tōloku-schō
Papiere	scholui
Personalausweis	mibun-schōmē-scho
Polizei	kēsatsu
~wagen	patokā
Polizist/in	omawali-san, kēsatsu-kan
Rauschgift	majaku
Rechtsanwalt/anwältin	bengo-schi
Reisepaß	pasᵘpōto
Richter/in	saiban-kan
Scheck	tchekku
Schlüssel	kagi
Schmuggel	mitsuju
Schuld	schakkin
Taschendieb	hittakuli, suli
Überfall	huiutchi, schin·njū, schūgeki
Übersetzer	hon·jaku-scha
Unfall	djiko
Untersuchungshaft	kōljū
Verbrechen	hanzai
Vergewaltigung	bōljoku
verhaften	taiho sulu
verlieren	nakusᵘ
zusammenschlagen	naguliai

Fundbüro

Ischitsubutsu-toliatsukaidjo

Wo ist das Fundbüro, bitte?	Ischitsubutsu-toliatsukai-djo wa do-ko desᵘ ka?
Ich habe … verloren.	… o nakuschimaschita.
Ich habe meine Handtasche im Zug vergessen.	hando-baggu o denscha no naka ni wasᵘlemaschita.
Benachrichtigen Sie mich bitte, wenn sie gefunden werden sollte.	Moschi mitsukalimaschitala, wataschi ni schilasete kudasai.
Hier ist meine Hotelanschrift/Heimatadresse.	Koko ga wataschi no hotelu/djikka no djūscho desᵘ.

10 Gesundheit
健康

In der Apotheke

Kusuli-ja de

Wo ist die nächste Apotheke?	Itchiban tchikai kusuli-ja wa doko desu ka?
Geben Sie mir bitte etwas gegen …	… ni kiku kusuli o kudasai.
● Dieses Mittel ist rezeptpflichtig.	Kono kusuli wa ischa no schohōsen go hitsujō desu.

Japanische Ärzte sind ihre eigenen Apotheker, d. h. Medikamente bekommen Sie normalerweise direkt vom Arzt.

Wortliste Apotheke   ▶ auch Wortliste Arzt/Zahnarzt/Krankenhaus

Abführmittel	gezai
Antibabypille	pilu
Antibiotikum	kōsē-busschitsu
Aspirin	asupirin
Augentropfen	me-gusuli
äußerlich	gaijō no
Beruhigungsmittel	tchinsēzai
Brandsalbe	jakedo jō nankō
Desinfektionsmittel	schōdoku-jaku
einnehmen	kusuli o nomu, huku jō sulu
Elastikbinde	schinschukusē no alu hōtai
vor dem Essen	schokudji no mae ni, schokuzen ni
nach dem Essen	schokudji no atode, schokugo ni
Fieberthermometer	taion-kē
Gegengift	gedokuzai
Gurgelwasser	ugai-gusuli
Halstabletten	nodo no kusuli
Hustensaft	sekidome-gusuli
innerlich	naihuku-jaku
Insektenmittel	sattchūzai
Insulin	inschulin
Jod(tinktur)	jōdo
Kopfschmerztabletten	zutsū-jaku
Kreislaufmittel	kekkōsokuschin-zai
auf nüchternen Magen	kūhuku-ji ni
Magenmittel	i-gusuli
Medikament	kusuli

Mittel (~ gegen)	(~ ni kiku) kus[u]li
Mückenstiche	muschisasale
Mullbinde	gāze no hōtai
im Mund zergehen lassen	kutchi no naka de tokas[u]
Nebenwirkungen	hukusajō
Ohrentropfen	mimi no kusuli
Pflaster	bansōkō
Präservativ	kondōmu, hinin-gu
Puder	paudā
Rezept	schohōsen
Salbe	nankō
Schlaftabletten	suimin-jaku
Schmerztabletten	itamidome
Sonnenbrand	hijake
Tablette	djōzai
Traubenzucker	budō-tō
Tropfen	tenteki
Watte	wata
Zäpfchen	zajaku

Arztbesuch

Ischa o tazunelu

Japans medizinische Versorgung und Einrichtungen befinden sich auf einem hohen Niveau. Viele Ärzte und Zahnärzte verstehen deutsch. Auch in den konfessionell geführten Krankenhäuser in den großen Städten werden ausländische Patienten behandelt. Englischsprachige Ärzte können Sie auch im Telefonbuch unter der Rubrik „Medizinische Versorgung" ausfindig machen.

Wenn Sie in Not geraten sind, wenden Sie sich am besten an:

Deutsche Botschaft:
4-5-10 Minami Azabu, Minato-ku, Tokyo 106   Tel.: (03) 3473-0151
Österreichische Botschaft:
1-1-20 Moto Azabu, Minato-ku, Tokyo 106   Tel.: (03) 3451-8281
Schweizerische Botschaft:
5-9-12 Minami Azabu, Minato-ku, Tokyo 106   Tel.: (03) 3473-0121

Generalkonsulat Deutschlands:
5. Stock, Kobe Kokusai Kaikan,
1-6 Goko-dori 8 chome
Chuo-ku, Kobe   Tel.: (078) 232-1212

Können Sie mir einen guten … empfehlen?	ĩoi … o schōkai schite kudasaimasen ka?
Arzt	ischa
Augenarzt	me-ischa, ganka-i
Frauenarzt	hudjinka-i
Hals-Nasen-Ohren-Arzt	djibi·inkōka-i
Hautarzt	hihuka-i
Internisten	naika-i
Kinderarzt	schōnika-i
Neurologen	schinkē ka-i
Praktischen Arzt	kaigjō-i
Urologen	hi·njōka-i
Zahnarzt	ha-ischa, schika-i
Wo ist seine Praxis?	Kale no schinljō-djo wa doko desᵘ ka?
Wann hat er Sprechstunde?	Schindan-djikan wa itsu desᵘ ka?
● Was für Beschwerden haben Sie?	Doko no guai ga walui no desᵘ ka?
Ich fühle mich nicht wohl.	Kibun ga joku alimasen.
Ich habe Fieber.	Netsu ga alimasᵘ.
Ich kann nicht schlafen.	Nelalemasen.
Mir ist oft schlecht/schwindelig.	Memai ga schimasᵘ.
Ich bin ohnmächtig geworden.	Kizetsu schimaschita.
Ich bin stark erkältet.	Hidoku kaze o hīte imasᵘ.
Ich habe Kopfschmerzen/Halsschmerzen.	Atama/nodo ga itai desᵘ.
Ich bin gestochen/gebissen worden.	Muschi ni sasale/kamale maschita.
Ich habe Husten.	Seki ga demasᵘ.
Ich habe mir den Magen verdorben.	I o kowaschimaschita.

Ich habe Durchfall/Verstopfung.	Geli/benpi o schite imas^u.
Ich vertrage das Essen nicht.	Schokudji o uketsukemasen.
Ich habe mich verletzt.	Kega o schimaschita.
Ich bin gestürzt.	Kolobi maschita.
Ich glaube, ich habe mir … gebrochen/verstaucht.	… ga oleta/nenza schita to omoimas^u.
● Wo tut es weh?	Doko ga itai des^u ka?
Ich habe hier Schmerzen.	Koko ga itai des^u.
● Tut es hier weh?	Koko ga itai des^u ka?
Ich habe einen hohen/ niedrigen Blutdruck.	Ketsuatsu ga takai/hikui des^u.
Ich bin Diabetiker/in.	Wataschi wa tōnjōbjō-kandja des^u.
Ich bin schwanger.	Ninschin schite imas^u.
● Bitte, machen Sie sich/ Ihren Arm frei.	Sode o makuliagete kudasai.
● Bitte tief einatmen. Atem anhalten.	Schinkokjū o schite, iki o tomete kudasai.
● Öffnen Sie den Mund.	Kutchi o akete kudasai.
● Zeigen Sie die Zunge.	Schita o misete kudasai.
● Husten, bitte.	Seki o schitemite kudasai.
● Wie lange fühlen Sie sich schon so?	Sono-jōna djōtai ga mō dono kulai tsuzuite ilu no des^u ka?
● Haben Sie Appetit?	Schokujoku ga alimas^u ka?
Ich habe keinen Appetit.	Schokujoku ga alimasen.
● Haben Sie einen Impfschein?	Jobōsesschu-tetchō o omotchi des^u ka?
Ich bin gegen … geimpft.	… no jōbō-tchūscha o schimaschita.
● Sie müssen geröntgt werden.	Rentogen o tolanakeleba nalimasen.

- Sie brauchen eine Blut-/ Urinprobe. — Ketsueki-kensa/njō-kensa ga hitsujō desu.

- Ich überweise Sie an einen Facharzt. — Senmon-i o schōkai schimasu.

- Sie müssen operiert werden. — Schudjutsu o schinakeleba nalimasen.

- Sie brauchen Bettruhe. — Ansē ni schitekudasai.

- Es ist nichts Ernstes. — Schinpai sulu hitsujō wa alimasen.

Können Sie mir bitte etwas gegen … geben? — Nani-ka … ni kiku kusuli o itadake masenka?

Normalerweise nehme ich … — Hutsū wataschi wa … o nonde imasu.

- Nehmen Sie eine Tablette vor dem Schlafengehen. — Nelu mae ni itchi-djō nonde kudasai.

Hier ist mein internationaler Versicherungsschein. — Kole wa wataschi no kokusai hokenschō desu.

Können Sie mir bitte ein Attest ausstellen? — Schindan-scho o daschite kudasai masen ka?

Beim Zahnarzt

Ha-ischa de

Ich habe (starke) Zahnschmerzen. — (Hidoku) ha ga itai desu.

Dieser Zahn (oben/unten/vorn/hinten) tut weh. — Kono ha (ue/schita/mae/oku) ga itai desu.

Ich habe eine Füllung verloren. — Ha no tsumemono o naku schimaschita.

Mir ist ein Zahn abgebrochen. — Ha ga kakemaschita.

- Ich muß ihn plombieren.

  Ha ni tsumemo o schinakeleba nali-masen.

- Ich behandle ihn nur provisorisch.

  Kalino schotchi o schite okimas.[u]

- Ich muß ihn ziehen.

  Ha o nukanakeleba nalimasen.

- Dieser Zahn muß eine Krone bekommen.

  Kono ha wa schikan o kabusenakeleba nalimasen.

  Geben Sie mir bitte eine/keine Spritze.

  Tchūscha o utte/schinaide kudasai.

- Bitte gut spülen.

  Joku jusuide kudasai.

  Können Sie diese Prothese reparieren?

  Kono ileba o naoschite kudasai masen ka?

- Kommen Sie in zwei Tagen bitte nochmal zum Nachsehen.

  Hutsuka go ni mō itchido mise ni kite kudasai.

- Suchen Sie dann gleich Ihren Zahnarzt auf.

  Suguni kakalitsuke no ha-ischa e itte kudasai.

Im Krankenhaus

Bjōin de

Wie lange muß ich hier bleiben?

Dono kulai koko ni inakeleba nali-masen ka?

Ich kann nicht einschlafen./Ich habe Schmerzen.

Nemule masen/itami ga alimas.[u]

Geben Sie mir bitte eine Schmerztablette/Schlaftablette.

Itamidome/suimin-jaku o kudasai.

Wann darf ich aufstehen/ausgehen?

Okitemo/gaischutsu schite mo ī des[u] ka?

Geben Sie mir bitte eine Bescheinigung über die Dauer des Krankenhaus-aufenthalts mit Diagnose.

Schindan to njūin-kikan no schōmē-scho o kudasai.

Wortliste Arzt/Zahnarzt/Krankenhaus

Abszeß	nōjō
Abtreibung	tchūzetsu
Ader	kekkan
Aids	e·izu
Alkoholiker/in	alukōlu-tchūdoku-scha
Allergie	alerugiē
allergisch sein gegen	… ni taischite alerugiē ga aru
Anfall	hossa
Angina	angĭna, hentōsen-en
Anspruchsausweis *(Krankenkasse)*	hokenschō
ansteckend	densensē no
Appetitlosigkeit	schokujoku-huschin
Arm	ude
Asthma	zensoku
Atembeschwerden	kokjū-kon·nan
atmen	iki o sulu, kokjū sulu
Attest	schindan-scho
Auge	me
Ausschlag	hossa
Bauch	onaka
Bein	aschi
Bescheinigung	schōmē-scho
Besuchszeit	schinsatsu-djikan
bewußtlos	ischiki-humē no
Bißwunde	kamikizu
Blähungen	onaka ga haru
Blase	bōkō
Blinddarm	mōtchō
~entzündung	mōtchō-en
Blut	tchi, ketsueki
~druck (hoher/niedriger)	(kō/tē) ketsuatsu
bluten	schukketsu sulu
Blut|erguß	aoaza
~gruppe	ketsueki-gata
~probe	ketsueki-kensa, saiketsu

~transfusion	juketsu
~ung	schukketsu
~vergiftung	nōdoku-schō, haiketsu-schō
Brechreiz	hakike
Bronchien	kikanschi
Bronchitis	kikanschi-en
Bruch	sekkotsu
Brust	mune
~korb	mune, kjōkaku
Bypass	baipasu
Chirurg/in	geka-i
Cholera	kolera
Darm	tchō
desinfizieren	schōdoku sulu
Diabetes	tōnjōbyō
Diagnose	schindan
Diät	daietto
Diphtherie	djihuteria
drogenabhängig	majaku-kandja
Drüse	sen
Durchfall	geli
Eiter	umi
eitern	kanō sulu
Ellbogen	hidji
Entzündung	enschō
Epilepsie	tenkan
erbrechen, sich	haku, ōto sulu
erkälten, sich	kaze o hiku
erkältet	kaze o hita
Erkältung	kaze
Facharzt/ärztin	senmon-i
Fehlgeburt	ljūzan
Fieber	netsu
Finger	jubi
Fuß	aschi
Gallenblase	tan·nō
gebrochen	olelu
Gehirn	nō
~erschütterung	nōschintō
~schlag	nōikketsu
Gehör	tchōljoku

Gelb|fieber	ōnetsu bjō
~sucht	ōdan
Gelenk	kansetsu
Geschlechts|krankheit	sēbjō
~organe	sēki
geschwollen	halelu
Geschwulst	dekimono, schujō
Geschwür	kaijō
Gesicht	kao
Gips	gipᵘsᵘ
Glieder	teaschi
Grippe	ljūkan
Hals	nodo
~schmerzen	nodo no itami
Hämorrhoiden	dji
Hand	te
Haut	hada, hihu
~krankheit	hihubjō
heiser sein	koe ga kaleteilu
Herz	schinzō
~anfall	schinzō-hossa
~beschwerden	schinzō-schōgai
~fehler	schinzō-kekkan
~infarkt	schinkin-kōsoku
~schrittmacher	shinpaku-tchōsēki
~spezialist	schinzō-senmon-i
Heuschnupfen	bien
Hexenschuß	jōtsū, gikkuligoschi
Hüfte	koschi
Husten	seki
impfen	jobō
Impfpaß	jobōsesschu-tetchō
Impfung	jobōseschu
Infektion	densen, kansen
Infusion	tenteki
Ischias	zakotsu-schinkētsū
Juckreiz	kajumi
Keuchhusten	hjakunitchi-seki
Kiefer	ago
Kinderlähmung	schōni-mahi

Knie	hiza
Knöchel	kulubuschi
Knochen	hone
~bruch	kossetsu
Kolik	sentsū
Kopf	atama
~schmerzen	zutsū
Krampf	kēlen
krank	bjōki
Kranken|haus	bjōin
~kasse	kenkō-hoken
~schein	hoken-schō
~schwester	kangohu
Krankheit	bjō-mē
Krebs	gan
Kreislaufstörung	djunkan-schōgai
Krone	schikan, kabuse
Lähmung	mahi
Lebensmittelvergiftung	schoku-tchūdoku
Leber	kanzō
Leistenbruch	helunia
Leukämie	hakketsubjō
Lippe	kutchibilu
Loch *(im Zahn)*	ana
Lunge	hai
Lungenentzündung	hai en
Magen	i
~schmerzen	itsū
Malaria	malaria
Mandelentzündung	hentōsen-en
Mandeln	hentōsen
Masern	haschika
Menstruation	gekkē, sēli, mensu
Migräne	henzutsū
Mittelohrentzündung	tchūdjien
Mumps	otahuku-kaze
Mund	kutchi
Muskel	kin·niku
nähen	nū, hōgō sulu
Narbe	kizuato

Narkose	mas^ui
Nase	hana
Nasenbluten	hana-dji
Nerv	schinkē
nervös	schinkē-schitsu na
Niere	djinzō
Nieren|entzündung	djin-en
~stein	djin-seki
Ohnmacht	kizetsu sulu, ki o uschinau
Ohr	mimi
Operation	schudjutsu
Plombe	djūtenzai
Pocken	hōsō
Praxis	schinljō-djo
Prellung	naischukketsu
Prothese	purotēze
Puls	mjaku
Quetschung	zaschō
Rheuma	rjūmatchi
Rippe	abalabone
röntgen	rentogen
Röntgenaufnahme	rentogen-schaschin
Röteln	hūschin
Rücken	senaka
~schmerzen	senaka no itami
Rückgrat	sebone
Rücktransport	gjaku-jusō
Salmonellen	salumonela-kin
Schädel	gaikotsu
Scharlach	schōkōnetsu
Schienbein	kēkotsu
Schiene	soegi
Schlaflosigkeit	humin-schō
Schlaganfall	sotcchū
Schlüsselbein	sakotsu
Schmerzen	itami
Schnittwunde	kilikizu
Schnupfen	hanakaze
Schulter	kata
Schüttelfrost	okan

Schwangerschaft	ninschin
Schweiß	ase
Schwellung	hale
Schwindel	memai
schwitzen	ase o kaku
Seitenstechen	sasu jō na itami
Sodbrennen	munejake
Sonnenstich	hijake
Speiseröhre	schokudo
Sprechstunde	schinsatsu-djikan
Spritze	tchūscha
Station	sutēschon, bjōtō
Stich	saschikizu, muschisasale
Stuhlgang	bentsū
Sucht	tchūdoku
süchtig	tchūdoku-schō no
Tetanus	tetanusu, haschōhū
Trommelfell	komaku
Typhus	tchihusu
Übelkeit	hakike
Ultraschalluntersuchung	tchō·onpa-kensa
Unterleib	kahukubu
Untersuchung	kensa, schinsatsu
Urin	njō
Verband	hōtai
verbinden	hōtai o sulu
Verbrennung	schōkjaku, jakedo
Verdauung	schōka
Verdauungsstörung	schōka-huljō
Vergiftung	doku
verletzen	kega o sulu, huschō sulu
Verletzung	kega, huschō
verschreiben	schidji sulu, schōhō sulu
verstaucht	nenza sulu
Verstopfung	benpi
Virus	bĩrusu
Wartezimmer	matchiai-schitsu
weh tun	itami o tomonau, itai
Windpocken	mizu-bōsō
Wirbelsäule	sebone
Wunde	kizu

Zahn	ha
Backen~	okuba
Schneide~	itokiliba
~fleisch	haniku
~schmerzen	haita, ha ga itamu
Zehe	aschi no jubi
Zerrung	sudjitchigai
ziehen *(Zahn)*	ha o nuku, basschi sulu
Zunge	schita

11 Geschäftsreise
出張

Der lange Weg zum Geschäftspartner

Tolihiki-aite to

Wo ist der Hauptein-
gang?

Tchūō-genkan wa doko desᵘ ka?

Wie komme ich bitte
zu …?

… e wa dono-jōni ittala ī desᵘ ka?

Mein Name ist … Ich
komme von der Firma …

Wataschi no namae wa … desᵘ, …
scha kala kimaschita.

Kann ich bitte Herrn/
Frau … sprechen?

… san to o-hanaschi dekimasᵘ ka?

Melden Sie mich bitte
bei … an.

… no tokolo ni mōschi de te kudasai.

Ich habe einen Termin
bei der Firma …

… scha to jakusoku ga alimasᵘ.

● … erwartet Sie bereits.

… ga sᵘdeni omatchi desᵘ.

● Herr/Frau … ist noch in
einer Sitzung.

… san wa mada kaigitchū desᵘ.

● Ich führe Sie zu …

… ni otsule itaschimasᵘ.

Entschuldigen Sie bitte,
daß ich zu spät komme.

Osoku nalimaschite sumimasen.

● Bitte setzen Sie sich.

Dozō osuwali kudasai.

● Darf ich Ihnen etwas zu
trinken anbieten?

Nani-ka o-nomimono wa ikaga desᵘ
ka?

● Hatten Sie eine angeneh-
me Reise?

Goljokō wa ikaga deschita ka?

● Wieviel Zeit haben Sie?

Dono kulai o-djikan ga alimasᵘ ka?

● Wann geht Ihre Maschi-
ne?

Hikōki wa nan-dji ni demasᵘ ka?

Ich brauche einen Dol-
metscher.

Tsūjaku ga hitsujō desᵘ.

Wo sind Sie zu errei-
chen?

Doko de anata ni lenlaku ga tolemasᵘ
ka?

Ich wohne im … -Hotel.

… hotelu ni tomatte imasᵘ.

● Ich möchte Ihnen gerne meine Mitarbeiter vorstellen.

Dōljō o go-schōkai itaschimasu.

Unser Unternehmen ist ein kleines/mittelständisches Unternehmen.

Wataschi-domo no kaischa wa lēsai-kigjō/tchūschō-kigjo desu.

Es war ein interessantes Treffen.

Totemo kjōmibukai kaigō deschita.

Essen wir zusammen zu Mittag/Abend?

Tchūschoku/jūschoku/o isscho ni tabemaschō ka?

Sehr gerne, danke.

Aligatō gozaimasu, jolokonde.

Wenn Sie in Japan auf einer Geschäftsreise sind, zu der Sie von dort aus eingeladen wurden, können Sie davon ausgehen, daß alles bestens organisiert ist.

Für einen europäischen Geschäftsmann ist es wichtig, viel Zeit zu haben. Aus japanischer Sicht ist eine gesamtheitlich gute Atmosphäre Voraussetzung für gute Geschäfte. Sie werden zum Essen eingeladen und vielleicht laden auch Sie ein. Wenn der Abend fortgeschritten ist, wird auch gerne gesungen. Japaner kennen und lieben deutsche Lieder. Genieren Sie sich nicht, mitzusingen. Es wäre undenkbar, zielstrebig auf die Verhandlungsinhalte zuzusteuern.

*Tritt man in die Verhandlungen ein, ist es wichtig, folgendes zu beachten: Japaner werden eine Rede nicht unterbrechen, da dies aus ihrer Sicht als sehr unhöflich gilt. Ablehnung oder Zustimmung werden weder verbal noch durch Gesichtsausdruck geäußert. Ein direktes **iie** – „nein" werden Sie von einem Japaner nie hören. Vielmehr wird eine ablehnende Haltung aus der Gesamtatmosphäre erspürbar und durch Redewendungen wie „das ist schwierig..." oder „das ist ein bißchen ungünstig..." umschrieben. Ein klares **hai** – „ja" bedeutet für den Japaner eine absolute Verpflichtung, die er unbedingt erfüllen muß, um nicht das Gesicht zu verlieren.*

Außer viel Zeit sollten Sie eine zweisprachige Visitenkarte mit genauer Angabe der Firma und Ihrer Position mitbringen. Die Kleidung sollte nicht legere sein. Auch bei hohen Temperaturen sind ein Anzug, helles Hemd und Krawatte unerläßlich. Bringen Sie Prospekte und Unterlagen auf japanisch oder englisch mit.

Treffen wir uns um …?	… dji ni o aischimaschō ka?
Es findet ein Geschäftsessen mit … statt.	… to schokudji-kai ga alimasᵁ.
Es gibt einen Empfang anläßlich …	… o kinenschite resepᵁschon ga alimasᵁ.

Wortliste Weg zum Geschäftspartner

Abteilung	bumon, … ka
Büro	djimuscho, ofuisᵁ
Dolmetscher/in	tsūjaku
Eingang	iligutchi, genkan
Empfang	resepᵁschon, pātī
Firma	kaischa, … scha
Gebäude	tatemono
Konferenz|raum	kaigi/kaigi-schitsu
Pförtner	schuē
Sekretariat	hischo-ka
Sekretär/in	hischo
Sitzung	kaigi
Stockwerk	kai
Termin	jakusoku kijitsu, kigen

Verhandlung/Konferenz/Messe

Tolihiki/Kaigi/Mihon-itchi

Ich suche den Messestand der Firma …	… scha no mihon-itchi-būsu o sagaschite imasᵁ.
Gehen Sie in Halle …, Stand Nr. …	Hōlu … no būsu … e itte kudasai.
Wir sind Hersteller von …	Watakuschi-domo wa … no sēzō o schite olimasᵁ.
Wir handeln mit …	Watakuschi-domo wa … to tolihiki o schite olimasᵁ.
Haben Sie Informationsmaterial über …?	… no schiljō ga alimasᵁ ka?
Wir können Ihnen ausführliches Material über … zusenden.	… ni tsuite no schōsai schiljō o ōkulischimasᵁ.

Wer ist Ansprechpartner für …?	Donata ga … no tantō-scha desu ka?
Könnten Sie uns ein Angebot zukommen lassen?	Mitsumoli o ōkuli itadakemasu ka?
Wir sollten ein Treffen vereinbaren.	Itchi-do oai sulu jakusoku o schimaschō.
Hier ist meine Visitenkarte.	Kole ga wataschi no mēschi desu.

Wortliste Verhandlung/Konferenz/Messe

Abteilungsleiter/in	katchō
Angestellte/r	kaischa-in, djūgjō-in
Angebot	tēkjō, mitsumoli-scho
Ansprechpartner	tantō-scha
Auftrag	tchūmon, ilai
Auftragsbestätigung	tchūmon-kakunin-scho
Aussteller	schuppin-scha
~verzeichnis	tendji-mokuloku
Ausstellungsmaterial	tendji-hin
Einzelhändler	kouli
Export	ju schutsu
Exporteur	ju schutsu-gjōscha
Fachmesse	senmon-mihon-itchi, messe
Finanzierung	schikin guli
Fracht	jusō
Garantie	hoschō
General|vertreter	sō-dailinin
~vertretung	sō-dailiten
Geschäfts|beziehungen	tolihiki-kankē
~partner	bisinesu-pātonā, tolihiki-aite
Großhändler	ton·ja
Halle	hōlu
Hallenplan	kaidjō-an·nai zu
Handelsvertreter	tolihiki-dailiten
Hersteller	sēsan-scha, sēzou-scha
Import	ju·njū
Importeur	ju·njū-gjōscha
Industriemesse	sangjō-mihon·ichi
Informations|material	schiljō, sanpulu
~stand	an·nai-scho, infomēschon
interessiert sein an	~ ni kjōmi ga alu

Joint-venture	gappē-djigjō, djointo-bentchā
Kabine	kjabin
Katalog	katalogu
Kaufvertrag	baibai-kējakuscho
Konditionen	djōken
Konferenz	kaigi
Konzern	konzerun
Kooperation	kjōljoku, kjōdō
Kosten	hijō
~voranschlag	mitsumoli
Kunde/Kundin	kjaku
Leasing	kaschitsuke
Lieferant	nōhin-scha
Liefer|bedingungen	nōki-djōken
~ung	nōhin
~zeit	nōki
Lizenz(vertrag)	tokkjo, laisensᵘ
Marketing	mākettingu
Meeting Point	matchiai-bascho
Mehrwertsteuer	schōhi-zē
Messe	mihon-itchi
~ausweis	mihon-itchi-njūdjō-ken
~hosteß	an·nai-djō, hosᵘtesᵘ
~leitung	mihon-itchi-sekinin-scha
~rabatt	mihon-itchi walibiki
~service	mihon-itchi-sābisᵘ
~stand	būsu
~zentrum	mihon-itchi-sentā/honbu
Mitarbeiter	djūgjō-in, dōljō
Muster	mihon
Öffentlichkeitsarbeit	kōhō-katsudō
Preis	kakaku
~liste	kakaku-hjō
~nachlaß	nebiki
Produktion	sēsan
Proforma-Rechnung	kali-kēsan-scho
Prospekt	katalogu
Protokoll	kiloku
Rechnung	sēkjū-scho
Schulung	kunlen, torēningu
Skonto	genkin walibiki
Tagesordnung	nittē
Tochtergesellschaft	kogaischa

Transport	jusō
~kosten	jusō-hijō
Treffen	schūkai, kaigō
Trend	kēkō, torendo
Umsatzsteuer	uliage-zē
Unternehmen	kigjō
Verkäufer/in	sēlusu-man, ten·in *(im Laden)*
Verkaufsförderung	hanbai-sokuschin
Verpackung	hōsō
Versicherung	hoken
Vertrag	kē jaku
Vertrags|bedingungen	kē jaku-djōken
~händler	daili-ten
Vertreter/in	daili-nin
Vertrieb	hanbai
Vertriebsnetz	hanbai-mō
Visitenkarte	mēschi
Vortrag	kōen
Ware	schōhin
Warenverzeichnis	schōhin-bangō
Werbe|kampagne	kjanpēn
~material	senden-schōhin
Werbung	kōkoku, senden, komāschalu
Wirtschaft	kēzai
Zahlungsbedingungen	schihalai-hōhō
Zentrale	honbu, sentā

Ausstattung

Setsubi

Könnten Sie mir hiervon einige Kopien machen?	Kole no kopĭ o nan-mai-ka schite itadakemasen ka?
Für meinen Vortrag benötige ich einen Tageslichtprojektor.	Wataschi no kōen no tame ni ōbāheddo-purodjekutā ga hitsujō desu.
Würden Sie mir bitte … besorgen?	… o djunbi schite itadakemasu ka?

Wortliste Ausstattung

Ausstellungsmaterial	tendji-hin, sanpᵘlu
Diskette	fuloppī-disᵘku
Drucker	pᵘrintā, insatsuki
Farbkopierer	kalā-kopī
Folienstift	madjikku-pen
Fotokopierer	kopī-ki
Katalog	katalogu
Kopie	kopī
Mikrofon	maiku
Modem	modemu
PC	pasokon
Rednerpult	endai
Schreibblock	memo-jōschi
Stift	enpitsu
Tageslichtprojektor	ōbāheddo-pᵘrodjekutā
Telefax	fakkusᵘ
Telefon	denwa
Telex	telekkusᵘ
Textverarbeitungssystem	wādo-pᵘrosessā-schisᵘtemu
Verlängerungsschnur	entschō-kōdo
Videorekorder	bĭdeo-rekōda

Kurzgrammatik

Satzbau

Ein einfaches Satzmuster führt in die japanische Sprache:

Subjekt	Objekt	Prädikat
Kore wa Dies	ringo (ein) Apfel	desu. ist.
Watashi wa ich	doitsu-jin Deutsche(r)	desu. bin.

Diese Satzstellung kann im Japanischen immer erhalten bleiben, da grammatische Informationen durch nachgestellte Partikel gegeben werden.

Zum Beispiel macht **ka** hinter dem Prädikat aus dem Satz einen Fragesatz:

Kore wa Dies	ringo (ein) Apfel	desu **ka?** ist?

o hinter dem Nomen macht daraus ein Akkusativ-Objekt:

Watashi wa Ich	ringo **o** **den** Apfel	kaimasu. kaufe.

● Das japanische Substantiv erscheint immer mit Platzzuweisung:
  – entweder durch die Partikel **wa** (oder **ga**), wenn es das Subjekt oder Thema des Satzes ist,
  – oder durch ein Anhängsel (**o, ni, no** usw.), das die Fälle klärt,
  – oder es wird gefolgt von **desu,** was so viel wie „ist" bedeutet.

Die Zeiten und auch Verneinungen derselben geschehen am Verb; die Satzstellung ändert sich nicht:

Anata wa Sie	ringo o den Apfel	kaimashita ka? kauften?
Watashi wa Ich	ringo o den Apfel	kaimasen deshita. nicht kaufte.

Fragewörter, Verhältniswörter und sogar Konjunktionen haben den Charakter von Substantiven und werden auf diese Weise in den Satz eingebaut. Das Fragewort **doko** wo? wird in den folgenden Sätzen behandelt wie das Substantiv **Kyōto** oder **eki** Bahnhof:

Eki wa (der) Bahnhof	doko wo	desu ka ? ist?
Anata wa Sie	doko e wohin	ikimasu ka? gehen?
Watashi wa Sie	Kyōto e woher	ikimasu. kamen?
Anata wa Ich	doko kara nach Kyoto	kimashita ka? gehe.
Watashi wa Ich	eki no mae ni vor dem Bahnhof	machimasu. warte.

Substantive (Hauptwörter)

Das Japanische verfügt weder über einen bestimmten noch einen unbestimmten Artikel.

Die grammatische Information, wie ein Substantiv verwendet wird, wird durch Anhängsel (kleine Partikelwörter) gegeben, die hinter das Substantiv bzw. Pronomen treten. Die Substantive selbst erfahren keine Veränderung. Da jedes Substantiv eine beliebige Position innerhalb des Satzes einnimmt, erscheinen die Substantive immer mit ihrer jeweiligen nachgestellten Zuweisung innerhalb des Satzes. Entweder durch die gefolgten Partikel oder durch das Wörtchen **desu** ist.

Fälle

wa, ga	verwende das Substantiv im 1. Fall (Nominativ, wer-Fall)
no	verwende das Substantiv im 2. Fall (Genitiv, wessen-Fall)
ni	verwende das Substantiv im 3. Fall (Dativ, wem-Fall)
o	verwende das Substantiv im 4. Fall (Akkusativ, wen-Fall)
wa, ga	hinter einem Substantiv bzw. Pronomen kennzeichnet nicht nur die Verwendung im 1. Fall, sondern hat auch die Aufgabe, das Satzthema herauszustellen, das häufig das Subjekt des Satzes ist, aber nicht sein muß.

Ashita wa	nani o	shimasu ka?
Morgen	was	machst du?
Kare wa	hikōki de	kimasu.
Er	mit (dem) Flugzeug	kommt.

wa und **ga** sind so gut wie austauschbar; die genaue Unterscheidung gehört zu den Feinheiten.

no	Die Partikel **no** nach einem Substantiv oder Pronomen gibt die Zugehörigkeit zu einer Person oder Sache an, also den Besitz. Der Besitzer steht jeweils vor, der besessene Gegenstand hinter dem Wörtchen **no**.

ie no	mado	Fenster des Hauses
chichi no	ie	das Haus des Vaters

Tritt die Partikel **no** hinter die Personalpronomen, erhält man dadurch die besitzanzeigenden Fürwörter mein, dein, sein usw.

watashi no	hon	
mein	Buch	(wessen Buch?)
anata no	kuruma	
ihr/dein	Auto	(wessen Auto?)

ni	1.	steht für den Dativ und antwortet auf die Frage „**wem**?"
		Kare wa okāsan ni agemasu Er der Mutter gibt
	2.	mit **ni** wird auch der Raum, Ort oder der Zeitpunkt bezeichnet, an dem sich jemand oder etwas befindet: **ni** antwortet auf die Fragen „**wo**?" und „**wann**?"
		Hoteru ni tomarimashita. „In einem Hotel (ich) gewohnt"; Ich wohnte in einem Hotel. Nanji ni kimasuka? „Wann (Sie) werden kommen?"; Um wieviel Uhr kommen Sie?
o		Die Partikel **o** nach einem Substantiv hat die Funktion des Akkusativs („**wen** oder **was**?").
		Tokei o kaimasu. „Eine Uhr (ich) kaufen." Ich kaufe eine Uhr.

Weitere Partikel (Anhängsel)

Im folgenden sind einige weitere Anhängsel aufgeführt, die nach dem gleichen Schema wie die „Fall-Anhängsel" funktionieren.

e	nach	gibt die Richtung an auf die Frage „**wohin**?"
		Depāto **e** ikimasu. Ich gehe **ins** Kaufhaus. Doitsu **e** kaerimasu. Ich gehe **nach** Deutschland zurück.
de	in, im	gibt den Ort einer Handlung an auf die Frage „**wo**?"
		Nihon **de** kaimashita **In** Japan gekauft.

de	mit, mittels	gibt das Mittel an, mit Hilfe dessen etwas geschieht: „**womit?**"
		Ohashi **de** tabemasu. Ich esse **mit** Stäbchen. Takushi **de** ikimasu. Ich fahre **mit** dem Taxi.
made	bis	gibt den zeitlichen oder räumlichen Punkt an, bis zu dem eine Handlung oder ein Zustand verläuft: „**Bis wann/wo?**"
		Baseru **made** ... **Bis** Basel ... Kyō **made** ... **Bis** heute ... Itsu kara itsu **made** ... ka? Von wann **bis** wann ...?
kara	von (her), ab	gibt den zeitlichen oder räumlichen Punkt an, von dem ab eine Handlung geschieht: „**Ab wann/wo?**"
		Kinō **kara** byōki desu. **Seit** gestern bin ich krank. Ima **kara** ginkō ni ikimasu. (**Ab**) jetzt gehe ich in die Bank. Itsu **kara** gakkō ni ikimasu ka? **Ab/Seit** wann gehst du in die Schule? Ashita **kara** ikimasu. **Ab** morgen gehe ich.
ka		am Ende eines Satzes bedeutet soviel wie ein Fragezeichen. Diese Partikel **ka** stellt den einzigen Unterschied zwischen einem Aussagesatz und einem Fragesatz dar.
		Ringo o kaimasu. Du kaufst einen Apfel. Ringo o kaimasu ka? Kaufst du einen Apfel?

Plural (Mehrzahl)

Im allgemeinen wird die Mehrzahl am Substantiv nicht ausgedrückt. Meist geht der Sinn aus dem Zusammenhang hervor, z. B. durch Mengenbezeichnungen wie **takusan** (viel) usw. Bei Menschen sind Mehrzahlendungen üblich, indem man ein **-tachi** oder **-gata** (höflich) oder **-ra** anhängt.

kodomo	Kind	→	kodomo-tachi	die Kinder
sensei	Lehrer	→	sensei-gata	die Lehrer
kare	er	→	kare-ra	sie

Personalpronomen (persönliche Fürwörter)

Sie werden im Japanischen seltener gebraucht als im Deutschen. Das konjugierte Verb benötigt nicht notwendig ein persönliches Fürwort wie im Deutschen.

| Kyōto e ikimasu. | Ich gehe nach Kyoto. *oder* Du gehst nach Kyoto. |
| „Nach Kyoto gehen." | *oder* Er geht nach Kyoto. *oder* Wir gehen nach Kyoto. *oder* … |

Da das konjugierte Verb meist ohne Personalpronomen benutzt wird und die Konjugationsendungen keine Rückschlüsse auf die Person zulassen, da sie für alle Personen gleich sind, kann nur aus dem Zusammenhang hervorgehen, ob **ich** oder **du** oder **Sie** gemeint ist.

Schematische Darstellung

Singular		Plural	
ich	watashi / watakushi	wir	watashi-tachi / watakushi-tachi
du/Sie	anata	ihr	anata-tachi
er	kare	sie *(m)*	kare-tachi
sie	kanojo	sie *(f)*	kanojo-tachi
		sie *(neutral)*	kare-ra

● Da die persönlichen Fürwörter in der Regel das Satzthema darstellen, steht danach meist die Partikel **wa**:

| Watashi wa doitsu-jin desu. | Ich bin Deutsche(r). |
| Anata wa nihon-jin desu ka? | Sind Sie Japaner(in)? |

Dieses Schema entspricht in etwa den deutschen grammatischen Vorstellungen und genügt zum „Hausgebrauch". Die japanische Sprachwirklichkeit ist jedoch komplizierter.

Dazu einige Anmerkungen:

Ein Japaner definiert sich nicht als Individuum, sondern in seiner sozialen Bezogenheit. Erwachsene reden anders mit Kindern, Kinder anders mit Erwachsenen als jeweils untereinander, Männer untereinander anders als mit Frauen. Angestellte reden anders mit ihren Chefs als mit einem anderen Angestellten usw. Dies findet u. a. in der Wahl der Personalpronomen seinen Ausdruck. Von daher verfügt die japanische Sprache über eine große Anzahl an Personalpronomen, um Respekt oder Höflichkeit, gleiches soziales Niveau oder z. B. die Anrede während eines Streitgesprächs zum Ausdruck zu bringen. Ein paar Beispiele:

ich

watakushi	höflich gegenüber Älteren, Ranghöhern
watashi	neutral für beide Geschlechter
boku	unter Männer gleichen Ranges
ore	niedere Umgangssprache unter Männern

Sie, du

anata-sama	sehr höflich für beide Geschlechter
anata	neutral
kimi	unter guten Freunden (nur von Männern)
omae	unter Männern gleichen Ranges

In der Anrede werden im Japanischen die Personalpronomen seltener benutzt als im Deutschen. Sobald man jemanden kennt, zieht man es vor, ihn mit seinem Namen oder Titel anzureden, auch wenn es der direkte Gesprächspartner ist.

Anata wa sensei desu ka?	Sind Sie Lehrer(in)?
Sumisu-san wa sensei desu ka?	Sind Sie (Herr/Frau Sumisu) Lehrer(in)?

● Übrigens: Man sollte niemals jemanden mit Namen anreden oder über ihn reden, ohne an den Vornamen oder Familiennamen ein **-san** („Herr/Frau/Fräulein") zu hängen. Bei Kindern fügt man ein **-chan** an den Namen. Von sich selbst spricht man ohne **-san**.

Anrede innerhalb der Familie

Jüngere Geschwister sprechen ihre älteren Brüder oder Schwestern nicht mit Namen, sondern mit ihrem Titel an, der den Altersunterschied ausdrückt:

z. B.

onii-san	älterer Bruder
onē-san	ältere Schwester

Es wird auch unterschieden, ob man von seiner Mutter spricht oder seine Mutter anspricht, ob man von seinen eigenen Kindern spricht oder von den Kindern seines Gesprächspartners.

haha	meine Mutter	okāsan	Mutter (*Anrede*) Ihre Mutter
chichi	mein Vater	otōsan	Vater (*Anrede*) Ihr Vater
kodomo	mein(e) Kind(er)	okosan	Ihre Kinder
musuko	mein Sohn	musuko-san	Ihr Sohn
musume	meine Tochter	musume-san	Ihre Tochter
kanai	meine Frau	okusan	Ihre Frau
shujin	mein Mann	goshujin	Ihr Mann

er, sie

Im Deutschen werden diese Personalpronomen der 3. Person gebraucht, wenn zwei Gesprächspartner über einen dritten reden. Wird im Japanischen schon in der Anrede (2. Person) Name oder Titel bevorzugt, so wird für die 3. Person das persönliche Fürwort noch seltener gebraucht. Kennt man den Namen nicht, so spricht man in der 3. Person von:

ano kata (*höflich*)	diese Person, dieser Mensch
ano hito	diese Person, dieser Mensch

Gebrauch der persönlichen Fürwörter in den Fällen

Es gelten dieselben Regeln wie für die Substantive: Die grammatische Information wird durch die Anhängsel ausgedrückt. Hängt man z. B. **no** an ein persönliches Fürwort, so drückt das den Genitiv aus, gibt also den Besitz an:

watashi no	mein
anata no	dein / Ihr
onēsan no	das … der älteren Schwester

Verben

Es gibt keine besonderen Formen für Zahl, Person und Geschlecht. Verben werden häufig ohne persönliche Fürwörter verwendet.

> kaimasu   ich kaufe, du kaufst, er/sie/es kauft,
> wir kaufen, ihr kauft, sie kaufen

Das Japanische kennt nur zwei echte Zeiten: Gegenwart und Vergangenheit. Die Zukunft wird durch andere Mittel ausgedrückt (s. S. 202).

Die Besonderheit der japanischen Verben liegt in der Vielfältigkeit der Endungen, mit denen man Feinheiten zum Ausdruck bringen kann, also z. B. eine Aufforderung zu gemeinsamem Handeln, einen Wunsch, ein Nichtwünschen usw. Außerdem gibt es auch Unterschiede in bezug auf die Höflichkeit. Die Formen unterscheiden sich, ob man von gleich zu gleich spricht oder mit einer höhergestellten Person. Viele dieser Feinheiten werden durch jeweils besondere Endungen ausgedrückt, die an den Verbstamm angehängt werden.

Verbgruppen

Entsprechend ihrer Endung in der Grundform werden die Verben in zwei Gruppen eingeteilt:

1. Gruppe: Verben, die **nicht auf -eru, -iru** enden
   yom**u** lesen   kak**u** schreiben

2. Gruppe: Verben, die auf **-iru** oder **-eru** enden
   dek**iru** können   hanas**eru** sprechen können

Bildung des Verbstamms

1. Gruppe: Bei dieser Gruppe fällt das **-u** weg, und man ist schon beim Verbstamm. Um die Endungen anhängen zu können, wird zwischen Stamm und Endung ein **-i-** eingeschoben.

Verb		Stamm
yomu	lesen	**yom-**
nomu	trinken	**nom-**
kaku	schreiben	**kak-**
kau	kaufen	**ka-**

2. Gruppe: Bei dieser Gruppe entfällt **-ru**, die Endungen können dann direkt angehängt werden.

Verb		Stamm
dekiru	können	**deki-**
yomeru	lesen können	**yome-**
taberu	essen	**tabe-**

Zeiten

Gegenwart

Das Japanische verfügt über
– eine bejahte Form der Gegenwart und
– zwei verneinte Formen, wobei eine höflich und die andere neutral ist.

Die bejahte Form der Gegenwart wird gebildet, indem man an den Verbstamm die Endung **-masu** hängt:

> deki**masu** ich kann, du kannst, er kann usw.

Die verneinte höfliche Form erhält man, indem an den Verbstamm -**masen** hängt:

> deki**masen** ich kann nicht, du kannst nicht usw.

Die verneinte neutrale Form wird gebildet:

bei der 1. Gruppe durch Anhängen von **-anai**,
> yom**anai** ich lese nicht, du liest nicht, ihr lest nicht usw.
> hatarak**anai** ich arbeite nicht, du arbeitest nicht usw.

bei der 2. Gruppe durch Anhängen von **-nai**.
> deki**nai** ich kann nicht, du kannst nicht usw.

Verb	Stamm	bejaht	verneint (höflich)	verneint (neutral)
yomu	yom-i-	yomi**masu**	yomi**masen**	yom**anai**
hataraku	hatarak-i-	hataraki**masu**	hataraki**masen**	hatarak**anai**
dekiru	deki-	deki**masu**	deki**masen**	deki**nai**

Vergangenheit

Das Japanische verfügt über zwei bejahte Vergangenheitsformen:
– eine zusammengesetzte Form, die immer anwendbar ist,
– eine verkürzte Vergangenheitsform, deren Anwendung etwas spezieller ist.
Wie bei der Gegenwart existieren auch hier zwei verneinte Formen: eine höfliche und eine neutrale.

Die bejahte Form wird gebildet, indem man **-mashita** an den Stamm anhängt:

> deki**mashita** ich konnte, du konntest, er hat gekonnt usw.

Die verkürzte bejahte Vergangenheitsform endet auf **-ta/-da**. Dieses **-ta/-da** wird an den Verbstamm angehängt, der sich bei der 1. Verbgruppe jedoch nicht immer ganz regelmäßig verändert:

> kai**ta** ich habe geschrieben
> yon**da** er hat gelesen
> tabe**ta** ich habe gegessen

Die Bildung der **-ta**-Form erfolgt nach den gleichen Regeln, die für die Bildung der **-te**-Form gelten, die im folgenden Kapitel behandelt wird.

Bei der verneinten höflichen Form nimmt man die **verneinte Gegenwartsform des Verbs + deshita**:

> dekimasen deshita ich konnte nicht,
> du hast nicht gekonnt usw.

Die neutrale Form wird gebildet, indem man
an den Stamm der 1. Verbgruppe **-anakatta** anhängt,

> yom**anakatta** ich habe nicht gelesen usw.

an den Stamm der 2. Verbgruppe nur **-nakatta**.

> deki**nakatta** ich habe nicht gekonnt usw.

Verb	Stamm	bejaht (Langform)	bejaht (ta-Form)	verneint (höflich)	verneint (neutral)
yomu	yom-i-	yomi**mashita**	yonda	yomi**masen deshita**	yom**anakatta**
kaku	kak-i-	kaki**mashita**	kaita	kaki**masen deshita**	kak**anakatta**
dekiru	deki-	deki**mashita**	dekita	deki**masen deshita**	deki**nakatta**

Die absolute Gegenwart (-te-Form)

Das Japanische verfügt über eine Form zum Ausdruck der absoluten Gegenwart, eines momentanen Zustands. Deutsch könnte man es mit „jetzt", „gerade", „im Moment" wiedergeben. Diese Form entspricht der englischen Verlaufsform („-ing"-Form).

Die -te-Form des Japanischen wird immer in Kombination mit einer Form von iru sein gebraucht, wobei diese Form wie jedes andere japanische Verb behandelt wird:

imasu	–	Gegenwart
imashita	–	Vergangenheit
imasen	–	Gegenwart verneint
imasen deshita	–	Vergangenheit verneint

Shinbun o yonde imasu.	Ich lese gerade die Zeitung.
Tegami o yonde imashita.	Ich habe den Brief gelesen.
Suzuki-san o shitte imasu ka?	Kennen Sie Herrn Suzuki?
Hai/E, shitte imasu.	Ja, ich kenne (ihn).
Kono koto o shitte imashita ka?	Haben Sie von dieser Sache gewußt?
Hai/E, shitte imashita.	Ja, ich wußte (es).

Die Bildung der -te-Form ist nicht ganz so regelmäßig wie bei den anderen Formen. Sie ist wichtig, da man die -te-Form auch zum Ausdruck der Befehlsform braucht und darüberhinaus zur Satzverknüpfung.

1. Verbgruppe: An den Verbstamm wird ein -te angehängt, wobei sich aber die jeweils letzten Konsonanten des Stammes verändern.

Verb		Stamm	Konsonanten-veränderung	-te-Form
kaku	schreiben	kak-	k → i	kaite
kiku	hören	kik-	k → i	kiite
aruku	zu Fuß gehen	aruk-	k → i	aruite
hanasu	sprechen	hanas-	s → shi	hanashite
kasu	leihen	kas-	s → shi	kashite
kaeru	zurückkehren	kaer-	r → tt	kaette
shiru	kennen, wissen	shir-	r → tt	shitte
matsu	warten	mats-	ts → tt	matte
motsu	haben	mots-	ts → tt	motte
yomu	lesen	yom-	m → nd	yonde
sumu	wohnen	sum-	m → nd	sunde

2. Verbgruppe: An den Stamm wird ein **-te** angehängt. Die Bildung dieser Formen ist ganz regelmäßig.

Verb		Stamm	-te-Form
iru	sein	i-	ite
miru	sehen	mi-	mite
dekiru	können	deki-	dekite
oboeru	sich erinnern	oboe-	oboete
tsutomeru	angestellt sein	tsutome-	tsutomete

Unregelmäßige Formen

kuru	kommen	kite
suru	tun, machen	shite
iku	gehen	itte
iu	sagen	itte

Formenübersicht

1. Verbgruppe

Verben, die nicht auf -**iru**, -**eru** enden		Stamm	-te-Form	-ta-Form	-anai-Form
kaku	schreiben	kak-	kaite	kaita	kakanai
yomu	lesen	yom-	yonde	yonda	yomanai
kaeru	zurückkehren	kaer-	kaette	kaetta	kaeranai

2. Verbgruppe

Verben auf -**iru**, -**eru**					-nai-Form
iru	sein	i-	ite	ita	inai
miru	sehen	mi-	mite	mita	minai
dekiru	können	deki-	dekite	dekita	dekinai
oshieru	lehren	oshie-	oshiete	oshieta	oshienai

Unregelmäßige Formen

suru	machen		shite	shita	shinai
kuru	kommen		kite	kita	konai

Endungen und Satzkonstruktionen zum Ausdruck von „Feinheiten"

Vorschlag für eine gemeinsame Handlung
Ausdruck der zukünftigen Handlung

„Laß uns!" „Laßt uns!"

Bildung:	**Verbstamm + -mashō**
iku gehen	iki -mashō

Yokohama e ikimashō.	Laß(t) uns nach Yokohama gehen!
Sukiyaki o tabemashō.	Laß(t) uns Sukiyaki essen!
Kimono o kaimashō.	Laß(t) uns einen Kimono kaufen!
Gorufu o shimashō.	Laß(t) uns Golf spielen!

Äußerung eines Wunsches

„Ich möchte gern!"

Bildung:	**Verbstamm + -tai desu**
taberu essen	tabe -tai desu

Sukiyaki ga tabetai desu.	Ich möchte gerne Sukiyaki essen!
Kabuki ga mitai desu.	Ich würde gerne das Kabuki-Theater sehen.

● In Verbindung mit diesen -**tai**-Formen immer die Partikel **ga** verwenden.

„Ich möchte nicht"

Höfliche Form:	**Verbstamm + -taku arimasen**
iku gehen	iki -taku arimasen

Kyōto e ikitaku arimasen.	Ich möchte nicht nach Kyoto gehen.

Neutrale Form:	**Verbstamm + -taku nai desu**
suru machen	shi -taku nai desu

Kyō wa benkyō shitaku nai desu.	Ich möchte heute nicht arbeiten.

Wunschform in der Vergangenheit
„Ich wollte"

Bildung:	**Verbstamm**	**+ -takatta desu**
iku gehen	iki	-takatta desu
Kyōto e ikitakatta desu.	Ich wollte nach Kyoto gehen.	

Höfliche Bitte (Befehlsform)

Höfliche Form:	**te- Form**	**+**	**kudasai**
yomu lesen	yonde		kudasai!
Yonde kudasai!	Lesen Sie bitte!		
Chotto matte kudasai!	Warten Sie bitte einen Moment!		

Unter Freunden:	**Verbstamm**	**+**	**-nasai**
kiku hören	kiki		-nasai
kikinasai	Höre! Hört!		
tabenasai	Iß! Eßt!		

Höfliche Ablehnung / Verneinte Befehlsform
„Bitte nicht!"

Bildung:	**Verbstamm + -nai de kudasai**	
taberu essen	tabe	-nai de kudasai
Kore o tabenai de kudasai!	Iß dies bitte nicht!	
Kore o wasurenai de kudasai!	Vergiß dies bitte nicht!	

Scharfe Ablehnung

Bildung:	**-te-Form +**	**wa ikemasen**
terebi o miru fernsehen	mi-te	wa ikemasen
Terebi o mite wa ikemasen!	Fernsehen kommt nicht in Frage!	

● Mit den Worten **-wa dame desu** geht überhaupt nicht – kann man auch eine scharfe Ablehnung zum Ausdruck bringen.

Höfliche Anfrage
„Darf ich?" „Ist es in Ordnung, wenn...?"

Bildung: **-te-Form + mo ii desu ka?**

Terebi o mite mo ii desu ka?	Darf ich Fernsehen?
Itte mo ii desu ka?	Darf ich sagen?

Höfliche Ablehnung auf eine höfliche Anfrage

In Japan geht man mit Ablehnung oder auch einem „nein" sehr delikat um. Man umschreibt dies, um niemandem zu nahe zu treten. Ein einfaches **„chotto"**, was so viel wie ein bißchen bedeutet, genügt schon. Ein **„chotto komarimasu"** oder **„muzukashii desune"** ist schon deutlicher und bedeutet das bringt mich in Verlegenheit.

müssen

Bildung: **-ta-Form + -nakute wa narimasen**
-ta-Form + -nakute wa ikemasen

Yūbinkyoku ni ika-nakute wa narimasen.	Ich muß zur Post gehen.
Narande mata-nakute wa narimasen deshita.	Ich mußte in der Schlange warten.
Genkin-futo o tsukawa-nakute wa ikemasen.	Sie müssen den Bargeldumschlag benützen.

● In bezug auf sich selbst gebraucht man **narimasen,** in bezug auf andere Personen **ikemasen.**

nicht müssen, nicht brauchen

Bildung: **nai-Verbstamm + nakute mo ii**

matsu warten, nai-Form: matanai ich warte nicht	
Mata nakute mo ii desu.	Sie brauchen nicht zu warten.

„Es ist besser, wenn ..."

Bildung: **-ta-Form + hō ga ii (desu)**

wörtlich:	„Richtung gut ist"
Watashi-tachi wa kaetta hō ga ii desu.	Es ist besser, wenn wir heimgehen.

„Es ist besser, wenn nicht …"

Bildung: **nai-Form + hō ga ii (desu)**

Osake wa nomanai hō ga ii desu.	Es ist besser, keinen Sake zu trinken.

● hō ist ein Substantiv und bedeutet „eine von zwei Seiten, Möglichkeiten". So kann man mit der Wendung … hō ga … vergleichen.

Chikatetsu no hō ga hayai.	Die Stadtbahn ist schneller.

Die Erfahrung von etwas schon einmal gemacht haben

Bildung: **-ta-Form + koto ga arimasu**

wörtlich:	„die Sache gibt es"
Kyōto ni itta koto ga arimasu.	Ich war schon einmal in Kyoto.

können

Bildung: **Verbstamm (Gruppe 1) + -eru**
Verbstamm (Gruppe 2) + -rareru

kiku	hören	kikeru	hören können
yomu	lesen	yomeru	lesen können
hanasu	sprechen	hanaseru	sprechen können
taberu	essen	taberareru	essen können

Eine andere Möglichkeit, **können** auszudrücken:

Grundform + koto ga dekiru

Dekiru können, koto Sache	
Nihongo ga hanasu koto ga dekimasu.	Ich kann japanisch sprechen.

Passiv

Das Passiv wird im Japanischen selten gebraucht.

Bildung: **Verbstamm (Gruppe 1)   + -areru**
              Verbstamm (Gruppe 2)   + -rareru

kiku	hören	kikareru	wird gehört
yobu	herbeirufen	yobareru	wird herbeigerufen
homeru	loben	homerareru	wird gelobt
miru	sehen	mirareru	wird gesehen
taberu	essen	taberareru	wird gegessen
Seito wa sensei ni homerare-ru.		Der Schüler wird vom Lehrer gelobt.	

● Ist ein Verb zum Passiv geworden, gehört es automatisch in die Verbgruppe 2, da alle Passivverben auf **-eru** enden.
Alle Formen, die für das Aktiv gelten, können auch für das Passiv gebildet werden.

Die Formen von **können** sind häufig identisch mit den Passivformen.

| Kore wa taberaremasu ka? | Kann man das essen?
Wird das gegessen? |

Bedingungsform

„wenn", „falls"

Bildung: **-ta-Form   + -ra**

| ame ga furu regnen | futta + -ra |

| Moshi ame ga futtara ikimasen. | Wenn es regnet, gehe ich nicht. |
| Moshi ojisan ga sore o kiitara bikkuri suru deshō. | Wenn der Onkel das hört, wird er wohl überrascht sein. |

Adjektive (Eigenschaftswörter)

Adjektive sind Wörter, die ein Substantiv näher bestimmen. Wie im Deutschen treten die japanischen Adjektive vor das Substantiv.

Es gibt 2 Gruppen von Adjektiven, die jeweils unterschiedlich behandelt werden.

1. i-Adjektive (echte Adjektive)

Sie enden immer auf -i, wobei diesem ein a, i, o oder u vorausgeht.

yasui	billig	omoshiroi	interessant
furui	alt	tōi	weit
atarashii	neu	chiisai	klein
ōkii	groß	takai	teuer

2. na-Adjektive (Quasi-Adjektive)

na-Adjektive sind Substantive, die erst durch Anhängen von **na** zu Adjektiven werden. Meistens enden sie nicht auf **-i**. Falls doch, dann geht dem **-i** ein **e** oder Konsonant voraus.

kirei	schön	iya	schlecht
suki	gern haben	benri	praktisch
shizuka	ruhig		

Attributiver Gebrauch: das schöne …, das große …

i-Adjektive

furui otera	ein alter Tempel
atarashii kuruma	ein neues Auto
tōi machi	weit entfernte Stadt

na-Adjektive werden durch Anhängen von na zu Adjektiven.

kirei na hana	eine schöne Blume
suki na hito	ein Mensch, den ich liebe/mag
yūmei na otera	ein berühmter Tempel

Prädikativer Gebrauch: … ist schön, … ist groß

Bildung: **wa + Adjektiv + desu**

Tatemono wa takai desu.	Das Gebäude ist hoch.
Kono hon wa omoshiroi desu.	Dieses Buch ist interessant.

wa + na-Adjektiv (ohne na) **+ desu**

Kono kissaten wa shizuka desu ne?	Dieses Cafe ist ruhig, nicht?
Kenchō-ji wa yūmei desu ka?	Ist der Kencho-Schrein berühmt?

Zeiten

Beide Gruppen von Adjektiven verfügen jeweils über eigene Formen für Gegenwart (bejaht, verneint) und Vergangenheit (bejaht, verneint).
Wie auch bei den Verben existieren verschiedene Formen für die verschiedenen sozialen Sprachebenen (Umgangssprache und höfliche Redeweise).

i-Adjektive

Umgangssprache

Gegenwart		Vergangenheit	
bejaht	verneint	bejaht	verneint
i-Adj. ohne -i	**+ -ku nai**	**+ -katta**	**+ -ku nakatta**
atarashi-i neu	atarashiku nai nicht neu	atarashikatta war neu	atarashiku nakatta war nicht neu
chiisa-i klein	chiisaku nai nicht klein	chiisakatta war klein	chiisaku nakatta war nicht klein
furu-i alt	furuku nai nicht alt	furukatta war alt	furuku nakatta war nicht alt
ii / yo-i gut	yoku nai nicht gut	yokatta war gut	yoku nakatta war nicht gut

● ii und yoi bedeuten beide gut. In Verbindung mit -ku oder -katta wird jedoch nur yoi gebraucht.

Höfliche Redeweise

	Gegenwart		Vergangenheit	
	bejaht	verneint	bejaht	verneint
i-Adj. ohne -i	**+ -ku arimasen**	**+ -katta**	**+ -ku arimasen deshita**
omoshi-ro-i interessant	omoshiroku arimasen nicht interessant	omoshirokatta war interessant	omoshiroku arimasen deshita war nicht interessant
muzuka-shi-i schwierig	muzukashiku arimasen nicht schwierig	muzukashikatta war schwierig	muzukashiku arimasen deshita war nicht schwierig

● Bei der Bildung der Formen entfällt das -i der i-Adjektive.
● Der Unterschied zwischen den Formen der Umgangssprache und der höflichen Redeweise besteht nur in den verneinten Formen.
Die jeweiligen Formen wurden schon bei den Verben aufgeführt (s. S. 202).

na-Adjektive

Umgangssprache

	Gegenwart		Vergangenheit	
	bejaht	verneint	bejaht	verneint
na-Adj. ohne na	**+ dewa nai**	**+ datta**	**+ dewa nakatta**
kirei na schön	kirei dewa nai nicht schön	kirei datta war schön	kirei dewa nakatta war nicht schön
benri na praktisch	benri dewa nai nicht praktisch	benri datta war praktisch	benri dewa nakatta war nicht praktisch

Höfliche Redeweise

	Gegenwart		Vergangenheit	
	bejaht	verneint	bejaht	verneint
na-Adj. ohne na	**+ dewa arima-sen**	**+ deshita**	**+ dewa arimasen deshita**
suki na gern haben	suki dewa arimasen nicht gern haben	suki deshita gerne gehabt haben	suki dewa arimasen deshita nicht gerne gehabt haben

Adverbien

i-Adjektive verwandelt man in Adverbien, indem man das **-i** durch ein **-ku** ersetzt.

Adjektiv		Adverb
chiisai	klein	chiisaku
atatakai	warm	atataku
yoi	gut	yoku
osoi	spät	osoku

Kyōto wa yoku shitte imasu.	Ich kenne Kyoto gut.
Yoru osoku nemashita.	Ich ging spät ins Bett.
Atataku narimasu.	Es wird warm.

Den **na-Adjektiven** wird ein **ni** nachgestellt, um aus ihnen ein Adverb zu machen.

Nihongo o **jōzu ni** hanashimasu ne.	Sie sprechen gut japanisch.
Sore wa **hontō ni** yokatta desu ne.	Das war wirklich gut.
Kinō **genki ni** kaette kimashita.	Gestern kam er gesund zurück.

Gebräuchliche Adverbien

Totemo omoshiroi desu.	Sehr interessant.
Taihen yorokonde imasu.	Ich freue mich sehr.
Amari oishiku arimasen.	Es schmeckt nicht gut.
Hontō ni dame desu ka?	Geht es wirklich nicht?
Yukkuri itte kudasai.	Sprechen Sie bitte langsam.

Steigerung

Die Steigerung wird mit den Adverbien **motto** und **ichiban** gebildet, die vor die Adjektive treten.

Adjektiv	Komparativ	Superlativ
yasui billig	motto yasui billiger	ichiban yasui am billigsten
furui alt	motto furui älter	ichiban furui am ältesten
yūmei berühmt	motto yūmei berühmter	ichiban yūmei am berühmtesten

Kore ga ichiban yasui desu.	Dieses ist am billigsten.
Sore wa ichiban yūmei na matsuri desu.	Das ist das berühmteste Fest.

Vergleich

Bei Vergleichen benutzt man nicht den Komparativ, sondern die Wendung **(no) hō (ga)** die Richtung von.
Der Vergleichspartner erscheint mit einem nachgestellten **yori** als.

Tōkyō no hō ga ōkii desu.	Tokyo ist größer.
Shikoku wa Kyūshū yori **chiisai desu.**	Shikoku ist kleiner als Kyushu.
Kyōto no hō ga Tōkyō yori **furui desu**.	Kyoto ist älter als Tokyo.
Tōkyō yori **Kyōto no hō ga furui desu**.	

● An den unterlegten Sätzen wird ersichtlich, daß es sich um einfache japanische Sätze handelt, der Vergleichspartner erscheint mit einem nachgestellten **yori**.

Demonstrativpronomen (Hinweisende Fürwörter)

Dies, das, jenes, hier, da dort, hierhin, dorthin

Demonstrativpronomen bieten für das Japanische vielfältige Möglichkeiten, einfache Sätze zu bilden. Sie bauen sich nach einem bestimmten Schema auf, das auch auf das Fragewort „wo" anwendbar ist.

Position des Sprechers in bezug auf das mit der folgenden Silbe Erfragte:

ko-	nahe dem Sprecher
so-	nahe dem Zuhörer
a-	sowohl vom Sprecher als auch vom Zuhörer weiter entfernt

An diese Silben wird angehängt:

-re	für Sachen, Gegenstände und Personen
-ko	für Ortshinweise
-chira	für Richtungs-/Ortshinweise

Sprecher-position	Ort		Sache/Person		Richtung/Ort	
ko-	koko	hier	kore	dies	kochira	hier(hin)
so-	soko	da	sore	das	sochira	dahin
a-	asoko	dort	are	das dort	achira	dorthin

● Demonstrativpronomen stehen anstelle von Substantiven und werden wie diese behandelt.

Koko wa Ginza desu.	Hier ist die Ginza.
Asoko wa koen desu.	Dort ist ein Park.
Kore o kudasai.	Dies bitte!
Kore wa hon desu.	Dies ist ein Buch.
Are wa Tōdai desu ka?	Ist jenes die Universität Tokio?

Diese, r, s; der, die, das da; jene, r, s;

Hängt man die Silbe **-no** an die Vorsilben **ko-, so-, a-,** erhält man Demonstrativpronomen, die stets zusammen mit einem Substantiv verwendet werden.

Kono kamera o kudasai.	Diese Kamera bitte.
Ano shinbun o kudasai.	Die Zeitung dort bitte.
Sono terebi wa ikura desu ka?	Wieviel kostet jenes Fernsehgerät?

Fragewörter

Einige Fragewörter sind nach dem gleichen Schema aufgebaut wie die Demonstrativpronomen.

doko?	wo?
dore?	welche, -r, -s
dochira?	wohin?
dono?	welche, -r, -s

Tōkyō eki **wa doko desu ka**?	Wo ist der Bahnhof von Tokyo?
Koko wa **doko desu ka**?	Wo sind wir hier?
Dore ga kaitai **desu ka**?	Welches wollen Sie kaufen?
Dono hon **desu ka**?	Welches Buch
Dono gurai?	Welches Ausmaß (Länge, Weite, Zeit ...)
Dono gurai tōi?	Wie weit?

● Dono kann nur zusammen mit einem Substantiv gebraucht werden.

Die Anwendung der Fragewörter ist einfach, da sie behandelt werden, als ob sie ganz normale Substantive wären. Daher kommt auch, daß man nicht einfach **doko** für die Frage wo? sagen kann, sondern „**doko desu ka?**", d. h. sie unterliegen auch den Satzbauregeln, die für die Substantive gelten.

214

doko + Anhängsel

Hängt man an doko die uns bekannten Anhängsel, so erhält man weitere Fragewörter; dies führt mitunter zu Bedeutungsüberschneidungen wie im Fall von **dochira** wohin und **doko e**, wobei **doko e** gebräuchlicher ist.

doko e?	wohin?
doko kara?	woher?
doko de?	wo?
doko no?	von wo (sein)?

Doko e ikimashō ka?	Wohin wollen wir gehen?
Doko kara kimashita ka?	Woher kommen Sie?
Doko de gohan o tabemashita ka?	Wo haben sie gegessen?
Doko no hito?	Woher stammt er?

dare? (höfliche Form: **donata?**) wer?

dare?	wer?
dare no?	wessen?
dare ni?	wem?

Kono hito wa dare desu ka?	Wer ist das?
Kore wa dare no hon desu ka?	Wessen Buch ist das?
Anata wa donata desu ka?	Wer sind Sie?

nan, nani? was?
nan vor d, t, n sonst meist nani

Kore wa nan desu ka?	Was ist das?
Nani o sashiagemashō ka?	Was darf es sein?
Nani ga mitai desu ka?	Was möchten Sie gerne sehen?
Hoka ni nani ka?	Außerdem noch etwas?

ka und **mo** hinter Fragewörtern

Die Partikel **ka** hinter einem Fragewort macht unbestimmt irgend-
Die Partikel **mo** + Verneinung macht die Negation davon nirgend-/
niemand/nichts etc.

doko	wo	doko ka	irgendwo	doko mo	nirgends
dare	wer	dare ka	irgendwer = jemand	dare mo	niemand
nani	was	nani ka	irgendetwas	nani mo	nichts

● Bei den Negationsformen mit **mo** wird das Verb verneint gebraucht:

Dare mo imasen.	Niemand ist da.

dō? wie?
sō?

Kore wa dō desu ka?	Wie wäre es damit?
Dō shimashō ka?	Wie wollen wir es machen?
Sō shimashō?	Wollen wir es so machen?
Dō itashimashite!	Bitte! Gerne geschehen! (*Anwort auf vorausgegangenes Danke!*)

itsu? wann?

Basu wa itsu kimasu ka?	Wann kommt der Bus?
Itsu kara itsu made?	Von wann bis wann?
itsuka	irgendwann
itsumo	immer

naze?, dōshite? warum?

Naze kimasen ka?	Warum kommt er/sie/es nicht?
Dōshite sore o shimasu ka?	Warum machen wir das?

!

Wieviel? + Kategoriewörter

Im Japanischen wird genau unterschieden, wieviel von was gemeint ist.

Frage nach dem Preis:

ikura desu ka?	Wieviel kostet? Wie teuer?
Hon wa ikura desu ka?	Wieviel kostet das Buch?

Frage nach der Uhrzeit:

nanji desu ka?	Wieviel Uhr ist es?

Neben den Wendungen für Preis und Uhrzeit wird ganz genau unterschieden, wie der Gegenstand, die Sache beschaffen ist, ob es Mensch oder Tier ist, von welchen eine Teilmenge gemeint ist. Man nennt dies auch **Kategoriewörter,** von denen hier eine kleine Auswahl vorstellt wird.

-nin	Menschen (drei oder mehr)
-hiki	Tiere
-mai	dünne, flache Dinge (Papier, Hemden, Fahrkarten)
-satsu	Bücher
-hon	lange, schmale Gegenstände (Stange, Bäume)
-dai	technische Geräte

Nicht nur in den Fragen wird genau unterschieden, sondern auch die zahlenmäßigen Antworten erscheinen mit derselben Endung.

nan-nin?	wie viele Menschen?	san-nin	3 Menschen
nan-satsu?	wie viele Bücher?	yon-satsu	4 Bücher
nan-bon?	wie viele Regenschirme?	rop-pon	6 Regenschirme
nan-mai?	wie viele Fahrkarten?	nana-mai	7 Fahrkarten
Otona, ichimai, kudasai			Eine Fahrkarte für Erwachsene.

● Bei der Zählweise für Menschen gibt es Unregelmäßigkeiten:
  hitori (1)   san-nin (3)
  furari (2)   yon-nin (4) und regelmäßig weiter.

Ito-san ni wa kodomo ga nannin	Wie viele Kinder hat Frau Ito?
imasu ka?	

● Bei dem Kategoriewort **-hon** wechseln h, b und p:
  ip-pon (1)   rop-pon (6)
  ni-hon (2)   nana-hon (7)
  san-bon (3)   hap-pon (8)
  yon-hon (4)   kyū-hon (9)
  go-hon (5)   jup-pon (10)

Banana sanbon onegai shimasu.	Drei Bananen, bitte.

ikutsu desu ka?

Wieviel von etwas, dessen Beschaffenheit man nicht mit dem Kategoriewort benennen will oder kann. Die Antwort auf eine Frage mit **ikutsu** erfolgt mit dem ursprünglichen japanischen Zahlensystem.

Tsukue ga ikutsu arimasu ka?	Wie viele Tische gibt es?
Tsukue ga itsutsu arimasu.	Es gibt 5 Tische.

Präpositionen

Präpositionen stellen die räumliche oder zeitliche Beziehung zwischen zwei Dingen dar. Im Japanischen werden sie als Substantive aufgefaßt und wie diese in den Satz eingebaut.

Wenn man die Präposition **mae** als Substantiv auffaßt und mit „Vorderseite" übersetzt, wird klar, warum sie zwischen **no** (Genitiv) und **ni** (Dativ) steht.

Tatemono	no	mae	ni	machimasu.
Gebäude	dessen	Vorderseite; vor/vorne	beim	(ich) warte

An der Vorderseite des Gebäudes warte ich.
→**Ich warte vor dem Gebäude.**

vor	mae	Eki no mae ni. Vor dem Bahnhof.
hinter	ushiro	Sono ushiro desu. Dahinter ist es.
jenseits	mukō	Gakkō wa mukō ni arimasu. Die Schule ist dort drüben.
diesseits	temae	Yūbinkyoku wa ginkō no temae desu. Das Postamt ist hier bei der Bank.
in der Nähe	chikaku	Kono chikaku ni. Hier in der Nähe.
neben	tonari	Ano depāto no tonari desu. Neben dem Kaufhaus dort.
rechts	migi	Migi ni magaru. Rechts abbiegen.
links	hidari	Hidari ni magaru. Links abbiegen.
innen	naka	Heya no naka ni. Im Zimmer.
außerhalb	soto	Kaisha no soto ni. Außerhalb der Firma.
auf, über	ue	Tsukue no ue ni. Auf dem Tisch.
unter	shita	Tsukue no shita ni. Unter dem Tisch.
gegenüber	mukai	Eki no mukai ni. Gegenüber des Bahnhofs.

Bindewörter

Hier einige der wichtigsten:

und	to	Hambāga **to** kōhi o kudasai. Einen Hamburger und einen Kaffee bitte.
mit	to	Kare **to** ikimasu. („er und ich gehe") Ich gehe mit ihm.
auch	mo	Kōhi o nomimasu. Kēki **mo** tabemasu. Ich trinke einen Kaffee. Ich esse auch einen Kuchen.
sowohl... **als auch**	mo... mo	Doitsujin **mo** furansujin **mo** imasu. Sowohl Deutsche als auch Franzosen sind da.
weder... **noch**	mo...mo + verneinte Verbform	Furansu ni **mo** Itaria ni **mo** iki**masen.** Ich gehe weder nach Frankreich noch nach Italien.
entweder **... oder**	ka	Kyōto **ka** Nara ni ikimasu. Ich gehe entweder nach Kyoto oder nach Nara.

● Bindewörter stehen immer hinter dem Substantiv.

Satzverknüpfung

Im Japanischen werden Sätze verknüpft, indem man zwei einfache Sätze (normaler japanischer Satzbau, s. S. 189) mit einem Wörtchen verknüpft, das zwischen beiden Sätzen steht bzw. am Ende des 1. Satzes. Diese Wörtchen sind uns teilweise als Partikel oder Präpositionen schon bekannt, andere sind Substantive. Für alle gilt, daß sie die Sätze durch ihre Wortbedeutung miteinander verknüpfen.

kara	*(präp)*	von, her; daher → **weil**
mae	*(präp)*	vor → **bevor, ehe**
made		bis → **bis**
ato		nach → **nachdem**
toki	*(subst)*	Zeit → **als**
aida	*(subst)*	Zwischenraum, Zeitraum → **während**

weil	kara/ node	Hon o kaimasu **kara,** okane o kudasai. ("Buch ich kaufe, **daher** Geld bitte") **Weil** ich ein Buch kaufe, bitte ich dich um Geld. Kyō wa doyōbi **da kara**, kaisha wa yasumi desu. **Weil** heute Samstag ist, habe ich frei (hat die Firma frei).
		● **da** ist eine Form für **desu**
		Tomodachi ga kuru **node**, uchi e kaerimasu. **Weil** Freunde kommen, gehe ich jetzt nach Hause.
bevor	mae ni	Koko ni kuru **mae ni**, Ōsaka ni sunde imashita. **Bevor** ich hierher kam, habe ich in Osaka gewohnt.
		● **mae** erfordert immer das Verb in der Grundform, im 2. Satz dann die Zeit am Verb.
bis	made	Goshujin ni au made, sore o shirimasen deshita. **Bis** ich ihren Mann traf, wußte ich es nicht.

nachdem	ato de	Benkyō shita **ato de** terebi o mimasu. **Nachdem** ich meine Arbeit gemacht habe, sehe ich fern.
		● **ato de** erfordert immer die **-ta/-da-Form** (Vergangenheitsform)
als, wenn	toki	Sore o kiita **toki,** bikkuri shimashita. **Als** ich das hörte, war ich überrascht.
während	aida	Gohan o taberu **aida** wa terebi wo mimasen. **Während** ich esse, sehe ich nicht fern.
und		● Im Japanischen stehen zwei vollständige Sätze hintereinander, die durch die **te-Form** im ersten Satz und die normale Verbform im zweiten Satz miteinander verbunden sind. Im Deutschen wird dies mit **und** wiedergegeben.
		Takushi ni **notte**, depāto e **ikimasu**. Ich steige ins Taxi **und** fahre zum Kaufhaus. Kaimono o **shite,** uchi ni **kaerimashita**. Ich machte die Einkäufe **und** fuhr nach Hause.
wenn	to	Takushi de iku **to,** gofun gurai desu. („Taxi mit gehen **wenn,** fünf Minuten etwa sein.") **Wenn** man mit dem Taxi fährt, dauert es etwa fünf Minuten.
		● **To** steht nach dem Verb des ersten Satzes und stellt die Bedingung für den zweiten Satz dar. Deutsch wird dies mit **wenn** übersetzt.
und, aber	ga	Jitaku no denwa bango wa 457-453 desu **ga,** jimusho wa 176-5684 desu. Meine Privatnummer ist 457-453, meine dienstliche 176-6684. Samui desu **ga**, soto e ikimasu. Es ist kalt, **aber** ich gehe nach draußen.

Zahlen

Das Zahlensystem stammt aus dem Chinesischen und ist einfach aufgebaut. Aus 15 Wörtern können alle Zahlen bis zu 100 Milliarden zusammengesetzt werden.

0	rei, zero	6	roku	100	hyaku
1	ichi	7	shichi (nana)	1 000	sen
2	ni	8	hachi	10 000	man
3	san	9	kuu (kyuu)	100 Milliarden	oku
4	shi (yon)	10	juu		
5	go				

11	juu-ichi	(zehn eins)
12	juu-ni	(zehn zwei)
14	juu-yon	
17	juu-nana	
20	ni-juu	(zwei zehn)
23	ni-juu-san	(zwei zehn drei)
30	san juu	(drei zehn)
31	san -juu- ichi	(drei zehn eins)
2 000	ni-sen	(zwei tausend)

- Bei **4 shi** oder yon und **7 shichi** oder **nana** werden bei den zusammengesetzten Zahlen nur **yon** und **nana** verwendet.
- Bei den folgenden Zahlen gibt es lautliche Unregelmäßigkeiten:

300	sam-byaku
600	rop-pyaku
800	hap-pyaku
3 000	san-zen
8 000	has-sen

Kore wa ikura desu ka?	Wieviel kostet das?
Sore wa ni-sen en desu.	Das kostet 2 000 yen.

Altes japanisches Zahlensystem

Neben diesem Zahlensystem, das aus dem Chinesischen stammt,
verfügt das Japanische über ein Zahlensystem, das schon existiert
hat, bevor die chinesische Schrift nach Japan kam. Es ist jedoch
nur in Fragmenten erhalten: Heute sind noch die Zahlen von 1–10
von Bedeutung und werden für gestaltlose Gegenstände verwendet (oder wenn man die passenden Kategoriewörter nicht kennt).

1	hitotsu	6	mutsu
2	futatsu	7	nanatsu
3	mitsu	8	yatsu
4	yotsu	9	kokonotsu
5	itsutsu	10	too

Tamanegi o yotsu to tomato o   4 Zwiebeln und 2 Tomaten bitte.
futatsu kudasai.

Wörterbuch Deutsch–Japanisch

In den Wortlisten der Kap. 1–11 finden Sie das themenbezogene Vokabular in einer dem Deutschen angepaßten Lautschrift. Im vorliegenden Wörterbuchteil sind diese Begriffe in der international gebräuchlichen Hepburn-Umschrift wiedergegeben, um Ihnen einen Vergleich mit den japanischen Silbenschriften, aber auch mit anderen Büchern, in denen Hepburn verwendet wird, zu erleichtern.

Bei Begriffen, die mit einem * gekennzeichnet sind, handelt es sich um ausländische Lehnwörter. Sie werden in Katakana geschrieben.

Bei mit · versehenen Begriffen handelt es sich zum einen um na- und i-Adjektive *(siehe Kurzgrammatik, S. 207 ff.)*, zum anderen signalisiert der Punkt einen unbedingt nötigen Stimmabsatz wie z. B. in *dt.* Bade·insel.

A

Aal unagi
ab *(von)* kara
abbestellen torikesu
abbiegen magaru
abblenden genkou suru
Abblendlicht genkou-*ra ito
abbrechen oru
Abend yoru
Abendessen yuushoku
Abendkleid yakai fuku
aber shikashi, demo
abfahren shuppatsu suru
Abfahrt shuppatsu
Abfahrtszeit shuppatsu-jikan
Abfall gomi
Abfallbeutel gomi-bukuro
Abflug tobidatsu, ririku suru
Abführmittel gezai
abgeben *(übergeben)* watasu
abgelegen henpi·na
abheben *(Telefon)* toru; *(Geld)* hikidasu
abholen *(etw.)* uketori ni iku; *(jdn)* mukaeni iku
Abkürzung *(Weg)* chikamichi
abladen ni wo orosu
ablaufen *(Flüssigkeit)* ryuushutsu suru; *(Gültigkeit)* owaru
ablehnen kyohi suru
abnehmen torisaru
Abreise tabidachi, shuppatsu
abreisen (nach) tabidatsu, shuppatsu suru

Absatz ureyuki; *(Schuhe)* kakato
Abschied wakare
Abschleppdienst *rekkā-gaisha
abschleppen ken·in suru
Abschleppwagen *rekkā-sha
abschließen *(die Tür)* doa ni kagi wo kakeru; *(den Vertrag)* keiyaku wo musubu
Abschnitt bubun
absenden hassou suru
Absender sashidashi-nin
Absicht ito, mokuteki
absichtlich keikaku·tekina
Abstand kankaku
abstellen *(stellen)* oku; *(anhalten)* tomeru
Abszeß nouyou
Abteil shashitsu
Abteilung bumon
Abtreibung chuuzetsu
abwärts kudaru
abwesend kesseki no
Achse *(Auto)* shajiku, jiku
achtgeben (auf) ki wo tsukeru
Achtung *(Warnung)* chuui; *(Verehrung)* sonkei
Adapter *adaputā
Ader kekkan
Adresse juusho
adressieren atena wo kaku
Agentur dairiten
ähnlich niteiru
Ahnung yokan, yosou
Aids eizu
Air Terminal *eā tāminaru

akklimatisieren, s. ~ junnou suru
Akt *(Theater)* maku
Alarmanlage keikoku-souchi
Algen kaisou
alkoholfrei *arukōru-bun nashi
Alkoholiker/in arukōru-
  chuudoku-sha
alle zenbu, subete
allein hitori de
Allergie *arerugī
allergisch sein gegen ... ni taishite
  *arerugī ga aru
alles zenbu
allgemein ippan·tekina
Allradantrieb zenrin-kudou
als to shite, *(Zeit)* no toki
also tsumari
alt furui
Altar saidan
Altenpfleger/in roujin-kango-shi
Alter toshi, nenrei
Altertum kodai
Altstadt kyushigai
Alufolie *arumi hoiru
Amerika *amerika
Amerikaner/in *amerika-jin
Ampel shingouki
Amt yakusho
amtlich koushiki no
amüsieren, s. ~ tanoshimu
an Bord kinai de
Ananas *painappuru
anbieten teikyou suru
Andenken omoide
andere, der, die, das ~ mou ippou
  no
andermal, ein ~ mata itsuka
ändern kaeru
anders hokano
anderswo dokoka hokade, yosode
anderthalb ichi to nibun no ichi
Anfall hossa
Anfang hajime, saisho
anfangen hajimeru
Anfänger/in shoshinsha
Angabe *(Meldung)* moushitate;
  (Hinweis) shiji
Angebot *(der Vorschlag)* teian;
  (anbieten) teikyou
Angel tsuri
Angelegenheit youji, youken
angeln tsuru

angenehm kokoyoi
Angestellte/r shain, shokuin, juu-
  gyouin
Angina hentousenen
Anglistik eibun-gaku
Angst fuan, kyoufu
anhalten tomeru
Anhänger *(Auto)* *toreirā;
  (Schmuck) pendanto
Animation *(comic)*animēshon,
  *manga
Anker *ankā
anklopfen tataku
ankommen touchaku suru
Ankunft touchaku
Ankunftszeit touchaku-jikan
Anlage *(Einrichtung)* setsubi
Anlaß *(Ursache)* gen·in; *(die Gele-*
  genheit) kikai
Anlasser shidou-souchi
anlaufen kaishi suru, shidou suru
Anlegeplatz funa tsukiba
anmachen *(einschalten)* tsukeru;
  (Salat) *saradawo mazeru
anmelden moushikomu
Anmeldung todokede, shinkoku
Annahme juryou
annehmen *(erhalten)* uketoru;
  (übernehmen) hikiukeru
Anorak *anorakku
anprobieren shichaku suru
Anreisetag ryokou-shuppatsu-bi
Anrufbeantworter rusuban-denwa
anrufen denwa wo suru, kakeru
anschauen miru
anscheinend mikakeno; *(adj)* douyara ... rashii
Anschluß setsuzoku
anschnallen, sich *shītoberuto wo
  shimeru
Anschnallgurt anzen-*beruto,
  *shīto-*beruto
Anschrift atena
ansehen miru
Ansicht *(Meinung)* iken, kenkai
Ansichtskarte ehagaki
Ansprechpartner tantou-sha
anspringen shidou suru
anstatt no kawari ni
ansteckend densesei no, hitoni
  utsuru
anstrengend tsukareru, ki wo haru

A/Z

Anstrengung *(Bemühung)* doryo-ku; *(Strapaze)* kurou
Antibabypille hinin-yaku
Antibiotikum kousei-busschitsu
antik kofuu na
Antike kodai-bunka
Antiquariat furuhon-ya
Antiquitätengeschäft kottou-shou, kottou-ya
Antwort henji, kaitou
antworten henji wo suru
anwenden mochiiru
Anwendung shiyou
anwesend shusseki shiteiru
Anzeige *(Meldung)* todokede; *(Annonce)* koukoku
anzeigen todokederu, koukoku wo dasu
anziehen mini tsukeru, fuku wo kiru
Anzug *sūtsu
anzünden hi wo tsukeru
Apfel ringo
Apfelsinen orenji
Apotheke kusuri-ya
Apotheker/in yakuzai-shi
Apparat kigu
Appartement *apāto
Appetit shokuyoku
Appetitlosigkeit shokuyoku-fus-hin
Aprikosen anzu
Arbeit shigoto
arbeiten shigoto wo suru
Arbeiter/in roudou-sha
arbeitslos shitsugyou
Archäologie kouko-gaku
Architekt/in kenchiku-ka
Architektur kenchiku
ärgern (sich ~) hara wo tateru
Arm ude
arm mazushi·i
Armband udewa
Armbanduhr ude-doke·i
Ärmel sode
Art *(Methode)* houhou; *(Sorte)* shurui
Artikel *(Waren)* shouhin; *(Zeitung)* kiji
Arzt/Ärztin ischi, ischa
Aschenbecher haizara
Asiate *ajia-jin

Asiatin *ajia-jin
asiatisch *ajia no, *ajia-jin·no
Asien *ajia
Aspirin *asupirin
Asthma zensoku
Atem iki, kokyuu
Atembeschwerden kokyuu-kon-nan
atmen iki wo suru
Attest shindan-sho
Auberginen nasu
auf *(darauf)* ~ no ne ni
auf *(offen)* akeru
aufbewahren hozon suru
aufbrechen kojiakeru
Aufenthalt taizai
Aufenthaltsraum danwa-shitsu
auffordern yousei suru
Aufführung *(Theater)* jouen, *(Film)* jouei, *(Konzert)* ensou
aufgeben dannen suru
aufhalten, jdn ~/s. ~ ~ wo hikito-meru
aufhängen kakeru
aufhören yameru
aufladen tsumikomu; *(Batterie)* juuden suru
aufmachen akeru
aufmerksam ki wo kubaru, chuui suru
Aufnahme ukeire
aufnehmen ukeireru
aufpassen (auf) ki wo tsukeru, chuui suru
aufpumpen fukuramasu
aufrufen yobikakeru
aufschieben enki suru
aufschreiben kakitomeru
Aufschub enki
Aufseher kantoku-sha
aufstehen tachiagaru
aufstellen *(liegen)* oku; *(Plan)* tateru
Auftrag chuumon
Auftragsbestätigung chuumon-kakunin
aufwachen me ga sameru
aufwärts ue e
aufwecken me wo samasu
Aufzeichnung kiroku
Aufzug *erebētā
Auge me

Augenblick isshun
Augenbrauen mayuge
Augentropfen megusuri
aus ~ kara
Ausbildung kyouiku
Ausdruck hyougen
ausdrücklich meikaku·na
Ausfahrt deguchi
Ausflug ensoku
Ausfuhr yushutsu
ausführen *(Export)* yushutsu suru
ausführlich kuwashi·i
ausfüllen mitasu
Ausgaben shishutsu
Ausgang deguchi
ausgeben shishutsu suru
ausgehen gaishutsu suru
ausgeschlossen fukanou·na
ausgezeichnet sugureta
Ausgrabungen hakkutsu
Auskunft annai
Ausland gaikoku, kaigai
Ausländer/in gaikoku-jin
ausländisch gaikoku no
Auslandsgespräch kokusai-tsuu-wa
auslaufen nagarederu
ausleihen kariru
Auslöser *suicchi
ausmachen kesu
Ausnahme reigai
auspacken (tsatsami o) hodoku
Auspuff haikikan
Ausreise shukkoku
ausreisen shukkoku suru
ausrichten *(Grüße)* tsutaeru; *(Ordnung)* totonoeru
ausrufen yobidasu
ausruhen, s. ~ yasumu
ausschiffen gesen suru
Ausschlag hossa
aussehen no youni mieru
außer no hoka
außerdem sono hoka ni
außergewöhnlich ijouna
außerhalb no hoka ni
äußerlich hyoumenteki·na, *(med.)* gaiyou no
Aussicht keshiki
Aussichtspunkt tenbou-dai
Aussprache hatsuon; *(Diskussion)* tougi

aussprechen hatsuon suru
Ausstattung soubi, setsubi
aussteigen gesha suru
Aussteller shuppin-sha
Ausstellung tenji-kai
Ausstellungsmaterial tenji-hin
aussuchen erabi dasu
Austausch koukan
austauschen koukan suru
Austern kaki
ausüben renshuu suru
Ausverkauf uritsukushi, urikire
Auswahl sentaku
Ausweis shoumei-sho
auszahlen shiharau
ausziehen nuku
Auto kuruma
Autobahn kousoku-douro
Autobahngebühren tsuukou-ryou-kin
Automat jidou-hanbaiki
Automatik(getriebe) jidou
automatisch jidoushiki no
Automechaniker jidousha-kou
Autoradio *kā-rajio
Autoreifen taiya
Autoschlüssel kuruma no kagi
Avocado *abogado

B

Baby akachan, *bebĭ
Babynahrung *bebĭ-*fūdo
Bäckerei *pan-ya
Bäcker/in *pan-ya
Backstein renga
Bad furo, *basu
Badeanzug mizugi
Badetuch *taoru
baden nyuuyoku suru, suiei suru
Badeort onsen-chi, kaisuiyokujou
Badewanne yokuson
Badezimmer *basu rūmu, furoba, yokushitsu
Badminton *badominton
Bahnhof eki
bald mamonaku
Balkon *barukonĭ, *terasu*
Ball *bōru
Ballett *barē
Bananen *banana

Band, das ~ *tēpu, himo
Band, der ~ kan
Bank *(Geldinstitut)* ginkou; *(Sitz~)* benchi
Bankkonto kouza-bangou
Bankleitzahl ginkou-bangou
bar *(Geld)* genkin, mukidashino
Bar *(Kneipe)** Bā
bar zahlen genkin de harau
Bargeld genkin
Barometer *baromētā
Barsch *(Fisch)* susuki
Bart hige
Basketball *basuketto bōru
Batterie *batteriē
Bauch onaka
bauen tateru
Bauer noumin
Bauernhof nouka
Baum ki
Baumwolle men, *kotton
Baustelle kouji-genba
Bauwerk kenchikubutsu
beabsichtigen mokuromu
beachten chuui wo harau
Beamter/Beamtin koumu-in
Beanstandung igi, kujou
beantworten kotaeru
bearbeiten kakou suru
Becher *koppu
bedauern zannen ni omou
Bedauern zannen
bedecken oou
bedeuten imi suru
bedeutend juuyou·na
Bedeutung imi
bedienen tsukaeru
bedienen, sich jibun de toru
Bedienung kyuuji
Bedingung jouken
beeilen, s. ~ isogu
beenden oeru, sumasu
befinden, s. ~ ni aru, ni iru
befolgen shitagau
befördern hakobu
befreundet sein shitashiku suru
befriedigt manzokushita
befürchten osoreru, kizuku
begegnen deau
begeistert (von) kandou suru
Beginn hajime
beginnen hajimeru

begleiten tsukisou
Begleitung tsukisoi-nin, douhan
begrüßen aisatsuwo suru
behalten hoji suru
Behälter youki, iremono
behandeln toriatsukau, *(Arzt)* chiryou suru
Behandlung toriatsukai, *(Arzt)* chiryou
behaupten shichou suru
behilflich tasakeninaru
Behörde kanchou, yakusho
bei no tokoro
beide ryouhou no
Beifall hakushu
beige *bēju
Beilage *(Essen)* tsukeawase; *(Zeitung)* furoku
Beileid kuyami
Bein ashi
beinahe hotondo, ayauku
Beispiel tatoe, rei
beißen kamu
bekannt yuumei·na
Bekannte, der, die ~ chijin
Bekanntschaft menshiki
beklagen, s. ~ **(über)** kujou wo iu
bekommen morau
Belagerung houi
belästigen meiwaku wo kakeru
belegen, einen Platz ~ shimeru
beleidigen kutsu joku suru
Beleidigung kutsujoku
Beleuchtung shoumei, akari
Belichtungsmesser roshutsu-kei
Belieben, nach ~ konomashi·i
belohnen mukuiru
Belohnung houshuu
bemerken kizuku
bemühen, s. ~ doryoku suru
benachrichtigen tsuuchi suru
Benehmen taido, furumai
benötigen hitsuyou to suru
benutzen tsukau
Benutzungsgebühr shiyou-ryou
Benzin *gasorin; ~**kanister** *gasorin-kan
beobachten kansatsu suru
bequem kokochiyoi
Bequemlichkeit kaiteki
berechnen keisan suru

berechtigt seitou·na, touzen no
bereit you ino dekita
bereits sudeni
Berg yama
bergab yama wo kudaru
bergauf yama ni noboru
Bergdorf sanson
Bergsteigen tozan
Bericht houkoku
Beruf shokugyou
beruflich shokugyou·gara
Berufsschule shokugyou-gakkou
beruhigen, s. ~ anshin suru
Beruhigungsmittel anteizai
berühmt yuumei·na
berühren ni fureru
Berührung sesshoku
Besatzung joumu-in
beschädigen hason suru
Beschädigung hason
beschaffen choutatsu suru
beschäftigt isogashi·i
Bescheid geben shiraseru
bescheinigen shoumei suru
Bescheinigung kakunin-sho
beschlagnahmen sashiosae
beschleunigen kasoku suru
beschließen ketsugi suru
beschreiben egaku
beschützen hogo suru
Beschwerde kujou
beschweren, s. ~ **(über)** kujou wo
iu
Besen houki
besetzt shiyou-chuu
besichtigen kengaku suru
Besichtigung kengaku
Besitz shoyuu
besitzen shoyuu suru
Besitzer shoyuu-sha
besondere(r, -s) tokushu na, tokubetsu na
besonders tokuni, toriwake
besorgen choutatsu suru
besorgt shinpai suru, ki o kubaru
Besorgung choutatsu
besser yoriyoi
bestätigen kakunin suru
bestehen aus kara naritatsu
bestellen *(Essen, Tisch)* chuumon
suru
Bestellung chuumon

beste(r, -s) ichiban yoi
bestimmt *(festgelegt)* sadamerareta; *(sicher)* tashikana
Bestimmungen kisoku
Bestimmungsort mokuteki-chi
Bestrahlung terasu
Besuch houmon
besuchen, jdn ~ wo otozureru,
houmon suru
Besuchszeit *(Arzt)* shindan-jikan;
(Krankenhaus) menkai-jikan
beten inoru
betrachten kansatsu suru
beträchtlich kanarino, soutouna
Betrag kingaku
betragen ni naru
betreffen kankei suru
betreten fumiireru, hairu
Betriebswirt/in keizai-keiei-gakushi
Betriebswirtschaft keizai-gaku
betrinken, s. ~ yopparau
Betrug sagi
betrügen damasu
betrunken yopparatta
Bett *betto; ~**decke** kakebuton;
~**laken** *sitsu
beurteilen handan suru
Beutel fukuro
bevor mae, izen
bewachen kanshi suru
bewegen ugoku
Bewegung ugoki
Beweis shouko
beweisen shoumei suru
Bewohner juumin
bewölkt kumori
bewundern kanshin suru
bewußt jikaku shiteiru
bewußtlos ishiki fumei no
bezahlen shiharau
bezaubernd miryou suru
Bezeichnung kankei
beziehen, s. ~ **auf** ni kanshite
Bibliothek toshokan
Bibliothekar/in toshokan-in, shisho
biegen magaru
Biene hachi
Bier *biru
bieten teikyou suru
Bikini bikini

Bild e
bilden tsukuru
billig yasui
binden musubu
Bindfaden musubi-himo
Biologe/in seibutsu-gakusha
Biologie seibutsu-gaku
Birne nashi
bis made
bißchen, ein ~ sukoshi
Bißwunde kamikizu
Bitte onegai
bitte dou itashimashite
bitten, jdn um etw ~ onegai suru
bitter nigai
Blähungen onaka ga haru
Blase boukou
Blatt ha, happa
blau ao
Blazer *burezā-kōto
bleiben todomaru
bleich aozameta
Bleistift enpitsu
Bleistiftspitzer enpitsu-kezuri
Blende hiyoke
blenden hikari wo saegiru
Blick shisen, nagame
blind moumoku
Blinddarm mouchou
Blinddarmentzündung mouchou-
  en
blinken pikapika *hikaru
Blinker *uinkā
Blitz inazuma
Blitzgerät *furasshu-souchi
blöd(e) manuke·na
blond kinpatsu no
blühen *(Blumen)* saiteiru; *(Ge-
  schäft)* sakaeru
Blume hana
Blumengeschäft hana-ya
Blumenkohl *karifurawā
Blumenstrauß hanataba
Bluse *burausu
Blut chi
  Blutdruck (hoher/niedriger) ket-
  suatsu (kou/tei)
bluten shukketsu suru
Bluterguß aoaza
Blutgruppe ketsueki-gata
Blutprobe ketsueki-kensa, saiketsu
Bluttransfusion yuketsu

Blütezeit kaika-jiki
Bö toppuu
Boden yuka, soko
Bohnen mame
Boiler *boirā
Boot *bōto
Bootsverleih kashi-*bōto
Bord, an ~ **gehen** fune, hikouki ni
  noru
Bordkarte toujou-ken
böse warui
Botanischer Garten shokubutsu-
  en
Botschaft taishikan
Boutique *butikku
Bowling *bōringu
Brand kaji, kasai
Brandsalbe yakedo-gusuri
braten yaku
Braten yakiniku, *rōsuto
brauchen hitsuyou to suru
Brauchtum fuushuu
braun cha-iro
Brechreiz hakike
breit haba
Bremsbelag *burēki-*rainingu
Bremse *burēki
bremsen *burēki wo kakeru
Bremsflüssigkeit *burēki oiru
brennen moeru
Brief tegami
Briefkasten posuto
Briefmarke kitte
Briefmarkenautomat kitte-jidou-
  hanbaiki
Briefpapier binsen
Brieftasche shorui-kaban, satsuire
Briefträger/in yuubin-haitatsu-nin
Briefumschlag fuutou
Briefwechsel buntsuu
Brille megane
bringen hakobu
Bronchien kikanshi
Bronchitis kikan-shien
Bronze dou
Brosche *burōchi
Brot *pan
Bruch *(Knochen)* sekkotsu; *(Ge-
  schirr)* wareru
Brücke hashi
Bruder kyoudai
Brunnen funsui, ido

Brust mune
Buch hon
buchen yoyaku suru
Buchhalter/in keiri-shi
Buchhandlung hon-ya
Büchse kanzume
buchstabieren tsuzuru
Bucht wan, irie
Buchung yoyaku
Bügeleisen airon
bügeln *airon wo kakeru
Bühne butai
Bummel sanpo
Bund doumei
Bungalow *bangarou
bunt iro-toridori
Burg shiro
Bürgermeister/in shichou
Büro jimu-sho
Büroklammern *kurippu
Bürste *burashi
bürsten *burashi wo kakeru
Bus *basu
Busch shigemi
Business class *bisinesu-kurasu
Bußgeld bakkin
Büste mune, *basuto
Büstenhalter *burajā
Butter *batā
Bypass *baipasu

C

Café kissaten
Camping *kyanpu
CD/Compactdisc *sīdī
Champignons *masshurūmu
Chauffeur unten-shu
Chef *chīfu
Chemie kagaku
Chemiker/in kagaku-sha
chemisch reinigen *dorai-*kuri-
ningu
China chuugoku
Chinese/in chuugoku-jin
chinesisch chuugoku-go
Chirurg/in geka-i
Cholera *korera
Chor gasshou-dan, *kōlasu
Christ *kirisuto

Christentum *kirisuto-kyou
Collage *korāju
Cousin/e itoko
Creme *kurīmu

D

da soko
Dach yane
Dachdecker/in yanefuki-shokunin
dafür sein ~ ni sansei dearu
dagegen sein ~ ni hantai dearu
daheim uchi ni īru
daher yotte, soreyueni
damals touji
Dame onna no hito, josei
Damenbinden gekkeitai, *napukin
Dämmerung *(am Abend)* yoake;
(am Morgen) yuugure
Dampfer kisen
danach sonoato
dankbar kansha shiteiru
danken kansha suru
dann soshite
Darm chou
dasselbe onaji
Datum hizuke
Dauer kikan
dauern tsuzuku
Dauerwelle *pāma
dazu sonotameni
Deck *dekki
Decke futon, tenjou
defekt koshou suru
Defekt koshou
Dekorateur/in shitsunai-
soushoku-ka
demnächst chikaiuchini
denken an ~ ni tsuite kangaeru
Denkmal kinen-butsu
Denkmalschutz bunkazai-hogo
denn nazenara
deshalb yueni, dakara
Design *dezain
Designer/in *dezainā
Desinfektionsmittel shoudoku-eki
desinfizieren shoudoku suru
deutlich akirakani
deutsch *doitsu-go
Deutsche, der, die ~ *doitsu-jin
Deutschland doitsu

Devisen *(Geld)* gaika
Dia *suraido
Diabetes tounyou-byou
Diabetiker/in tounyou-kanja
Diagnose shindan
Diät *daietto
dicht mitsu·na, koi
Dichtung tsumeru
dick *(Mensch)* futotta; *(Buch)* at-sui
Dieb dorobou
Diebstahl tounan
dienen tsukaeru
Dienst kinmu
diese(r, -s) kono
diesig donyoritoshita
Ding mono
Diphtherie *jifuteria
direkt chokusetsu, chokutsuu
Direktflug chokkou-bin
Direktion kanribu
Direktor torishimariyaku, shachou
Dirigent shiki-sha
Diskette *furoppī-*desuku
Diskothek *disuko
D-Mark *doitsu-*maruku
doch yappari
Doktor hakase
Dokument kiroku, shorui
Dolmetscher/in tsuuyaku
Dom daiseidou
Donner kaminari
Doppel nijuu
doppelt nijuuno
Dorf mura
dort soko
dorthin sokoe
Dose kan
Dosenöffner kan-kiri
Dozent/in sensei
Drachenfliegen takoage
Draht harigane
Drama dorama
draußen soto
drehen mawasu
drin, drinnen no naka ni
dringend kyuuno
Drittel, ein ~ sanbun no ichi
drittens mittsu-me ni
dritte(r, -s) sanban-me
Drogerie kusuri-ya
drüben mukou-gawa, achira-gawa

drücken osu
Drucker insatsu-ki, *purintā
Drucksache insatsu-butsu
Drüse sen
dumm baka·na, oroka·na
Düne sakyuu
dunkel kura·i
dünn hoso·i; *(Kaffee)* usu·i
durch wo tooshite
Durchfahrt toori nukeru
Durchfall geri
Durchgang nukemichi
durchschnittlich heikin no
durchwählen chokutsuu, *daire-kuto-kōru
dürfen wo yurusu
Durst nodo no kawaki
durstig nodo ga kawaita
Dusche *shawā
Düse *nozuru
Düsenmaschine hikouki, jettoki

E

Ebbe hikishio
eben *(flach)* taira·na; *(zeitlich)* choudo ima
Ebene *(Land)* heiya; *(Stufe)* *rebe-ru
echt honmono
Ecke kado
Economy class *ekonomī-kurasu
EDV-Fachmann/frau *puroguramā
Ehe kekkon
Ehefrau tsuma
Ehemann otto
Ehepaar fuufu
eher yori mae ni
Ehering kekkon-yubiwa
Ehre meiyo
Ei tamago
eigen *(Besitz)* jibun no
Eigenschaft tokusei
eigentlich jissai
Eigentümer shoyuusha
Eilbrief sokutatsu
eilig isogi no
Eimer *baketsu
einander tagaini
einbiegen (nach rechts/links ~) magaru (migi e/hidari e)

Eindruck inshou
ein(e) hitotsu no
einfach kantan·na
Einfahrt iriguchi
Einfluß eikyou
Einfuhr yunyuu
Eingang iriguchi
einheimisch sono tochi koyuuno
einig sein icchi suru
einige ikutsuka no
einigen, s. ~ icchi shita
einkaufen kaimono wo suru
einladen shoutai suru
Einladung shoutai
einmal ichido, ikkai
einnehmen *(Medikament)* nomu, fukuyaku suru
einpacken tsutsumu
Einreise nyuukoku
einreisen nyuukoku suru
eins hitotsu
einsam kodoku na
einschalten *suicchi wo ireru
einschiffen jousen suru
einschlafen nemurikomu, nemuru
einschließen *(einsperren)* tojikomeru; *(inklusive)* fukumeru
Einschreibebrief kakitome
einsteigen norikomu
eintreffen touchaku suru
eintreten hairu
Eintritt nyuujou
Eintrittskarte nyuujou-ken
Eintrittspreis nyuujou-ryoukin
Einverständnis ryoukai
einwerfen nageireru
einwickeln tsutsumu
einwilligen doui suru
Einwohner juumin
einzahlen haraikomu
Einzel kobetsu
Einzelhändler kouri-gyousha
Einzelheiten shousai
einzeln kobetsu no
einzig yuiitsu
einzigartig murui·no, hokani nai
Eis *aisu, kouri
Eisen tetsu
Eisenbahn tetsudou
Eisenbahner tetsudou-in
Eisenwarengeschäft kanamono-ya

Eiter umi
eitern kanou suru
Elektriker/in denki-setsubi-kou
elektrisch denki no
Elektrohandlung denki-ya
Ellbogen hiji
Eltern ryoushin, oya
emanzipiert jiritsu shita
Empfang kangeikai, *resepushon
empfangen *(erhalten)* uketoru, mukaeru
Empfänger uketori-nin
Empfangsbestätigung ryoushuusho
Empfangshalle *genkan-hōru, *robi*
empfehlen susumeru
Empfehlung suisen
Ende owari
enden oeru
endgültig ketteiteki·na
endlich tsuini
Endstation shuuchaku-eki
eng semai
englisch eigo
Enkel/in mago
entdecken hakken
entfernt hanareta
Entfernung kyori
entgegengesetzt hantai no
enthalten fukumu
entkorken *koruku wo nuku
entlang ni sotte
entscheiden kettei suru
entschließen, s. ~ kesshin suru
entschlossen sein kesshin shita
Entschluß kesshin
entschuldigen ayamaru; **s.** ~ shazai suru
Entschuldigung *(Ausrede)* benkai, shazai
enttäuscht shitsubou shita
entweder … oder moshiku wa …
entwickeln hatten suru
Entwicklung kaihatsu
entzückend miryoku·teki·na
Entzündung enshou
Epilepsie tenkan
Epoche jidai
er kare
erbrechen, sich haku

Erbsen mame
Erdbeeren ichigo
Erde *(Boden)* tsuchi, jimen; *(Erd-kugel)* chikyuu
Erdgeschoß ikkai
ereignen, s. ~ okoru, hassei suru
Ereignis dekigoto, jiken
erfahren *(adj)* jukuren shita
erfahren *(Verb) (lernen)* shiru; *(erleben)* keiken suru
Erfahrung keiken
erfinden hatsumei suru
Erfolg seikou
erfreut (über) yorokondeiru
Erfrischung kibun-soukai
Ergebnis seika, kekka
ergreifen tsukamu
erhalten uketoru, hozon suru
erhältlich nyuushudekiru, te ni hairu
erhöhen ageru
erholen, s. ~ kaifuku suru
Erholung kaifuku
erinnern, jdn an etw. ~ omoidasaseru; **s.** ~ wo omoidasu
erkälten, sich kaze wo hiku
erkältet kaze wo hiiteiru
Erkältung kaze
erkennen ninshiki suru
Erker demado
erklären setsumei suru
erkundigen, s. ~ tazuneru
erlangen eru; *(erreichen)* tassuru
erlauben kyoka suru
Erlaubnis kyoka-shou
erledigen katazukeru
Ermäßigung waribiki
ermöglichen kanouni suru
erneuern ninmei suru
ernst shinken·na, majime·na
Ernte shuukaku
erreichen tassuru, todoku
Ersatz *supea
Ersatzrad yobi*taiya
Ersatzteile yobi-buhin
erscheinen *(verlegt werden)* arawareru, hakkou suru
erschöpft tsukareta
erschrecken odoroku
ersetzen *(wechseln)* torikaeru, benshousuru
erst saisho no

erstklassig ichiryuu no
ertragen gaman suru
Erwachsene(r) otona
erwarten kitai suru
erwidern henji suru, kotaeru
erzählen hanasu
erzeugen seisan suru
Erzeugnis seisan-butsu
Erzieher/in kyouiku-sha
Erziehung kyouiku
es gibt *(Lebewesen)* ga iru; *(Dinge)* ga aru
Esel roba
eßbar taberareru
Essen shokuji
essen taberu, shokuji wo suru
Essig su
Etage kai
etwa yaku, ooyoso
etwas ikuraka no
Europa *yōroppa
Europäer/in *yōroppa-jin
europäisch *yōroppa no
eventuell hyotto shitara
Exponat chinretsu-hin, tenjihin
Export yushutsu
Exporteur yushutsu-gyousha
extra *ekisutora, tokubetsu ni

F

Fabrik koujou
Facharzt/ärztin senmon-i
Fachmesse sangyou-mihon·ichi
Faden ito
fähig yuunou·na
Fähre *ferī
fahren unten suru
Fahrer/in unten-shu
Fahrplan jikoku-hyo
Fahrpreis unchin
Fahrkarte jousha-ken
Fahrlehrer/in jidousha-kyoushuu-jo-shidouin
Fahrrad jitensha
Fahrradweg jitensha-senyou-douro
Fahrstuhl *erebētā
Fahrt soukou, *doraibu
fair *feā
Fall *kēsu

fallen ochiru, korobu
falls ~ no baai
Fallschirmspringen rakkasan
falsch machigai, ayamari
Familie kazoku
Familienname myouji
Familienstand kazoku-kousei
fangen tsukamaeru
Farbe iro
färben chakushoku suru
farbig tasai·na
Farbkopierer *karā-kopī
Farbstift iro-enpitsu
Faß taru
fast hotondo
Fata Morgana shinkirou
faul namake·na
Feder hane
fehlen kakeru, tarinai
Fehler ayamari, ketten, kekkan
Fehlgeburt ryuuzan
feierlich genshuku·na
Feiertag shukujitsu
Feigen ichijiku no mi
feilschen negiru
fein komaka·i; *(elegant)* jouhin·na
Feld *(Heide)* nohara; *(Acker)* hata-ke
Fell kegawa
Fels iwa
Fenster mado
Fensterplatz mado gawa no zaseki
Ferien kyuuka
Ferienhaus bessou
Ferngespräch choukyori-tsuuwa
Fernglas bouenkyou
Fernlicht *hai-bīmu
fernsehen *terebi wo miru
Fernseher *terebi
Fernsehraum *terebi-shitsu
fertig shuuryou
fest katamatta
Fest omatsuri
Festival *fesutibaru
Festland tairiku
festsetzen sadameru
Festung yousai, toride
fett aburakko·i
feucht shimetta
feucht-kühl jimejimeshite samui
feucht-warm jimejimeshite atsui
Feuer hi

feuergefährlich kaki genkin
Feuerlöscher shoukaki
Feuermelder kasai-honchiki
Feuerwehr shoubou-sho
Feuerwerk hanabi
Feuerzeug *raitā
Fieber netsu
Fieberthermometer taion-kei
Filiale shiten
Film *firumu, eiga
Filmschauspieler/in *(m)* haiyuu; *(w)* joyuu
Filter *firutā
Filzstift *fueruto-pen
Finanzierung yuushi, zaisei-kanri
finden mitsukeru
Finger yubi
finster *(dunkel)* makkuro·na; *(düster)* inki·na
Firma kaisha
Fisch sakana
fischen tsuru
Fischerhafen gyokou
Fischer/in ryou-shi
Fischgeschäft sakana-ya
fit taichou ga i·i
flach taira·na
Flamme honou
Flasche bin
Flaschenöffner sennuki
Flaute *suranpu
Fleck shimi; *(Ort)* basho
Fleisch niku
fleißig nessin·na
flicken *(nähen)* nuu; *(reparieren)* shuuri suru
Flickzeug *(Nähzeug)* saihou-dou-gu, shuuri-dougu
Fliege hae
fliegen tobu
fließen nagareru
Flip-chart *furō-chāto
Flirt tawamure
flirten ichatsuku
Flohmarkt kottou-ichi
Florist/in *furawā-*dezainā
Flug hikou
Fluggesellschaft koukuu-gaisha
Flughafen kuukou
Flughafengebühr kuukou-shiyou-ryou
Flugzeug hikouki

A/Z

Flügel hane
Fluß kawa
flüssig ekitai no
Flut michishio; *(Überwasser)* kouzui
folgen ni shitagau
Folienstift *majikku-pen
Folklore minzoku
Folkloremusik minzoku-ongaku
Fön *doraiä
fönen *doraiä wo kakeru
fordern youkyuu suru
Forderung youkyuu
Form keishiki, kata
Format saizu, ookisa
Formular youshi
Förster/in shinrin-kanri-sha
fort tooku ni
Fortgeschrittener joukyuusha
Fortschritt shinpo
fortsetzen tsuzukeru
forttragen hakobisaru
Foto shashin
Fotoapparat kamera
Fotogeschäft kamera-ya
fotografieren shashin wo toru
Fotograf/in shashin-ka, *kamera-*man
Fotokopierer *kopĭ-ki
Fracht kamotsu
Frage shitsumon
fragen shitumon wo suru
frankieren kitte wo haru
französisch furansu-go
Frau *(Anruf)* san; *(Dame)* josei; *(eigene)* tsuma
Fräulein *(Anruf)* san; ojousan
frei jiyuu·na; *(kosten)* muryou no
Freilichtbühne yagai-gekijou
Freizeichen yobidashi-on
Freizeitpark yuuenchi
fremd *(Ausland)* gaikoku no, mishiranu
Fremde, der, die ~ gaikoku-jin
Fremdenführer *(Person)* *gaido; *(Buch)* *gaido-*bukku
Freude yorokobi
freuen, s. ~ **auf/über** ~ wo tanoshimini suru
Freund/in tomodachi
freundlich shinsetsu·na
Freundlichkeit shinsetsu

Freundschaft yuukou
Friede heiwa
Friedhof bochi
frieren samui
frisch shinsen
Frischhaltefolie *rappu
Friseur, Friseuse biyou-shi
frisieren kami wo totonoeru
Frisur kamigata, *heyäsutailu
froh yorokobashi·i, ureshi·i
Frost kanki, touketsu, shimo
Frostschutzmittel futou-eki
früh hayaku, haya·i
früher izen
Frühstück choushoku, asa-gohan
frühstücken choushoku wo toru
Frühstücksbüfett choushoku-*byuffe
fühlen kanjiru
führen michibiku
Führer shidou-sha; *(Stadt-)* *gaido
Führerschein unten-menkyo-shou
Führung shidou; *(Stadt-)* annai
füllen mitasu
Füllfederhalter mannenhitsu
Füllung tsumemono
Fundament kiso, dodai
Fundbüro ishitsubutsu-toriatsukai-jo
Funke hibana
funktionieren kinou wo hakki suru, ugoku
für ~ no tameni
Furcht osore
fürchten osoreru
fürchterlich hido·i, osoroshi·i
Fürst koushaku
Fuß ashi
Fußball *sakkä; *(~mannschaft)* *sakkä *chimu*; *(~platz)* *sakkä-jou*
Fußbremse *burēki
Fußgänger hokou-sha
Fußgängerzone hokousha-tengoku
Futter esa; *(Stoff)* uraji

G

Gabel *fōku
gähnen akubi wo suru

Galerie *gyararī
Gallenblase tannou
Gang *(Essen)* *kōsu
Gangschaltung *gia
ganz zenbu no
Ganze, das ~ zentai
gar mattaku, zenzen
gar nicht mattaku …dewanai, zen-
zen …dewanai
Garage shako
Garantie hoshou
Garderobe *kurōku
Garnelen ebi
Garten niwa
Gärtner/in niwa-shi
Gaspedal *akuseru
Gasse roji
Gast kyaku
Gastfreundschaft motenashi
Gastgeber/in shujin, *hosuto
Gasthaus, Gasthof ryokan, *resu-
toran
Gastwirt/in *resutoran no *ōnā
Gebäck *kukkī
gebacken yaku
Gebäude tatemono
geben *(übergeben)* ataeru, wata-
su
Gebet inori
Gebirge sanmyaku
Gebläse soufuuki
geboren umareno
gebraten yaku
Gebrauch shiyou
gebrauchen shiyou suru
gebräuchlich yoku tsukawareru
gebrochen oreta
Gebühr ryoukin
Geburt shussei
gebürtig aus … … umare
Geburtsdatum seinen-gappi
Geburtsstadt shussei-chi
Geburtstag tanjou-bi
Gedanke kangae
Gedeck shokki
Gedenkstätte kinen no chi
Geduld nintai, gaman, shinbou
geduldig shinbou zuyoi
Gefahr kiken
gefährlich kiken·na
gefallen kini iru
Gefallen konomu

Gefälligkeit shinsetsu, koui
Gefängnis keimu-sho
Gefäß youki, iremono
Gefühl kankaku
gefüllt tsumatta
gegen *(ca.)* goro, … ni hanshite
Gegend kinpen, chiiki
Gegengift gedokuzai
Gegenstand taishou
Gegenteil hantai
gegenüber mukaigawa
geheim himitsu no
Geheimzahl anshou-bangou
gehen iku
Gehirn nou
Gehirnerschütterung noushin-
tou
Gehirnschlag nousocchuu
Gehör chouryoku
gehören … ni zokusuru
Gehsteig hodou
Geistlicher seishoku-sha
gekocht ryourizumi no
Gelände youchi, shikichi
Gelb ki-iro
Gelbsucht oudan
Geld o-kane, kahei; ~**anwei-
sung** kawase; ~**automat**
*kyasshu-*kōnā; ~**börse** *saifu;
~**schein** shihei; ~**strafe** bakkin;
~**stück** kouka; ~**wechsel** ryougae
Gelegenheit kikai, *chansu
gelegentlich oriomite
Gelenk kansetsu
gelten tsuuyou suru
Gemälde kaiga
gemein hiretsu·na, hidai
gemeinsam *(adv)* isshoni, kyoudou no
gemischt kongoushita, mazeta
Gemüse yasai
Gemüsehändler yao-ya
gemütlich kokochiyo·i, kutsurogeru
genau seikaku·na; *(adv)* choudo
Genauigkeit genmitsusa
genehmigen kyoka suru
Generalvertreter sou-dairinin;
~**vertretung** sou-dairiten
genießen tanoshimu
genug juubun

Genuß tanoshimi
geöffnet aite iru
Geographie chiri-gaku
Geologie chishitsu-gaku
Gepäck nimotsu
Gepäckabfertigung tenimotsu-hassou-*kauntā
Gepäckausgabe tenimotsu-hiki-watashijo
Gepäckschließfach *koin-rokkā
Gepäckträger akabou, *pōtā
gerade *(zeitlich)* choudo; *(räumlich)*
geradeaus massugu
geräuchert kunsei
Geräusch souon, zatsuon
gerecht kousei·na
Gericht saiban-sho
gering sukuna·i, wazuka no
gern yorokonde
geröstet yaita
Geruch nioi, kaori
Gesang uta
Geschäft shoubai, torihiki
Geschäftsbeziehungen torihiki-kankei
Geschäftspartner *bijinesu-*pātōnā
Geschäftsführer/in shihai-nin, torishi mariyaku
geschehen okoru
Geschenk okurimono
Geschenkpapier housoushi
Geschichte rekishi
geschickt jouzu·na
Geschlechtskrankheit seibyou
Geschlechtsorgane seiki
geschlossen heisateki·na
Geschmack aji, kankaku, konomi
geschmacklos mazu·i; *(Stil)* shu-mino waru·i
Geschwindigkeit jisoku
geschwollen hareta
Geschwulst dekimono
Geschwür kaiyou
Gesellschaft *(Welt)* shakai; *(Verein)* kyoukai
Gesicht kao
Gespräch kaiwa
gestreift shima
gesund kenkou·na
Gesundheit kenkou

Getränk nomimono
getrennt betsu betsu no
Getriebe unten-souchi
gewähren ataeru
gewaltig hidoku, kyouretsu·na
Gewebe orimono
Gewerbe soshiki
Gewicht omosa
Gewinn *(Sieg)* shouri; *(Vorteil)* rieki
gewinnen *(Sieg)* katsu; *(Vorteil)* moukeru
gewiß kakujitsuna, kanarazu
gewissenhaft ryoushinteki·na
Gewitter raiu
gewöhnen, s. ~ an ~ ni nareru
Gewohnheit shuukan
gewöhnlich tuujou no, arifureta
gewohnt nareteiru
Gewürz choumiryou
Gift doku
giftig doku no aru
Gipfel choujou
Gips *gipusu
Gitarre *gitā
Gitter koushi-mado/gaki
glänzen hikaru, kagayaku
glänzend koutaku no aru
Glas *gurasu, *koppu; *(Fenster)* *garasu
Glaser *garasu-ya
glatt taira·na, nameraka·na
Glatteis touketsu shita
Glaube shinnen
glauben shinjiru, omou
gleich *(sofort)* suguni; *(identisch)* douyou ni
gleichen niteiru
gleichfalls douyou ni
gleichwertig taitou ni
gleichzeitig doujini
Gleis bansen *rēru
Glieder teashi
Glocke kane
Glockenspiel shikake-dokei
Glück kouun
glücklich shiawase·na
Glückwunsch oiwai wo noberu
Glühbirne denkyuu
Gold kin
golden kin no
Goldschmiedekunst choukin

Golf *gorufu
Golfplatz *gorufu-jou
Gott kami
Gottesdienst reihai
Grab haka
Grabstein hakaishi
Grad *(Standard)* teido; *(Temperatur)* do
Graphik *gurafikku
Gräte sakana no hone
gratis muryoude, tadade
gratulieren iwau
Grau haiiro
Graupel arare
Grenze sakai, kokkyou
Grenzübergang kenmon-jo
Griechen *girisha
griechisch *girisha no
Griff totte, tegakari
Grill *bābekyū
Grippe ryuukan, kaze
groß ooki·i; *(Flächeninhalt)* hiro·i
großartig kandai·na
Größe ookisa
Großhändler tonya
Großmutter sobo, obaasan
Großvater sofu, ojiisan
grün midori
Grund *(Ursache)* riyuu; *(Erde)* tochi
Grundriß mitorizu
Grundschule shougakkou
Gruppe *gurūpu
grüßen aisatsu wo suru
gültig yuukou·na
Gültigkeit yuukou-kigen
Gummistiefel *gomu-nagagutsu
günstig yuuri·na, tsugou no yo·i
Gurke *kyūri
Gürtel *bando
gut yo·i, i·i
Güter kamotsu
Gutschein hikikae-ken
Gymnasium koutou-gakkou
Gymnastik taisou

H

Haar kaminoke
Haarbürste *burashi
Haarspray *supurē

Haarwaschmittel *shanpū
haben motsu
Hackfleisch hikiniku
Hafen minato
Hagel hyou
Hahn ondori
Hähnchen tori-niku
Haken kake-kugi, tomegane
halb hanbun no
Halbpension nishoku-tsuki
Halbzeit *hāfu-*taimu
Hälfte hanbun
Halle *hōru
Hals nodo, kubi
Halsschmerzen nodo no itami
Halstabletten nodo no kusuri
Halstuch *nekkachifu, *mafurā
halt! tomare!
haltbar hozon-kikan
halten tomaru
Haltestelle teiryuu-jo
Hammer *hanmā, kanazuchi
Hämorrhoiden ji
Hand te
Handball *handobōru
Handbremse *hando-*bureki
handeln torihiki wo suru
Handelsschule shougyou-gakkou
Handelsstadt shougyou-toshi
Handelsvertreter dairi-shou, *ējento
Handfeger te-bouki
handgemacht *handomeido, tezukuri no
Handgepäck tenimotsu
Handschuhe tebukuro
Handtasche *hando-*bakku
Handtuch *taoru
Handwerker/in shoku-nin
Hang *(Berg)* shamen
hängen kakeru
hart *(Material)* kata·i, kibishi·i
Härte koudo
häßlich miniku·i
häufig yoku
Hauptbahnhof chuuou-eki
Haupteingang chuuou-guchi
Hauptpostamt chuuou-yuubinky-oku
hauptsächlich toriwake
Hauptsaison *haishīzun
Hauptspeise *mein

Hauptstadt shuto
Hauptstraße *mein-*sutoríto, chuuou-doori
Haus ie, uchi
Hausnummer bonchi
Hausbesitzer yanushi
Haustiere *petto
Hause, nach ~ uchi e kaeru
Hausfrau shufu
hausgemacht *hōmumeido no
Haushaltswarengeschäft katei-youhinten, nichiyou-zakkashou
Hausschuhe *surippa
Hauseingang genkan
Haut hada, hifu
Hautkrankheit hifubyou
Hebamme sanba
Hebel teko
heben mochiageru
Heft *nōto
heilig shinseinaru
Heilmittel chiryou-yaku
Heimat furusato, kokyou
heimlich hisokani
Heimreise kikyou
Heirat kekkon
heiraten kekkon suru
heiser sein kare ta koe
heiß atsu·i
heißen … to iu
Heißluft nekki
heiter kaisei, hare
heizen danbou wo ireru, atatame-ru
Heizung danbou
hektisch memagurushi·i
helfen, jdm ~ … wo tasukeru
hell akaru·i
Hemd *shatsu
herabsetzen *(Preis)* sageru, kena-su
heraufsetzen hikiageru
herb shibumi, nigami
Herbergseltern *pearentsu
Herd *renji, konro
Herd *(Elektro~)* denki-*renji; *(Gas~)* gasu-*renji
herein! ohairi!
hereinkommen haitte kuru
Hering *(Fisch)* nishin
Herr *(Anruf)* san, otoko no hito, dansei

herrlich subarashi·i
Hersteller seisan-sha
Herz shinzou, kokoro
Herzanfall shinzou-hossa
Herzfehler shinzō-kekkan
Herzinfarkt schinkin-kousoku
Herzspezialist shinzou-senmoni
herzlich kokorokara no
Herzlichkeit magokoro, shinsetsu
Heuschnupfen bien
heute kyou
Hexenschuß youtsuu, gikkuri-goshi
hier koko
hierher kochira e
Hilfe (a. Erste ~) kyunjo
Himmel sora, tengoku
hinaufgehen agaru
hinausgehen deteiku
hindern samatageru, kobamu
hineingehen haitte iku
hinlegen *(liegen)* oku
hinsetzen, s. ~ suwaru
hinten ushiro ni
hinter … no ushiro ni
hinterlassen nokosu
hinterlegen azukeru
Hinterrad kourin
hinuntergehen orite iku
hinzufügen tsuketasu
Hitze nekki; ~**welle** atsusa
Hobby shumi
Hoch *(Wetter)* koukiatsu
hoch taka·i
Hochgeschwindigkeit kousoku
Hochschule daigaku
Hochseefischen enyou-gyogyou
höchstens saikou
Hochzeit kekkon-shiki
Hockey *hokkē
Hof nakaniwa
hoffen nozomu
höflich reigi tadashii, teinei·na
Höflichkeit reigi tadashisa, teinei-sa
Höhe takasa
Höhepunkt chouten
Höhle doukutsu
holen *(Dinge)* torini iku; *(Person)* tsurenei iku
Holz mokuzai, ki
Holzschnitt kibori

Holzschuhe kigutsu
Honig hachimitsu
Honorar sharei
hören kiku
Hörer choushuu; *(Telefon)* juwaki
Hose *zubon
Hose, kurze han-*zubon
Hotel *hoteru
hübsch kawai·i, suteki·na
Hubschrauber *herikoputā
Hüfte koshi
Hügel oka
Hund inu
hundert hyaku
Hunger kuufuku
hungrig kuufukuno
hungrig sein onaka ga suku
Hupe *kurakushon
Husten seki
husten seki wo suru
Hustensaft seki dome-gusuri
Hut boushi
hüten, s. ~ (vor) keikai suru
Hütte koya

I

ich watashi
Idee *aidea, kangae
Illustration sashie, zukai
Illustrierte *gurafu-zasshi
Imbiß keishoku
immer itsumo, tsuneni
impfen yobou-sesshu wo suru
Impfpaß yobou-seschu-techou
Impfung yobousesshu
Import yunyuu
Importeur yunyuu-gyousha
Impressionismus inshou-ha
imstande sein nouryoku ga aru
in no naka ni/de
inbegriffen fukumareteiru, komi, fuhumu
Industriemesse sangyou-mihon·ichi
Infektion kansen, densen
Informatik jouhou-shori-gaku
Informationsmaterial jouhou-shi·ryou
Informationsstand an·nai-jo
informieren shiraseru, oshieru

Infusion tenteki
Ingenieur/in gishi, *enjinia
Inhalation kyuunyuu
inhalieren kyuunyuu suru
Inhalt naiyou
Inland kokunai
Inlandsflug kokunai-sen
innen naibu de, naka de
Innenhof naka-niwa
Innenstadt shinai
Innere, das ~ naibu
innerhalb inaini
innerlich kokoro no nakade, naibu de
Insekt konchuu
Insel shima
Inselrundfahrt shima-meguri
Inserat koukoku
Installateur/in setsubi-kouji-shi
Institut kenkyuu-jo
Insulin *inshurin
Inszenierung enshutsu
interessant omoshiro·i, kyoumibu-ka·i
Interesse kyoumi
interessieren, s. ~ (für) ni kyoumi ga aru
interessiert sein an ni kyoumi ga aru
international kokusai no
inzwischen sono aida ni
irgendwie dounika·shite
irgendwo dokoka·de
irgendwohin dokoka·e
irren, s. ~ omoichigai wo suru
Irrtum omoichigai
Ischias zakotsu-schinkētsū

J

Jacht *yotto
Jacke uwagi
Jahr nen, toshi
Jahreszeit kisetsu
Jahrhundert seiki
jährlich maitoshi
Japan nihon
Japaner/in nihon-jin
japanisch nihon-go/jin no
Jazztanz *jazu-*dansu
je katsute, ni tsuki

Jeans *jīnzu
jede(r, -s) kaku·jin
jedesmal maikai
jedoch keredomo, soredemo
jemals katsute
jemand dareka
jene(r, -s) ano
jenseits mukou-gawa, achira-gawa
jetzt ima
Jod(tinktur) *yōdo
Jogging *jogingu
Jogginganzug *jogingu-*sūtsu
Joghurt *yōguruto
Joint-venture *jointo-*benchā,
   goudou-jigyou
Journalist/in *jānarisuto, kisha
jucken kayu·i
Juckreiz kayumi
Jude *yudaya-jin
Judo juudou
Jugend seishun-jidai/ki
Jugendherberge *yūsu-*hosuteru
Jugendherbergsausweis *yūsu-
   *hosuteru-kaiinshou
Jugendherbergsführer *yūsu-*ho-
   suteru-*gaidobukku
jung waka·i
Junge shounen
Junggeselle dokushin
Jura houritsu-gaku
Juwelier houseki-shou,
   kikinzoku-shou

K

Kabarett yose
Kabel *kēburu
Kabine (a. Umkleide~) kouishitsu
Kaffee *kōhī
Kahn *bōto
Kai futou
Kaiser koutei, tennou
Kajüte senshitsu
Kakerlake *gokiburi
Kalbfleisch koushi-niku
kalt samu·i
Kamm kushi
kämmen kami wo tokasu
Kanadier kanada-jin
Kanal unga, kan, suiro
Kaninchen anausagi

Kanu *kanū
Kapelle *chaperu
Kapitän *kyaputen
kaputt kowareta
Karate karate
kariert chekku no
Karosserie shatai
Karotten ninjin
Karte *toranpu
Kartoffeln jagaimo
Käse *chizu
Kasse kaikei
Kassette *kasetto
Kassettenrekorder *kasetto-
   rekōdā
Kassierer/in kaikei-gakari
Kastanien *maronie, tochi
Katalog *katarogu
Kategorie kategorī
Katholik *katorikku
Katze neko
Kauf kounyuu
kaufen kau
Käufer kounyuu-sha
Kaufhaus *depāto, hyakka ten
Kaufmann/frau *sērusu-man,
   *bijinesu-man
Kaufvertrag baibai-keiyaku
Kaugummi *gamu
kaum hotondo ~ nai
Kaution hoshou-kin
kegeln *bōringu
Kehrblech chiritori
Keilriemen v-beruto
keinesfalls kesshite ~ nai
Kekse *kukkī
Kellner *ueitā
kennen shitte·iru
kennenlernen shiriau
Kenntnis chishiki
Kennzeichen mejirushi
Keramik touki
Kerze rousoku, *kyandoru
Ketchup *kechappu
Kette kusari
Keuchhusten hyakuni chizeki
Kfz-Schein jidousha-tourokushou
Kiefer matsu
Kies jari
Kiesel koishi
Kilometerpreis *kiromēta-ryoukin
Kind kodomo

Kinderbetreuung komori, bebĭ-shittä
Kinderfahrkarte kodomo-jousha-ken
Kinderlähmung shounimahi
Kinderschuhe kodomo gutsu
Kinderspielplatz yuuenchi, asobi-ba
Kino eiga-kan
Kiosk baiten
Kirche kyoukai
Kirschen sakuranbo
Kissen *kusshon
Kiste hako
Klang hibiki
klar hakkiri shita, sunda
Klasse *kurasu
Klebstoff secchakuzai
Kleid *wanpĭsu
Kleiderbügel *hangä
Kleiderbürste you-fuku-*burashi
Kleidung irui, fukusou
klein chiisa·i
Kleingeld kozeni
Klima kikou
Klimaanlage *kūrä
Klingel *beru
klingeln *beru wo narasu
klopfen tataku
Kloster shuudouin
klug kashiko·i
Kneipe nomiya
Knie hiza
Kniestrümpfe *hai-*sokkusu
knipsen oru
Knoblauch ninniku
Knöchel kurubushi
Knochen hone
Knochenbruch kossetsu
Knopf *botan
Knopf drücken botan wo osu
Knoten musubime; *(Schiff)* *notto
Kochbuch ryouri no hon
kochen ryouri wo suru
Koch/Köchin ryouri-nin, *kokku
Kochtopf nabe
Koffer kaban
Kohl *kyabetsu
Kohle sekitan
Kokosnuß *kokonattsu
Kolben *pisuton
Kolik sentsū

Kollege, Kollegin douryou
Kölnisch Wasser *ödekoron
kommen kuru
Komödie *komedĭ
Kompaß *konpasu
Komponist/in *sakkyoku-ka
Konditionen choushi, *kondishon
Konditorei okashi-ya, *kēki-ya
Konditor/in kashi-shokunin
Kondom *kondōmu
Konferenz kaigi
Konferenzraum kaigi-shitsu
König ou
Königin jou-ou
können dekiru
Konserven kanzume
Konsulat ryoujikan
konsultieren soudan suru
Kontakt *kontakuto
Konto kouza
Kontrolleur kensa-kan
kontrollieren kensa suru
Konzern *konzerun
Konzert *konsäto
Kooperation kyoudou
Kopf atama
Kopfschmerzen zutsuu
Kopfhörer *hēddohōn
Kopfkissen makura
Kopfschmerztabletten zutsuu-yaku
Kopie *kopĭ
Koralle sango
Korb kago
Korea kankoku
Koreaner/in kankoku-jin
koreanisch kankoku no
Korkenzieher *koruku-sennuki
Körper karada
korrekt seikaku·na
Kosmetiksalon biyouin
Kosten hiyou
Kostenvoranschlag mitsumori
kostenlos muryou
kostspielig kouka·na
Kostüm *kosuchūmu
Kotelett *kōtoretto, katsuretsu
Koteletten momiage
Kotflügel *fendä
Krabben ebi
Kraft chikara
Kraftfahrer unten-sha/shu

A/Z

Kraftfahrzeugmechaniker/in jidou-sha-seibi-kou
kräftig takumashi·i
Kragen eri
Krampf keiren
krank byouki
Krankenhaus byouin
Krankenkasse kenkou-hoken
Krankenschein kenkou-hoken-shou
Krankenschwester kangofu
Krankenwagen kyuukyuu-sha
Krankheit byouki
Kräuter yakusou, *hābu
Krawatte *nekutai
kreativ souzou·tekina
Krebs gan
Kredit kashitsuke
Kreditkarte *kurejitto-*kādo
Kreislaufmittel junkanki-zai
Kreislaufstörung junkan-shougai
Kreuzfahrt *kurūzu
Kreuzung kousaten
Krieg sensou
Kristall *kurisutaru
kritisieren hihan suru
Krone kanmuri, shikan
Küche daidokoro, *kicchin
Kuchen *kēki
Kugelschreiber *bōrupen
Kuh ushi
kühl tsumeta·i, samu·i
Kühler *kūra
Kühlschrank reizouko
Kühlwasser reisui
Kultstätte reihaijo
Kultur bunka
Kummer nayami
kümmern, s. ~ um ~ nitsuite naya-mu
Kunde, Kundin okyaku
Kunst geijutsu
Kunstakademie bijutsu-daigaku
Kunstgeschichte bijutsu-shi
Kunstfaser kagaku-sen·i
Kunstgewerbe kougei
Kunsthändler bijutsu-shou
Künstler/in geijuts-ka
Kupferstich dou-hanga
Kuppel *dōmu
Kupplung *kuracchi
Kur hoyou
Kurort hoyou-chi

Kürbis kabocha
Kurs *kōsu
Kurve *kābu
kurz mijika·i
kurzfristig *(Dauer)* tankikan no
Kurzschluß *shōto
Kuß *kisu
küssen *kisu wo suru
Küste kaigan

L

Laborant/in jikken-shitsu no joshu
lachen warau
lächerlich okashi·na
Laden mise
Lage joukyou
Lähmung mahi
Lammfleisch *ramu-niku
Lampe *ranpu
Land *(auf dem ~)* riku, inaka; *(Staat)* kuni
landen chakuriku suru
Landkarte chizu
Landschaft fuukei
Landschaftsmalerei fuukei-ga
Landsmann doukoku-jin
Landstraße kaidou
Landung chakuriku
Landwirt/in noumin
lang nagai
Länge nagasa
langsam yukkuri
Languste ise-ebi
langweilig hima·na, tsumarana·i
Lärm souon
lassen ~saseru, okiwasareru
Last kamotsu
lästig wazurawa shii
Lastwagen *torakku
Lauch negi
laufen hashiru
Laune kigen
laut oogoe no, urusa·i
läuten naru
Lautsprecher *supīkā
Lava yougan
Leasing *rīsu-gyou
leben ikiru
Leben jinsei, seimei
lebend ikiteiru

Lebensmittel shokuhin
Lebensmittelgeschäft shokuhin-ten
Lebensmittelvergiftung shoku-chuudoku
Leber kanzou
lebhaft kappatsu·na
Leder kawa
Lederjacke kawa-*jaketto
Lederwarengeschäft kawa-seihin-ten
ledig dokushin
leer kara no
legen oku; *(Haare)* uēbu o tsukeru
lehren oshieru
Lehrer/in sensei
Lehrling minarai
leicht karu·i
Leichtathletik rikujou-kyougi
leider zannen-nagara
leihen kasu
Leihgebühr karichin
Leinen *lin·neru, asa
leise shizuka·na
Leistenbruch heruniya
Leiter, die ~ hashigo
Leiter/in sekinin-sha, shidou-sha
Leitung shidou, shiki
Lenker *(Zweirad)* *handoru
Lenkrad *handoru
lernen narau, manabu
lesen yomu
letzte(r, -s) saigo no
leuchtend hikaru
Leuchter rousoku tate
Leuchtturm toudai
leugnen hitei suru
Leukämie hakketsubyou
Leute hitobito
Licht hikari
Lichtmaschine hatsu denki
Lichtschalter *suicchi
Lidschatten *aishadō
lieb shinsetsu·na, konomashi·i
Liebe ai
lieben aisuru
liebenswürdig shinsetsu·na
Liebenswürdigkeit shinsetsu
Liebling okiniiri
Lied uta
Lieferant nouhin-sha
Lieferbedingungen hikiwatashi-jouken
Lieferung nouhin
Lieferzeit nouki
liefern nouhin suru
liegen yokotawatte·iru
liegenlassen oitamamani shiteoku, okiwasareru
Liegewagenkarte shindaiken
lila murasaki
Limonade remonēdo
Linie sen
Linienflug teiki-koukuubin
linke(r, -s) hidari no
links hidari
Linse *renzu
Lippe kuchibiru
Lippenstift kuchi-beni
Liste *risuto, hyou
Live-Musik nama-ensou, *laibu
Lizenz *raisensu, ninkasho
loben homeru
Loch ana
Loch *(im Zahn)* mushiba
Locken *käru
Lockenwickler *karā
Löffel *supūn
logisch touzen no
Lohn houshuu, kyuuryou
Lokal inshoku-ten
Lokomotive jouki-kikansha
Lorbeer gekkeiju
löschen kesu
lösen toku, yurumeru, hodoku
lösen *(Fahrschein) (kippawo)* kau
Luft kuuki
Luft; ~**druck** kuuki-atsu
lüften kaze wo toosu
Luftpost koukuu-bin
Luftzug sukimakaze
Lüge uso
Lunge hai
Lungenentzündung haien
Lust yorokobi, tanoshimi
lustig yukai·na
luxuriös *derakkusu·na, gouka·na
Luxus *derakkusu, gouka

M

machen suru, tsukuru
Mädchen onnanoko

Magen i
Magenschmerzen itsuu
Magenmittel i-gusuru
mager yaseta, abura no sukunai
Mahlzeit shokuji
Mais toumorokoshi, *kōn
Makler/in assen-gyousha
Makrele saba
Mal kai
Malaria *mararia
Malbuch nurie-chou
malen egaku
Malerei kaiga
Maler/in ga-ka
malerisch kaigateki·na
man hito
Mandarinen mikan
Mandelentzündung hentousen-en
Mandeln *āmondo; *(Gaumen~)* hentousen
Mangel fusoku
Mann otokono-hito
Mannequin *fasshon-moderu
männlich *(Mensch)* otoko; *(Tier)* osu
Mannschaft *chīmu
Mantel *kōto
Mappe *fairu
Margarine *māgarin
Marketing *mākettingu
Markt *(Wirtschaft)* shijou; ichiba
Marmelade *jamu
Marmor dairiseki
Maschine kikai
Maschinenbau kikai-seisaku
Masern hashika
Maß *saizu, youseki
Massage *massāgi
Masseur/in *massāgi-shi
massieren massāgi wo suru
mäßig doori
Material genryou, zairyou
Mathematik suugaku
Matratze *mattoresu
Matrose sen·in
Mauer jouheki
Maurer sakan
Mayonnaise *mayonēzu
Mechaniker/in kikai-kou
Medikament kusuri
Medizin igaku

Meer umi
Meeting Point chiai-basho
Mehl komugiko
mehr motto, yori ijou
Mehrwertsteuer shouhizei
meinetwegen watashi no tameni
Meinung iken
Meisterschaft senshuken
melden *(anmelden)* moushi ko-mu; *(mitteilen)* houkoku suru
Melone *(Honig~)* * meron; *(Was-ser~)* suika
Menge ryou
Mensch ningen
menschlich ningen·tekina
Menstruation gekkei, *mensu
merken kizuku
Messe mihon-ichi
Messestand būsu
messen hakaru
Messer *naifu
Meteorologe/in kishou-gakusha
Metzgerei niku-ya
Metzger/in niku-ya
Miete yachin
mieten kariru
Migräne henzutsuu
Mikrofon *maiku
Milch gyuunyuu, *miruku
mild odayaka·na, *mairudo·na
mindestens sukunakutomo
Mineralwasser *mineraru-sui
Minibar *mini-*bā
Minirock *mini-*sukāto
Ministerium shou, naikaku
minus *mainasu
Minute fun, pun
Mißbrauch *(Frau, Kinder)* bou-kou, akuyou
mißbrauchen akuyou suru, bou-kou suru
mißtrauen shin·youshinai
Mißverständnis gokai
mißverstehen gokai suru
mit to, de
mitbringen *(Dinge)* motte kuru; *(Person)* tsurete kuru
Mitglied kai·in
Mitgliedskarte kai·in-shou
Mitleid doujou
mitnehmen *(Dinge)* motte iku; *(Person)* tsurete iku

Mittag shougo
Mittagessen hiru-gohan, chuusho-ku
Mitte chuou, mannaka
mitteilen shiraseru
Mitteilung tsuuchi
Mittel *(Art)* shudan; *(Arznei)* ku-suri
Mittelalter chuusei
mittelalterlich chuusei no
Mittelohrentzündung chuujien
Mitternacht mayonaka
Möbel kagu
Möbelgeschäft kagu-ya
Mode hayari, ryuukou
Modell *moderu, mokei
Modem modemu
Modenschau *fasshon-*shou
modern *modan·na
mögen konomu, suki·na
möglich kanou·na
Möglichkeit kanou·sei
Moment shunkan
Monat tsuki
monatlich tsuki zuki
Mond tsuki
Monteur kumitate-in
Morgen, das ~ ashita; **der ~** asa
Moslem *isuramu-kyouto
Motor *enjin
Motorboot *mōtā-*bōto
Möwe kamome
Mücke ka
Mückenstiche mushi ni sasare
müde tsukareta
Mühe kurou
Müll gomi
Mülleimer gomi-bako
Mullbinde *gāze no houtai
Mumps otafuku-kaze
Mund kuchi
münden sosogu
Mündung kakou
Münze kouka
Münzfernsprecher koushuu-denwa
Muscheln kai
Museum hakubutsukan
Musical myūjikaru
Musik ongaku
Musiker/in ongaku-ka
Muskel kinniku

müssen shinakereba naranai
Muster mihon
Mutter okāsan, haha
Mütze boushi

N

Nabe *habu
nach e
nach dem Essen shokuji no ato
Nachbar/in tonorino hito, kin·jo
nachher atode
nachlässig darashi no nai
Nachmittag gogo
Nachmittagsvorstellung gogo no kouen
Nachnahme, per daikin-hikikae
nachprüfen shiraberu
Nachricht shirase
Nachrichten nyūsu
nachsehen shiraberu
nachsenden atokara okuru, tensou suru
nächste(r, -s) tsugi no
Nacht yoru
Nachtclub *naito-*kulabu
Nachteil tansho
Nachthemd nemaki
Nachtisch *dezāto
nackt hadaka no
Nadel hari
Nagel tsume
Nagellack *manikyua
Nagellackentferner jokou-eki
Nagelschere tsume-kiri
nahe chika·i
Nähe kinpen, chikasa
nähen nuu
nahrhaft koeta, eiyou aru
Nahrung shokumotsu, eiyou
Nahrungsmittel shokuhin
Nahverkehrszug kinkou-futsuu-ressha
Name namae
Narbe kizuato
Narkose masui
Nase hana
Nasenbluten hanaji
naß nureta
Nation *(Volk)* kokumin; *(Staat)* kokka

Nationalitätskennzeichen kokuse-ki
Nationalpark kokuritsu-kouen
Natur shizen
Naturheilverfahren shizen-ryou-hou
natürlich shizen no
Naturschutzgebiet shizen-hogo-kuiki
Nebel kiri
neben no yoko
Nebenkosten tsuika-hiyou, zappi
Nebenstraße wakimichi
Nebenwirkungen fukusayou
neblig kiri no kakatta
Neffe oi
negativ mainasu no, hiteiteki·na
nehmen toru
Nelken *(Blumen)* *kānēshon; *(Ge-würz)* *chōuji
nennen nazukeru
Nerv shinkei
nervös shinkei shitsu no
nett yasashi·i, shinsetsu·na
Netz ami, kairo
Netzkarte shuuyuu-ken
neu atarashi·i
neugierig koukishin no aru
Neuheit atarashisa
Neuigkeit *nyūsu
neulich senjitsu
Nichte mei
Nichtraucher ni·kitsuen-sha
nie keshite ... nai
nieder, niedrig hikui
Niederlage haiboku
Niederschlag kousuiryou
niemand daremo ... nai
Niere jinzou
Nierenentzündung jinen
Nierenstein jinseki
Nieselregen kirisame
niesen kushami wo suru
nirgends dokonimo ... nai
noch mada
nochmal mouichido
Nonne shuudoujo
Norden kita
nördlich kita no
normal futsuu no
normalerweise tsuujou
Notar/in koushou-nin

Notausgang hijou-guchi
Notbremse hijou-*burēki
Notfall, im ~ kinkyuu no baai
notieren kakitomeru
nötig hitsuyou·na
Notizblock; ~buch *memo-you-shi
Notrufsäule kinkyuu-renraku-souchi
notwendig hitsuzenteki·na
Notwendigkeit hitsuzen·sei
nüchtern reisei·na
Nudeln men, *nūdoru
numerieren bangou zuke suru
Nummer bangou
Nummernschild *nanbā-*purēto
nun *(jetzt)* ima, sate
nur dake
Nüsse; Erd~ *nattsu, *pinattsu
nützlich yakunitatsu
nutzlos yakunitatanai

O

ob ka douka
oben ue
Ober *uētā
Objektiv *renzu
Obst kudamono
Obsthandlung kudamono-ya
obwohl nimo kakarawazu
oder soretomo
Ofen *sutōbu; *(kochen)* ōbun-renji
offen aiteiru
offenbar akirakana
öffentlich koukai no, koukyou no
Öffentlichkeitsarbeit kouhou-kat-sudou
offiziell koushiki no
öffnen akeru
Öffnungszeit aiteiru-jikan, eigyou-jikan
oft yoku
ohne nashi ni
Ohnmacht shisshin, ishiki-fumei
ohnmächtig shisshin suru
Ohr mimi
Ohrentropfen mimino kusuri
Ohrringe *mimi-kazari, *iaringu
Oktanzahl *oktan-ka
Öl *oiru, abura

Ölwechsel oiru-koukan
Ölmalerei abura-e
Onkel ojisan, oji
Oper *opera
Operation shujutsu
operieren shujutsu wo suru
Opernglas operagurasu
Optiker megane-ya
Optiker/in gankyou-shi
orange *orengi
Orangensaft *orengi-*jūsu
Orchester ōkesutora
ordentlich kichinto shita
Ordnung seiton, chitsujo
Orgel paipu-*orugan
Orient *oriento
orientalisch oriento no
Original orijinaru, *honmono no
Originalfassung gensaku
Ort basho
Ortschaft machi
Ortsgespräch shinai-tsuuwa
Osten higashi
Österreich *ōsutoria
Österreicher/in *ōsutoria-jin
Ozean kaiyou

P

Paar, ein ~ hitokumi
paar, ein ~ ikutsuka no
Päckchen kozutsumi
packen tsumeru
Packung housou
Paket tsutsumi
Palast kyuuden
Panne *(Reifen)* kosshou; *panku
Pannendienst koshou-*sābisu
Panorama *panorama
Papier kami
Papiere shorui
Papierservietten kami-*napukin
Papiertaschentücher chirigami,
  *tishū
Paprika *(Gemüse)* *piman
Parfüm kousui
Parfümerie keshouhin-ten
Park kouen
parken chuusha suru
Parkplatz chuusha-jou
Party *pātī

Paß *(Ausweis)* *pasupōto; *(Gebir-
ge)* touge
Passagier ryokyaku
Paßbild *pasupōto-you-shashin
passen au
passieren *(entstehen)* tsuuka suru,
  okoru
Paßkontrolle pasupōto-kensa
Pauschale sougaku, ikkatsu
Pause kyuukei
Pavillon *pabirion
PC *pasokon
Pedal *pedaru
Pelz kegawa
Pelzmantel *kegawa-kōto
Pension *penshon, nenkin
Perle shinju, *pāru
Perser *perusha-jin
persisch *perusha no
Person hito
Personal shokuin, juugyouin
Personalausweis mibun-shoumei-
sho
persönlich kojinteki na
Perücke katsura
Petroleum touyu
Petroleumlampe sekiyu-*ranpu
Pfad komichi
Pfand hoshou-kin
Pfarrer/in bokushi
Pfeffer koshou
Pfeife *paipu
Pfeilwerfen yari-nage
Pferd uma
Pferderennen keiba
Pfirsiche momo
Pflanze shokubutsu
Pflaster bansoukou
Pflaumen sumomo
Pflicht gimu
Pförtner/in monban, shuei
Pharmazie yakugaku
Philosophie tetsugaku
Physik butsuri-gaku
Physiker/in butsuri-gaku-sha
Physiotherapie butsuri-ryouhou
Pilot/in *pairotto
Pilze kinoko
Pinzette pinsetto
Plakat *posutā
Plan *puran
planmäßiger Abflug yoteidoori no

hikou
Plastik *purasutikku
Platte *purēto
Plattenspieler *rekōdo-*pureiyā
Plattfuß henpeisoku, *(Reifen)* *panku shita taiya
Platz basho
platzen haretsu suru
Platzkarte zaseki-shiteiken
Plombe *(Zahn)* juutenzai
plötzlich totsuzen no
plus *purasu
Pocken housou
Politik seiji
Politikwissenschaft seiji-gaku
Polizei keisatsu
Polizist/in keisatsu-kan
Pommes frites *furaido-poteto
Pony *ponī
Portier kanri-nin, *doa-man
Portion ichinin-mae
Porto yuubin-ryoukin
Porzellan touki
positiv purasu no, koutei·teki·na
Post yuubin-kyoku
Postleitzahl yuubin-bangou
Postanweisung yuubin-furikomi
Postbeamter/beamtin yuubinkyoku-in
Poster *posutā
praktisch jitsuyou·teki·na
Präservativ hiningu
Praxis jikkou, jisshuu
Praxis *(Arzt)* shinryou-jo; jissen
Predigt sekkyou
Preis ryoukin
Preisliste ryoukin-hyou
Prellung naishukketsu
Premiere shoen
Priester shinpu
privat *puraibēto
pro ~ ni tsuki
Probe kari, kokoromi
probieren tamesu
Produkt seihin
Produktion seisan
Professor/in kyouju
Programm *puroguramu
Promille *pāmiru
Propangas *puropan-gasu
Prospekt *panfuretto
Protestant *purotesutanto

protestieren *(gegen)* ~ ni kougisu-ru
Prothese purotēze
Protokoll kiroku
Provision tesuuryou
provisorisch karino
Prozent *pāsento
Prozentsatz wariai
prüfen kensa suru, shiraberu
Prüfung shiken, kensa
PS bariki
Psychologe/in shinri-gakusha
Psychologie shinri-gaku
Publikum kanshuu
Puder *paudā
Pullover *sētā
Puls myaku
Pulver kona
Pulverschnee kona-yuki
Punkt ten
pünktlich jikandoori no
Puppe ningyou
putzen souji suru
Pyjama *pajama

Q

Qualität hinshitsu
Qualle kurage
Quelle izumi
quer durch yokogiru
Quetschung zashou
quittieren ryoushuusho wo kaku
Quittung ryoushuu-sho

R

Rabatt nebiki, waribiki
Rad sharin
Radarkontrolle *rēdā-*kontorōru
radfahren jitensha ni noru
Radiergummi keshi-*gomu
Radio *rajio
Radrennen jitensha-kyousou
Rand fuchi
Rang chii, kaikyuu
rasch haya·i
Rasen shibafu
Rasierapparat kamisori
rasieren hige wo soru

Rast kyuukei
Raststätte kyuukei-jo
Rat jogen, chuukoku
raten jogen suru, chuukoku suru
Rathaus shichousha, shiyakusho
Rauch kemuri
rauchen *(Zigarette)* *tabako wo suu
Raucher kitsuen-sha
Raucherzimmer kitsuen-shitsu
Rauchfleisch kunsei no niku
Raum heya
Rauschgift mayaku
Realismus genjutsu-shugi
rechnen keisan suru
Rechnung kanjou-sho, seikyuu-sho
Recht *(Anspruch)* kenri; *(Gesetz)* hou
recht haben tadashi·i
rechte(r, -s) migi no
rechts migi
Rechtsanwalt/anwältin bengo-shi
rechtzeitig choudo yoi toki ni
Redakteur/in henshuu-sha
reden hanasu
Rednerpult endai
regelmäßig kisokuteki·na
regeln chousei suru
Regen ame
Regenzeit tsuyu
Regenmantel *reinkōto
Regie enshutsu
Regierung seifu
Regisseur/in kantoku
regnen amega furu
regnerisch amemoyou no
reich kanemochi no
reichen todoku
reichlich juubun na
Reichtum shisan
reif jukushita
Reifen *taiya
Reihe retsu
reinigen kireini suru, *kurīningu suru
Reinigung souji
Reinigung, chemische *dorai-kurīningu
Reis kome
Reise ryokou
Reiseandenken omyage

Reisebegleiter/in tenjou-in
Reisebüro ryokou-gaisha
Reiseführer *(Buch)* *gaido-*bukku
Reisegesellschaft ryokou-dantai
Reiseleiter/in *gaido
reisen (nach) ~ e ryokou suru
Reisende, der, die ~ ryokou-sha
Reisepaß *pasupōto
Reiseroute *ryokou-koutei
Reisescheck *toraberāzu-*chekku
Reisetasche ryokou-kaban
Reiseziel ryokou-mokutekichi
reißen hikisaku
Reißverschluß *chakku, *fasunā
Reißzwecken gabyou
reiten uma ni noru, jouba
Reitsport jouba-*supōtsu
reizen shigeki suru
Reklame koukoku, senden
reklamieren kujou wo moushitate-ru
rekonstruieren fukugen suru
Religion shuukyou
Rennen *rēsu
rennen kakeru, hashiru
Rentner/in nenkin-seikatsu-sha
Reparatur shuuri
reparieren shuuri suru
Reservereifen yobi-*taiya
reservieren yoyaku suru
Reservierung yoyaku
Rest nokori
Restaurant *resutoran, shokudou
Restaurator/in resutoran no *ōnā
restaurieren shuufuku suru
retten kyuujo suru
Rettungsboot kyuujo-*bōto
Rezept shohousen
Rezeption uketsuke, resepushon
Rheuma *ryūmachi
Richter/in saiban-kan
richtig tadashi·i
richtigstellen teisei suru
Richtung houkou
riechen niou
Riemen himo, *beruto
Riff *rīfu
Rindfleisch gyuuniku
Ring *ringu
Ringkampf *resuringu
Rippe abarabone

Risiko kiken
Ritter kishi
Rock *sukāto
roh nama
Rohr *paipu
Rolle; Haupt~ shuyaku
Rollschuhe *rōrā-*sukēto
Roman shousetsu
Romanik romanesuku
romanisch romanesuku no
röntgen *rentogen
Röntgenaufnahme *rentogen-shashin
rosa pinku-iro no
Rose bara
Rosinen hoshibudou
Rost sabi
Rot aka
Röteln fuushin
Rouge beni
Route *rūto, *kōsu*
Rücken senaka
Rückfahrkarte kaeri no kippu
Rückfahrt kaeri-michi
Rückgrat sebone
Rückkehr fukki, kikan
Rückspiegel *bakku-mirā
Rucksack *ryukku sakku
Rücksicht kouryo
rücksichtslos omoiyari no nai
Rücktransport yusou
rückwärts ushiro e
Ruder ōru; *(Steuer)* kaji, rādā
rudern kogu
rufen yobu
Rufnummer denwa-bangou
Rugby *ragubī
Ruhe shizuke sa
ruhen yasumu
ruhig shizuka·na
Ruine haikyo
rund *(adv)* yaku, marui
Runde isshuu; *(Kreis)* *sākuru
Rundfahrt shuuyuu
Rundreisefahrschein shuuyuu-ken
Russe *roshia-jin
russisch *roshia-go
Rußland *roshia
Rutschbahn suberidai

S

Saal *hōru
Sache koto, mono
Sack fukuro
Safe kinko
saftig mizuke no oo·i
sagen iu
Sahne *kurīmu
Saison kisetsu, *shīzun
Sakko sebiro
Salami *sarami
Salat *sarada
Salbe nankou
Salmonellen *sarumonera-kin
Salz shio
sammeln atsumeru
Sammlung shuushuu-hin, *kore-kushon
Sanatorium *sanatoriumu
Sand suna
Sandalen *sandaru
sandig suna darake no, sunaji no
Sandstein sagan
Sänger/in kashu, seigaku-ka
Sardellen *anchobi
Sardinen *sādin, iwashi
satt manpuku shita, akiaki shita
Sattel *sadoru
Satz bun; *(Musik)* gakusetsu
sauber kirei·na, seiketsu·na
sauer suppa·i
Saugflasche honyuu-bin
Säule hashira
Sauna *sauna
Schachtel hako
schade, es ist ~ zan·nen
Schädel zugaikotsu
Schaden songai
schaden songai wo ataeru
Schadenersatz songai-baishou
schädlich yuugai·na
Schaf hitsuji
schaffen tsukuru
Schaffner shashou
Schal *shōru, *mafurā*
Schallplatte *rekōdo
Schallplattengeschäft *rekōdo-ten
Schalter suicchi; *(Rezeption)* madoguchi; ~**stunden** uketsukejikan
scharf *(Gewürz)* karai

Scharlach shoukou netsu
Schatten kage
schätzen suitei suru
Schatzkammer houko
schauen miru
Schaufenster *shōuindou
Schaum awa
Schauspiel engeki
Schauspieler haiyuu
Schauspielerin joyuu
Scheck kogitte, *chekku
Scheibenwischer *waipā
Schein *(Geld~)* shihei
scheinen teru, kagayaku
Scheinwerfer *heddo-raito
Scheitel wakeme
schenken okuru
Schere hasami
Scherz joudan
schicken okuru
Schiebedach *san-*rūfu
schieben osu
Schiedsrichter shinpan
Schienbein keikotsu
Schiene *rēru, soegi
schießen utsu
Schiff fune
Schild hyousatsu
Schilling shiringu
schimpfen nonoshiru, okoru
Schinken *(gekocht)* *hamu; *(roh)*
nama-*hamu
Schirm kasa
Schlaf nemuri
Schlafzimmer shinshitsu
schlafen nemuru
Schlaflosigkeit fuminshou
Schlafsack nebukuro
Schlaftabletten suiminyaku
Schlafwagenkarte shindaiken
Schlag utsu
Schlaganfall socchuu
schlagen utsu
Schläger *raketto
Schlamm doro
Schlange hebi
schlank hossoritoshita
schlau zurugashiko·i
Schlauch *hōsu
Schlauch *(Reifen)* *chūbu
Schlauchboot *gomu-bōto
schlecht waru·i

schließen tojiru
schlimm hido·i
Schlitten sori
Schlittschuhe *sukēto-gutsu
Schloß shiro
Schlosser/in seibi-kou
Schlucht keikoku
Schluß owari
Schlüssel kagi
Schlüsselbein sakotsu
schmal sema·i
schmecken aji ga suru
Schmerzen kutsuu
schmerzen itamu
schmerzhaft ita·i
Schmerzmittel itami dome
schmieren nuru
schminken, s. ~ keshou wo suru
Schmuck kazari, *akusesarī
Schmuggel mitsuyu
schmuggeln mitsuyu suru
Schmutz yogore
schmutzig kitana·i
schnarchen ibiki wo kaku
Schnee yuki
Schneesturm fubuki
schneiden kiru
Schneider/in shitate-ya
schneien yuki ga furu
schnell haya·i
Schnelligkeit hayasa, *supīdo
Schnellimbiß keishoku
Schnellstraße kousokudouru
Schnittwunde kirikizu
Schnitzerei choukoku
Schnorchel *shunōkeru
Schnuller oshaburi
Schnupfen hanakaze
Schnur himo
Schnurrbart kuchi·hige
Schnürsenkel kutsu-himo
Schokolade *chokorēto
schön utsukushi·i
schon sudeni, mou
Schönheit utsukushisa
Schonkost *daietto-shoku
Schrank todana, tansu
Schraube neji
Schraubenmutter *natto
Schraubenschlüssel *supana
Schraubenzieher *doraibā
schrecklich osoroshi·i

schreiben kaku
Schreibwarengeschäft bunbougu-ya
schreien sakebu
Schrift moji
schriftlich bunshou de
Schriftsteller/in sakka
Schritt ayumi
schüchtern hazukashigariya no
Schuh kutsu
Schuhgeschäft kutsu-ya
Schuld tsumi, sekinin, shakkin
schulden sekinin ga aru, shakkin ga aru
Schule gakkou
Schüler/in seito
Schulter kata
Schulung kunren, *torēningu
Schuß *(Waffe)* shageki; *(Fußball)* shūto
Schüssel *bōru, hachi
Schüttelfrost okan, samuke
Schutz hogo
schwach yowa·i
Schwäche yowasa
Schwager *(älter)* giri no ani; *(jünger)* giri no otouto
Schwägerin *(älter)* giri no ane; *(jünger)* giri no imouto
Schwamm *suponji
schwanger ninshin shiteiru
Schwangerschaft ninshin
schwarz kuro
Schwarzweiß-Film shirokuro-*firumu
schweigen damaru
Schweigen chinmoku
Schweinefleisch buta-niku
Schweiß ase
Schweiz *suisu
Schweizer Franken *suisu-furan
Schweizer/in *suisu-jin
Schwellung hare
schwer *(Gewicht)* muzukashi·i, omo·i
Schwester imouto, ane
schwierig muzukashi·i
Schwierigkeit konnan, muzukashisa
Schwimmbad *pūru
schwimmen oyogu
Schwimmer/in suiei-senshu
Schwimmflossen ashihire

Schwimmen suiei
Schwindel memai
schwindeln memai ga suru
Schwindler sagi-shi
schwindlig memai ga suru
schwitzen ase wo kaku
schwül mushiatsu·i
See, die ~ umi
See, der ~ mizuumi
Seebad kaisui yoku
Seegang umi no jōsu
seekrank funayoi
Segelboot *yotto
segeln *sēringu
sehen miru
Sehenswürdigkeiten meisho, midokoro
sehr totemo
Seide kinu
Seife sekkeen
Seil nawa, *rōpu
Seilbahn *kēburu-*kā
sein ~ de aru
seit ~ irai
seitdem sore·irai
Seite *(Buch)* *pēji
Seitenstechen sasuyou na itami
Sekretariat jimukyoku
Sekretär/in hisho
Sekunde byou
selbst jibun·jishin
Selbstauslöser *serufu-*taimā
Selbstbedienung *serufu-*sābisu
Sellerie *serori
selten mezurashi·i
senden okuru
Sendung hassou
Senf karashi
Serviette *napukin
Sessel *āmu-*cheā
setzen suwaraseru
Setzer/in shokuji-kou
Sex *sekkusu, sei
Shampoo *shanpū
Shorts shōtsu
Show *shou
sich rasieren lassen hige wo soru
sicher anzen·na
Sicherheit anzen
Sicherheitsgurt anzen-*beruto
Sicherheitskontrolle anzen kakunin
Sicherheitsnadeln anzen-*pin

Sicherung hyūzu
Sicht shikai
sichtbar me ni mieru, akiraka·na
Sichtvermerk *biza
sie kanojo
Sie anata
Sieg shouri, kachi
siegen katsu
Signal *shigunaru
Silber gin, *shirubā
silbern *shirubā no
singen utau
Sinn imi
Sitz seki
sitzen suwaru
Sitzung kaigi
Ski *sukī
Skonto genkin-waribiki
Skulptur choukoku
Slip *shōtsu, *pantī
so sono-youni
Socken kutsushita
Sodbrennen muneyake
sofort suguni
sogar desaemo, soredokoroka
Sohle ashino-ura
Sohn musuko
solange no aidawa
solch sono-youna
Solist/in solo
sollen subekide aru
Sommerkleid natsu-fuku
Sonder . . . tokubetsu·na
Sondermarke kinen-kitte
sondern dewanaku te
Sonne taiyou
Sonnenaufgang hinode
Sonnenuntergang nichibotsu
Sonnenbrand hiyake
Sonnenschirm higasa
Sonnenbrille *sangurasu
Sonnenöl *san-oiru
Sonnenschirm higasa
Sonnenstich nisshabyou
sonnig hareta
sonst samonaito
Sorge shinpai, fuan
sorgen, ~ für, s. ~ um shinpai suru
Sorgfalt menmitsu
sorgfältig menmitsu·na
Sorte hinshu
Soße *sōsu

Sozialarbeiter/in *soshiaru-*wākā
Soziologie shakai-gaku
Spaghetti *supagetti
sparen ken·yaku suru
Spargel *asuparagasu
Spaß tanoshimi, joudan
spät oso·i
später atode
spazierengehen sanpo wo suru
Spaziergang sanpo
Speck *bēkon
Speise ryouri
Speiseröhre shokudou
Speisesaal shokudou
Speisewagen shokudou-sha
Sperre *barikēdo
Spesen ryouri
Spezialität meibutsu
speziell tokubetsu·na
Spiegel kagami
Spiel asobi
Spielcasino *kajino
spielen asobu
Spielkarten *toranpu
Spielplan jouen-yoteihyou
Spielwarengeschäft omocha-ya
Spielzeug omocha
Spirituosengeschäft sakaya
Spiritus arukōru
spitz surudo·i
Spitze saki, *rēsu
Sport *supōtsu
Sportartikel *supōtsu-youhin
Sportler/in *supōtsu-*man
Sportplatz undou-jou
Sprache kotoba
sprechen hanasu
Sprechstunde shinsatsu-jikan
springen tobu
Spritze chuusha
Spülmittel senzai
Spur ashiato
Staat kokka
Staatsangehörigkeit kokuseki
Stadt machi
Stadtbus shinai-*basu
Stadtplan shigai-chizu
Stadtrundfahrt shinai-kankou
Stadtteil machi no ikkaku
stammen (Person) no shusshin de
aru
Ständer *sutando, gakufu-dai

Standlicht *pākingu-*raito
Stange bou
stark tsuyo·i
Stärke tsuyosa; *(Vorteil)* chousho
Start *sutāto
starten *sutāto suru
Station eki, byoutou
Stativ sankyaku
statt ~ no kawarini
stattfinden okonawareru
Statue ritsuzou, chouzou
Stau juutai
Staub hokori
Stausee chosuichi
stechen sashikomu
Steckdose *konsento, *soketto, sashikomi
Stecker *puragu
Stecknadel *pin
stehen tatsu
stehenbleiben tachidomaru, tomaru
stehlen nusumu
steigen noboru
steil kewashi·i, *chāmingu na
Stein ishi
steinig ishi darake no
Steinzeit sekki-jidai
Stelle *(Ort)* basho; *(Beruf)* shoku
stellen oku
Stellung ichi
Stempel *sutanpu
sterben shinu
Stern hoshi
Sternwarte tenmondai
stets itsumademo
Steuerberater/in zeirishi
Steward *suchuwādo
Stewardeß *suchuwādesu
Stich sasu, sashikizu
Stiefel nagagutsu
Stift enpitsu
Stil youshiki
still shizuka·na
Stimme koe
stimmen au
stinken kusa·i, nioi ga suru
Stock bou, *sutekki
Stockwerk kai
Stoff kiji; *(Material)* zairyou
stören jama wo suru
stornieren torikesu
Störung koshou

Stoß shoutotsu
stoßen tsuku
Strafe batsu
Strahl kousen
Strand hama, kaigan
Strandbad kaisui-yoku
Straße michi
Straßenbenutzungsgebühr tsuu-kou-ryoukin
Straßenkarte douro-chizu
Strauß hanataba
Strecke michinori
Streichholz *matchi
Streichholzschachtel *matchi-bako
Streit kenka
streiten kenka wo suru
streng kibishi·i
Strom nagare; *(elektr.)* denryuu
Strömung nagare
Strümpfe kutsushita, *sokkus
Strumpfhose *panti-*sutokkingu
Stück ko, bubun
Studentenwohnheim gakusei-ryou
Student/in gakusei
Studienfach senkou
Studienreise kenshuu-ryokou
studieren benkyou suru
Studio *sutajio
Studium gakugyou
Stuhl isu
Stuhlgang bentsuu
Stunde jikan
Sturm arashi
Sturz rakka, tenraku
stürzen rakka suru, tenraku suru
Sturzhelm *herumetto
suchen sagasu
Sucher *faindā
Sucht chuudoku
süchtig chuudokushou no
Süden minami
südlich minami no
Summe goukei
Sumpf numachi
Supermarkt *sūpā-māketto*
Suppe *sūpu
Suppenteller *sūpu-zara
surfen sāfin
süß ama·i
Süßigkeiten okashi
Süßstoff kanmiryou
Süßwarengeschäft okashi-ya

Swimmingpool *pūru
sympathisch koukan no moteru

T

Tabak *tabako
Tabakladen *tabako-ya
Tablette jouzai
Tachometer *takomētā
Tag hi, nitchuu
Tagesausflug higaeri-ryokou
Tagesgericht; ~menü higawari-
    *menyu
Tageskarte ichinichi-joushaken
Tageslichtprojektor ōbāheddo-
    *purojekutā
Tagesordnung giji-nittei
Tagespaß ichinichi-ken
Tal tani
Tampons *tanpon
Tank; ~stelle *gasorin-*sutando
tanken gasorin wo ireru
Tante oba, obasan
Tanz odori, *dansu
tanzen odoru, dansu wo suru
Tänzer/in *dansā, odoriko
Tasche kaban
Taschenbuch poketto-ban no hon
Taschendieb suri
Taschenlampe kaichuu-dentou
Taschenmesser *pokketo-*naifu
Taschenrechner dentaku
Taschentuch *hankachi
Tasse *kappu
Tat koudou, okonai
Tätigkeit katsudou
Tatsache jijitsu
tauchen moguru
Taucheranzug sensui-fuku
tauschen koukan suru
täuschen, s. ~ kanchigai wo suru
Tauwetter yukidoke
Taxi *takushī
Taxifahrer/in *takushi-*doraibā*
Taxistand *takushi-noriba
Techniker/in gishi
Technische Hochschule kouka-
    daigaku
Technische(r) Zeichner/in seizu-kou
Tee o-cha
Teil bubun

teilen wakeru
teilnehmen (an) sanka suru
Telefax *fakkusu
Telefon denwa
Telefonbuch denwachou
Telefongespräch tsuuwa
Telefonkarte *terehon-*kādo
Telefonnummer denwa-bangou
Telefonzelle denwa-*bokkusu
telefonieren denwa wo kakeru/suru
Telegramm denpou
Teleobjektiv bouen-*renzu
Telex *terekkusu
Teller sara
Tempel otera
Temperatur ondo
Tennis *tenisu
Teppich juutan
Termin yakusoku
Terrasse *terasu
Tesafilm® *serofan-*tēpu*
Tetanus *tetanusu, hashoufun
teuer taka·i
Textverarbeitungssystem *wādo-
    *purosessā-*shisutemu
Theater geki, geki-jou
Theaterstück kyaku-hon, *dorama
Theologie shingaku
Therapeut/in chiryou-shi
Thermalbad/becken *onsui-pūru
Thunfisch maguro
tief fuka·i
Tief (Wetter) teikiatsu
Tier doubutsu
Tierarzt/ärztin juui
Tip *hinto
Tisch tsukue
Tischtennis *pinpon, takkyuu
Tischtuch *tēburu-*kurosu
Toast *tōsuto
Toaster *tōsutā
Tochter musume
Tochtergesellschaft kogaisha
Tod shi
Toilette *toire
Toilettenpapier *toiretto-*pēpā
Tollwut kyokenbyou
Tomaten *tomato
Ton oto
tönen hibiku, (Haare) kami wo
    someru
Tonwaren toujiki

Topf nabe
Töpferei tougei
Tor mon; *(Spiel)*gōlu
tot shinde iru
Tour *tsuā
Tourist/in *tsūrisuto
Tracht minzoku-ishou
tragen hakobu
Träger unpan-nin
Tragödie higeki
trampen *hitchihaiku
Tramper *hitchihaikā
Transferbus norikae-*basu
Transport yusou
Transportkosten yusou-hiyou
transportieren yusou suru
Traubenzucker budoutou
Traum yume
träumen yume wo miru
traurig kanashi·i
treffen au
Treffen shuukai, kaigou
trennen wakareru
Treppe kaidan
treu seijitsu·na
trinkbar nomeru
trinken nomu
Trinkgeld *chippu
Trinkwasser nomimizu
trocken kawaku
trocken *(Wein)* karakuchi
Trockenheit kansou
trocknen kawakasu
Trödler kobutsu-shou
Trommelfell komaku
tropfen shitataru
Tropfen shizuku
trotz ~ nimo kakawarazu
trotzdem ~ nimo kakawarazu
trüb nigotta
tschüß *baibai
T-Shirt *T-*shatsu
Tube chuubu
Tuch *taoru
tüchtig yuunou·na
tun suru
Tunnel *tonneru
Tür *doa
Turm tou
Turnen taisou
Turnschuhe *supōtsushūzu
Tüte kamibukuro

Typhus *chifusu
typisch tenkeiteki·na

U

U-Bahn chikatetsu
übel fukai·na
Übelkeit fukai kan
üben renshuu suru
über ~ ni tsuite
überall itarutokorode
überbringen todokeru
Überfahrt
Überfall shuugeki, shinnyuu, fuiuchi
überfallen shuugeki suru
überflüssig yokei·na
überfüllt tsumatta
Übergang utsurikawari
übergeben watasu
überholen oikosu
übernachten tomaru
Übernachtung shukuhaku
übernehmen hikitsugu
überqueren yokogiru
überrascht odoroku
überreden settoku suru
überschreiten koeru
Überschwemmung kouzui
Übersee kaigai
übersetzen hon·yaku suru
Übersetzer/in hon·yaku-sha
übertragbar ouyou dekiru
übertrieben oogesa·na
überweisen furikomu
Überweisung furikomi
überzeugen kakushin saseru
üblich tsuujou no
übrig nokori no
übrigbleiben nokotte iru
übrigens tokorode
Übung renshuu
Ufer kishi
Uhr tokei
Uhrmacher/in tokei-ya
Ultraschall chouonpa
umarmen daku
umbuchen henkou suru
Umgebung shuui, atari
umgekehrt hantai no
umkehren hikikaesu
Umkleidekabine kouishitsu

Umleitung ukairo
Umrechnung kansan
Umsatzsteuer uriage zei
umsehen mimawasu
umsonst muryou de
Umstände joukyou
umsteigen norikaeru
umtauschen torikaeru
Umweg mawari michi
Umwelt kankyou
umziehen hikkosu
unangenehm fukai·na
unanständig bushitsuke·na
unbedingt zettai ni
unbegreiflich fukakai·na
unbekannt shirarete inai
unbequem kaiteki denai
unbeständig fuantei·na
unbestimmt hakkiri shinai
und to, soshite
undankbar onshirazu·na
unecht nise no
unentbehrlich fukaketsu·na
unentschieden hikiwake
unentschlossen yuujuu·fudan no
unerfahren keiken no nai
unerfreulich fuyukai·na
unerträglich gaman dekinai
unerwartet omoigakena·i
unerwünscht nozomarete inai
unfähig munou·na, nouryoku no nai
Unfall jiko
unfreundlich fushinsetsu·na
ungeeignet futekitou·na
ungefähr ooyoso
ungenau fuseikaku·na
ungenügend fujuubun·na
ungerecht futou·na
Ungerechtigkeit fusei
ungern kirai·na
ungesund fukenkou·na
ungewiß futashika·na
ungewöhnlich futsuudena·i
unglaublich shinjirarena·i
Unglück fukou
unglücklich fukou·na
unglücklicherweise fukouna kotoni
ungültig mukou no
ungünstig futsugou·na
unhöflich burei·na
Universität daigaku
Unkosten shuppi

unmittelbar chokusetsu no
unmodern jidai okure no
unmöglich fukanou·na
unnötig fushitsuyou·na
unnütz muda·na
Unordnung muchitsujo
unpraktisch hi·jitsuyouteki·na
Unrecht fusei
unrecht haben machigatte iru
unregelmäßig fukisoku·na
unruhig sawagashi·i
unschuldig tsumi no nai
unser, unsere watashitachi no
unsicher futashika·na
unten shita ni
unter ~ no shita ni
unterbrechen chuudan suru
Unterführung *gādo shita no michi
unterhalb shita ni
unterhalten, s. ~ hanashiau
unterhaltend omoshiro·i
Unterhaltung hanashiai
Unterhemd; ~wäsche *andāshatsu
Unterkunft yado
Unterleib kafukubu
Unternehmen kigyou
unterrichten oshieru
unterscheiden kubetsu suru
Unterschied chiga·i
unterschreiben shomei suru
Unterschrift *sain, shomei
Unterstützung enjo
untersuchen kensa suru, shiraberu
Untersuchung kensa, chousa
Untersuchungshaft kouryuu
Untertitel *(Film)* jimaku
unterwegs ryokou·chuu
unverbindlich gimu no nai
unvermeidlich sakerare nai
unverschämt zuuzuushi·i
unvollständig fukanzen·na
unvorsichtig fuchuui·na
unwahrscheinlich totetsumona·i
unwichtig juuyou dewana·i
unwohl fuyukai·na
unzufrieden fumanzoku
Urin nyou
Urlaub kyuuka
Ursache genin
Urteil hanketsu
urteilen hanketsu wo kudasu

V

Vase kabin
Vater chichi, otousan
Vaterland sokoku
vegetarisch saishoku-shugi
Ventil *pisuton
Ventilator senpuuki
verabreden, s. ~ yakusoku suru
Verabredung yakusoku
verabschieden, s. ~ wakare wo
tsugeru
verändern kaeru, henkou suru
Veränderung henkou
veranstalten moyousu
Veranstaltung moyoushi-mono
Veranstaltungskalender moyoushi-
mono-*puroguramu
verantwortlich sekinin no aru
Verband (Vereinigung) renmei;
(med.) houtai
Verbandszeug houtai-youhin
verbessern kaizen suru
verbieten kinshi suru
verbinden musubitsukeru, houtaino
Verbindung ketsugou, musubi tsuki
Verbot kinshi
verboten kinshi suru
Verbrauch shouhi
verbrauchen shouhi suru
Verbrechen hanzai
Verbrennung shoukyaku
Verdacht kengi
Verdauung shouka
Verdauungsstörung shouka furyou
verderben kusaru
verdienen kasegu
Verdienst, das ~ kouseki; **der** ~
shuu·nyuu
Verein kyoukai
vereinbaren kyoutei suru
Verfassung kenpou
Vergangenheit kako
Vergaser *kyaburētā
vergehen sugisaru
vergessen wasureru
vergewaltigen gyoukan suru
Vergewaltigung gyoukan
Vergiftung chuudoku
Vergleich hikaku
vergleichen hikaku suru
Vergnügen tanoshimi

Vergoldung kin-mekki
verhaften taiho suru
Verhandlung koushou
verheimlichen himitsu ni suru
verheiratet kekkon shiteiru, kikon no
verhindern samatageru
Verhütungsmittel hinin yaku
verirren, s. ~ michi ni mayou
Verkauf hanbai
verkaufen uru
Verkäufer/in *sērusu-*man; (im
Laden) ten-in, uriko
Verkaufsförderung hanbai sokushin
Verkehr koutsuu
Verkehrsamt kankou-annaisho
verlangen motomeru
verlängern nobasu
Verlängerungsschnur entchō-*kōdo
verlassen hanareru
verletzen kega wo suru, kizutsuku
Verletzte, der, die ~ kega-nin
Verletzung kega
verlieren nakusu
verloben, s. ~ konyaku suru
Verlobte, der, die ~ konyaku-sha
Verlust sonshitsu
vermeiden sakeru
vermieten kasu
Vermittler *burōkā, chuukai-nin
Vermittlung chuukai
vermuten suisoku suru
Vermutung suisoku
vernachlässigen orosoka ni suru
vernünftig hunbetsu no aru
verpacken housou suru, tsutsumu
Verpackung housou
Verpflegung makanai
verpflichtet sein gimuzuke rareta
Verpflichtung gimu
verrechnen, s. ~ gosan suru, seisan suru
verreisen tabi ni deru
verrückt kichigai
versäumen nogasu
verschaffen sewa wo suru
verschieben nobasu, enki suru
verschieden kotonatta
verschließen shimeru, kagi wo
kakeru
Verschluß kagi; (Kamera) shattā
verschwinden kieru
Versehen, aus ~ ukkari suru

versenden okuru
versichern hoken wo kakeru
Versicherung hoken
Versicherungskarte hoken shou
versilbert gin-mekki
versorgen mit wo ataeru
verspäten, s. ~ okureru
Verspätung okure
Versprechen yakusoku
Verstand rikai ryoku, risei
verständigen, jdn ~ ni shiraseru
verstauchen nenza suru
verstecken kakusu
verstehen rikai suru
verstopft tsumaru
Verstopfung benpi
Versuch tameshi, kokoromi
versuchen tamesu, kokoromu
vertauschen torikaeru
verteidigen bougyo suru
verteilen wakeru, kubaru
Verteilung bunpai
Vertrag keiyaku
vertragen
Vertragsbedingungen keiyaku jouken
Vertragshändler dairi ten
Vertrauen shin·you
vertrauen auf wo shin·you suru
Vertreter/in dairi-nin
Vertrieb hanbai
Vertriebsnetz hanbai mou
verunglücken fukou ni au
verursachen gen·in ni naru
Verwaltung gyousei
verwandt shinseki no
verwechseln machigaeru
verwenden shiyou suru
Verwendung shiyou
verwirklichen jitsugen suru
verwitwet yamome no
Verzeichnis mokuroku
verzeihen yurusu
verzögern nobasu
verzollen zeikin wo kakeru
verzweifelt zetsubou suru
Video *bideo
Videokamera *bideo *kamera
Videorekorder *bideo-*rekōdā
viel takusan no
vielleicht tabun
viereckig shikakkei no

Viertel, ein ~ yonbun no ichi
violett murasaki
Virus *bīrusu
Visitenkarte meishi
Visum *biza
Vogel tori
Volk minzoku
Volksstück taishuu-engeki
Volkstracht minzoku-isshou
voll ippai
vollenden shiageru
Volleyball *bārē-*bōru
vollkommen kanzen ni
Vollmacht dairi ken, ininjou
Vollpension sanshoku-tsuki
vollständig kanpeki ni
Volt *boruto
von kara
vor no mae ni
vor dem Essen shokuji no mae ni
Voranmeldung yoyaku
voraus, im ~ sakidatte
vorbei sugite
vorbeigehen wo sugite iku
vorbeikommen soba wo tooru, ni tachiyoru
vorbereiten junbi suru
vorbestellen yoyaku suru
Vordruck kinyuu youshi
Vorfahrt yuusen soukou
Vorfall jiken
vorgehen susumu
Vorhang *kāten
vorher izen
vorläufig toriaezu
Vorlesungen kougi
Vormittag gozen
vorn mae ni
Vorname namae
vornehm jouryuu no
Vorort, Vorstadt kougai, kinkou
Vorrat takuwae
Vorsaison kisetsu mae
Vorschlag teian
vorschlagen teian suru
Vorschrift kisoku
Vorsicht shuui
vorsichtig ki wo tsukeru
Vorspeise zensai
vorstellen shoukai suru
Vorteil choushou
vorteilhaft yuuri·na

Vortrag kouen
vorüber sugite
vorübergehen toori sugiru
vorübergehend ichiji·tekina
Vorverkauf mae uri
Vorwahlnummer shigai kyokuban
Vorwand iiwake
vorwärts mae e
vorzeigen teiji suru
vorziehen yuusen suru
Vorzug chousho
Vulkan kazan

W

Waage hakari
wach okite iru
wachsen seichou suru
Wagen kuruma
wagen omoikitte suru
Wagenheber *jakki
Wagenwäsche senscha
Wagennummer (*Zug*) schaljō-bangō
Wahl senkyo
wählen erabu
wahr jijitsu
während ~ no aida ni
Wahrheit shinjitsu
wahrscheinlich osoraku
Wahrscheinlichkeit kakuritsu
Währung tsuuka
Wahrzeichen (*Symbol*) shouchou
Wald mori
Waldbrand yamakaji
Walkman *wōkuman
Wand kabe
wandern *haikingu wo suru
Wanderweg *haikingu-dou
Ware shouhin
Warenverzeichnis buppin hyou
warm atataka·i
Wärme atatakasa
wärmen atatameru
Warnblinker uinkā
warnen (vor) keikoku suru
warten matsu
Wartesaal machiaishitsu
Wartezimmer machiaishitsu
Waschbecken senmen dai
Wäsche sentakumono
waschen arau

Wäscherei *kurīningu-ya
Wäschetrockner kansouki
Waschlappen zoukin
Waschmittel senzai
Waschmaschine sentakuki
Waschraum senmenjo
Wasser mizu
Wasserhahn jaguchi
Wasserfall taki
Watt *watto
Watte wata
Wechsel koukan
Wechselgeld kozeni
wechselhaft kawariyasu·i
Wechselkurs *rēto
wechseln koukan suru
wecken okosu
Wecker mezamashi dokei
weder ... noch ... mo ... monai
weg hanareru
Weg michi
wegen ~ no tameni
weggehen tachisaru, gaishutsu suru
wegnehmen tori ageru
wegschicken (*Post*) hassou suru
Wegweiser hyoushiki
weh tun itamu
weiblich (*Tier*) mesu; (*Mensch*) josei
weich yawaraka·i
weigern, s. ~ kobamu
weil nazenara
Wein *wain
weinen naku
Weintrauben budou
Weise houhou
weiß shiro
weit (*fern*) tooi, (*Flächeninhalt*) hiroi
Welle nami
Welt sekai
wenden hikkuri kaesu
wenig sukoshi
wenigstens sukunakutomo
Werbekampagne kōkoku-*kyanpēn
werben senden suru
Werbung senden, koukoku
werden ~ ni naru
werfen nageru
Werk sakuhin
Werkstatt koujou

Werkzeug dougu
werktags heijitsu
Wert kachi
wert kachi ga aru
Wertangabe kakaku hyouji
wertlos kachi no nai
Wertsachen kouka na mono
Wespe hachi
Weste *besuto
Westen nishi
westlich nishi no
Wettbewerb *kontesuto
Wette kakegoto
wetten kakeru
Wetter tenki
Wetterbericht kishoutsuuhou
Wettkampf shiai
wichtig juuyou
wie donoyouni
wieder mata
wiederaufbauen saiken suru
wiederbekommen kaeshite morau
wiedergeben kaesu
wiederholen kurikaesu
wiederkommen kaettekuru
wiedersehen saikai suru
wiegen hakaru
wild yasei no
Willkommen kangei
Wind kaze
Windeln oshime
windig kaze no tsuyoi
Windpocken mizubousou
Windschutzscheibe *furonto-*ga-rasu
Winkel kakudo
winken te wo furu
Winterreifen fuyuyou-*taya, *sunō-taya
wir watashitachi
Wirbelsäule sebone
wirklich (adv) hontou ni
Wirklichkeit genjitsu
wirksam kouka ga aru
Wirkung kouka
Wirt/in shujin
wissen shitte iru
Wissen chishiki
Wissenschaftler/in kagaku-sha
Witz joudan
Woche shuu
Wochentage youbi

wöchentlich shuu goto ni
wohl genki ni
Wohl kenkou, shiawase
Wohlbefinden kenkou de aru
wohlhabend yuufuku·na
wohlwollend kouiteki·na
wohnen sumu
Wohnort juusho
Wohnung sumai
Wolke kumo
Wolkenkratzer chou·kousou-*biru
Wolldecke moufu
Wolle *ūru
Wort tango
Wunde kizu
wunderbar subarashi·i
wundern, s. ~ (über) odoroku
Wunsch negai
wünschen negau
Wurf toukyuu
Würfel saikoro
Wurm mimizu
Wurst *sōsēji
würzen aji wo tsukeru
Wut ikari
wütend gekido shiteiru

Z

zäh katai
Zahl kazu
zahlen shiharau
zählen kazoeru
zahlreich oozei no, takusan no
Zahlung shiharai
Zahlungsanweisung shiharai-sashi-zusho/kawase
Zahlungsbedingungen shiharai-jouken
Zahn ha
Zahnarzt/ärztin ha-isha
Zahnbürste ha-*burashi
Zahnpasta nerihamigaki
Zahnstocher tsumayouji
Zange *penchi
zanken, s. ~ kouron suru
zart sensai·na
zärtlich yasashi·i
Zehe ashi no yubi
Zeichen shirushi
Zeichenblock *sukketchi-*bukku

zeichnen egaku
Zeichnung suketchi
zeigen miseru
Zeit jikan
Zeitlang, eine ~ shibaraku no aida
Zeitschrift zasshi
Zeitung shinbun
Zelt *tento
zelten *tento wo haru
zentral chuuou no
Zentrale honbu
Zentrum chuushinbu
zerbrechen wareru
zerbrechlich wareyasu·i
zerreißen hikisaku
Zerrung kinniku
zerstören kowareru
Zeuge shou-nin
Zeugnis shoumei-sho
ziehen hiku; *(Zahn)* nuku
Ziel mokuteki
ziemlich kanari
Zigarette *tabako
Zigarillo hamaki
Zigarre hamaki
Zimmer heya
Zimmermädchen *meido
Zirkus *sākasu
Zitrone *remon
zögern tamerau
Zoll zeikan
Zollerklärung zeikan-shinsei sho
zollfreier Laden menzei-ten
Zoo doubutsu-en
zornig rippuku shita
zu *(Richtung)* e; *(geschlossen)* shimatte iru; *(mit adj)* sugiru
zubereiten chouri suru
Zucker satou
zudecken oou
zuerst hajimeni
Zufall guuzen
zufällig guuzen ni
zufrieden manzoku suru
Zug densha
Zugang iriguchi
Zugpersonal joumuin
zugunsten no tameni
zuhören, jdm ~ mimi wo katamu-keru
Zukunft shourai
zukünftig shourai no

zulassen kyoka suru
zulässig kyoka sarete iru
zuletzt saigoni
zumachen shimeru
zunächst saishoni
Zündkerze *supāku-*pulagu
Zündung tenka
zunehmen fueru
Zunge shita
zurück ushiro e
zurückbringen modosu
zurückfahren kaeru
zurückgeben kaesu
zurückkehren kaeru
zurücklassen kaeraseru
zurückweisen shirizokeru
zurückzahlen hensai suru
zurückziehen shirizoku
zusagen shoudaku suru
zusammen isshoni
zusammenrechnen goukei suru
zusammenschlagen uchiawase suru
Zusammenstoß shoutotsu
zusätzlich tsuika no
Zuschauer kankyaku
Zuschlag warimashi-ryoukin
zuschließen kagi wo shimeru
Zustand joukyou
zuständig tantou
zusteigen norikomu
zustimmen sansei suru
zuverlässig shin·you dekiru
zuviel oosugiru
Zwang kyousei
Zweck mokuteki
zwecklos muimi·na
zweckmäßig yakuni tatsu
Zweifel utagai
zweifelhaft utagawashi·i
zweifellos utagainashi ni
zweifeln, an etw ~ utagau
zweitens futatsu me ni
Zwiebel tamanegi
zwingen kyou sei suru
zwischen no aida ni
Zwischendeck santou-senshitsu
Zwischenfall toppatsu-jiken
Zwischenlandung chuukan-cha-kuriku
Zwischenstecker *adaputā
Zylinder *shirindā

Wörterbuch Japanisch–Deutsch

A

abarabone Rippe
*abogado Avocado
abura Öl; **abura-e** Ölmalerei
abura no sukunai mager
aburakko·i fett
achira-gawa drüben; jenseits
*adaputā Adapter; Zwischenstecker
agaru hinaufgehen
ageru erhöhen
ai Liebe
  ~ **no aida ni** während; zwischen
  ~ **no aidawa** solange
*aidea Idee
*airon Bügeleisen; ***airon wo kakeru** bügeln
aisatsu suru grüßen, begrüßen
*aishadō Lidschatten
*aisu Eis
aisuru lieben
aite iru geöffnet, offen; **aiteiru-jikan** Öffnungszeit
aji Geschmack; **aji ga suru** schmek-ken; **aji wo tsukeru** würzen
*ajia Asien; ***ajia-jin** Asiate; Asiatin; ***ajia-jinno** asiatisch
akabou Gepäckträger
akachan Baby
aka Rot
akari Beleuchtung
akaru·i hell
akeru aufmachen; öffnen
akiaki shita satt
akiraka·na sichtbar; offenbar
akirakani deutlich
akubi wo suru gähnen
*akuseru Gaspedal
*akusesarī Schmuck
akuyou Mißbrauch; **akuyou suru** mißbrauchen
ama·i süß
ame Regen
amega furu regnen
amemoyou no regnerisch
*amerika Amerika; ***amerika-jin**

Amerikaner/in
ami Netz
*āmondo Mandeln
*āmu-*cheā Sessel
ana Loch
anata Sie
anausagi Kaninchen
*anchobi Sardellen
*andāshatsu Unterhemd, Unterwäsche
ane ältere Schwester
*animēshon Animation
*ankā Anker
annai Auskunft; (Stadt-) Führung; **annai-jo** Informationsstand
ano jene(r, -s)
*anorakku Anorak
anshin suru s. beruhigen
anshou-bangou Geheimzahl
anteizai Beruhigungsmittel
anzen Sicherheit; **anzen-*beruto** Anschnallgurt; Sicherheitsgurt; **anzen kakunin** Sicherheitskontrolle; **anzen-*pin** Sicherheitsnadeln
anzen·na sicher
anzu Aprikosen
ao Blau
aoaza Bluterguß
aozameta bleich
*apāto Appartement
arare Graupel
arashi Sturm
arau waschen
arawareru (verlegen) erscheinen
*arerugī Allergie; ~ **ni taishite** ***arerugī ga aru** allergisch sein gegen ~
arifureta gewöhnlich
  ~ **ni aru** s. befinden
arukōru Spiritus; **arukōru-chuu-doku-sha** Alkoholiker/in; ***aru-kōru-bun nashi** alkoholfrei
*arumihoiru Alufolie
asa (der) Morgen; Leinen; **asa-gohan** Frühstück
ase Schweiß; **ase wo kaku** schwitzen

ashi Bein; Fuß; **ashi no-ura** Sohle; **ashi no yubi** Zehe
ashiato Spur
ashihire Schwimmflossen
ashita *(das)* Morgen
asobi Spiel; **asobi-ba** Kinderspielplatz
asobu spielen
assen-gyousha Makler/in
*****asuparagasu** Spargel
*****asupirin** Aspirin
ataeru *(übergeben)* geben; gewähren; ~ **wo ataeru** versorgen mit
atama Kopf
atarashi·i neu
atarashisa Neuheit
atari Umgebung
atataka·i warm
atatakasa Wärme
atatameru wärmen; heizen
atena Anschrift; **atena wo kaku** adressieren
shokuji no ato nach dem Essen
atode nachher; später
atokara okuru nachsenden
atsu·i heiß; *(Buch)* dick
atsumeru sammeln
atsusa Hitzewelle, Hitze; *(Buch)* Dicke
au passen; stimmen; treffen
akeru offen, auf
awa Schaum
ayamari Fehler; falsch
ayamaru entschuldigen
ayauku beinahe
ayumi Schritt
azukeru hinterlegen

B

*****bābekyū** Grill
bachi Strafe
*****badominton** Badminton
*****baibai** tschüß
baibai-keiyaku Kaufvertrag
*****baipasu** Bypass
baiten Kiosk
baka·na dumm
baketsu Eimer
bakkin Bußgeld; Geldstrafe
*****bakku-mirā** Rückspiegel

*****banana** Bananen
banchi Hausnummer
*****bando** Gürtel
*****bangarou** Bungalow
bangou Nummer; **bangou zuke suru** numerieren
bansen *****rēru** Gleis
bansoukou Pflaster
bara Rose
*****barē** Ballett
*****bārē-*bōru** Volleyball
*****barikēdo** Sperre
bariki PS
*****baromētā** Barometer
*****barukonī** Balkon
basho Ort; Platz; Stelle
basu Bus; Bad; *****basu-*rūmu** Badezimmer
*****basuketto-*bōru** Basketball
*****basuto** Büste
*****batā** Butter
batsu Strafe
*****batteriē** Batterie
*****bebī** Baby; *****bebī-*fūdo** Babynahrung; *****bebī-*shittā** Kinderbetreuung
*****bēju** beige
*****bēkon** Speck
benchi *(Sitzbank)* Bank
bengo-shi Rechtsanwalt/anwältin
beni Rouge
benkai *(Ausrede)* Entschuldigung; **benkai suru** entschuldigen
benkyou suru studieren
benpi Verstopfung
benshousuru ersetzen
bentsuu Stuhlgang
*****beru** Klingel; *****beru wo narasu** klingeln
*****beruto** Riemen
bessou Ferienhaus
*****besuto** Weste
betsu betsu no getrennt
*****betto** Bett
*****bideo** Video; *****bideo *kamera** Videokamera; *****bideo-*rekōdā** Videorekorder
bien Heuschnupfen
*****bijinesu-*pātōnā** Geschäftspartner
bijutsu-daigaku Kunstakademie; **bijutsu-shi** Kunstgeschichte; **bi**

jutsu-shou Kunsthändler
bijutsukan *(Kunst)* Museum
bikini Bikini
bin Flasche
binsen Briefpapier
*__bīru__ Bier
*__bīrusu__ Virus
*__bisinesu-*kurasu__ Business class
biyou-shi Friseur, Friseuse
biyouin Kosmetiksalon
*__biza__ Sichtvermerk; Visum
bochi Friedhof
*__boirā__ Boiler
bokushi Pfarrer/in
*__bōringu__ Bowling; kegeln
*__bōru__ Ball; Schüssel
*__bōrupen__ Kugelschreiber
*__boruto__ Volt
*__botan__ Knopf; **botan wo osu** Knopf drücken
*__bōto__ Boot; Kahn
bou Stange; Stock
bouen-*renzu Teleobjektiv
bouenkyou Fernglas
bougyo suru verteidigen
boukou Blase; Mißbrauch; **boukou suru** mißbrauchen
boushi Hut; Mütze
bubun Abschnitt; Teil; Stück
budou Trauben
budoutou Traubenzucker
bumon Abteilung
bun Satz
bunbougu-ya Schreibwarengeschäft
bunka Kultur
bunkazai-hogo Denkmalschutz
bunpai Verteilung
bunshou de schriftlich
buntsuu Briefwechsel
buppinhyou Warenverzeichnis
*__burajā__ Büstenhalter
*__burashi__ Bürste; Haarbürste; *__burashi wo kakeru__ bürsten
*__burausu__ Bluse
burei·na unhöflich
*__burēki__ Bremse; Fußbremse; *__burēki-*oiru__ Bremsflüssigkeit; *__burēki-*rainingu__ Bremsbelag; *__burēki wo kakeru__ bremsen
*__burezā-kōto__ Blazer
*__burōchi__ Brosche

*__burōkā__ Vermittler
bushitsuke·na unanständig
būsu Messestand
buta-niku Schweinefleisch
butai Bühne
*__butikku__ Boutique
butsuri-gaku Physik; **butsuri-gaku-sha** Physiker/in; **butsuri-ryouhou** Physiotherapie
byou Sekunde
byouin Krankenhaus
byouki krank; Krankheit
byoutou Station

C

chai-ro braun
*__chakku__ Reißverschluß
chakuriku Landung; **chakuriku suru** landen
chakushoku suru färben
*__chāmingu·na__ steil
*__chansu__ Gelegenheit
*__chaperu__ Kapelle
*__chekku__ Scheck
chekku no kariert
chi Blut
chichi Vater
*__chīfu__ Chef
*__chifusu__ Typhus
chiga·i Unterschied
chii Rang
chiiki Gegend
chiisa·i klein
chijin der, die Bekannte
chika·i nahe
chikaiuchini demnächst
chikamichi *(Weg)* Abkürzung
chikara Kraft
chikasa Nähe
chikatetsu U-Bahn
chikyuu *(Erdkugel)* Erde
*__chīmu__ Mannschaft
chinmoku Schweigen
chinretsu-hin Exponat; Ausstellungsgegenstand
*__chippu__ Trinkgeld
chiri-gaku Geographie
chirigami Papiertaschentücher
chiritori Kehrblech
chiryou *(Arzt)* Behandlung; **chiry-**

ou-shi Therapeut/in; **chiryou su-ru** behandeln; **chiryou-yaku** Heilmittel

chishiki Kenntnis; Wissen

chishitsu-gaku Geologie

chitsujo Ordnung

*__chīzu__ Käse

chizu Landkarte

chokkou-bin Direktflug

*__chokorēto__ Schokolade

chokusetsu direkt; **chokusetsu no** unmittelbar

chokutsuu *(Telefon)* durchwählen; *(Zug)* direkt

chosuichi Stausee

chou Darm

choudo *(adv)* genau; *(zeitlich)* gerade; **choudo ima** eben; **choudo yoi toki ni** rechtzeitig

chōuji *(Gewürz)* Nelken

choujou Gipfel

choukin Goldschmiedekunst

choukoku Schnitzerei; Skulptur

chou·kousou-*biru Wolkenkratzer

choukyori-tsuuwa Ferngespräch

choumiryou Gewürz

chouonpa Ultraschall; **chouonpa-kensa** Ultraschalluntersuchung

chouri suru zubereiten

chourui-hogo-chiiki Vogelschutzgebiet

chouryoku Gehör

chousa Untersuchung

chousei suru regeln

choushi Konditionen

chousho Stärke; Vorteil; Vorzug

choushoku Frühstück; **choushoku-*byuffe** Frühstücksbüfett; **choushoku wo toru** frühstücken

choushuu Hörer

choutatsu Besorgung; **choutatsu suru** beschaffen; besorgen

chouten Höhepunkt

chouzou Statue

*__chūbu__ *(Reifen)* Schlauch

*__chuubu__ Tube

chuudan suru unterbrechen

chuudoku Sucht; Vergiftung

chuudokushou no süchtig

chuugoku China; **chuugoku-go** chinesisch; **chuugoku-jin** Chinese/in

chuui Warnung; Achtung; **chuui suru** aufmerksam; aufpassen (auf); **chuui wo harau** beachten

chuujien Mittelohrentzündung

chuukai Vermittlung; **chuukai-nin** Vermittler

chuukan-chakuriku Zwischenlandung

chuukoku Rat; **chuukoku suru** raten

chuumon Auftrag; Bestellung; **chuumon-kakunin** Auftragsbestätigung; **chuumon suru** *(Essen, Tisch)* bestellen

chuuou Mitte

chuuou-doori Hauptstraße; **chuuou-eki** Hauptbahnhof; **chuuou-guchi** Haupteingang; **chuuou no** zentral; **chuuou-yuubinkyoku** Hauptpostamt

chuusei Mittelalter; **chuusei no** mittelalterlich

chuusha Spritze

chuusha-jou Parkplatz; **chuusha suru** parken

chuushinbu Zentrum

chuushoku Mittagessen

chuuzetsu Abtreibung

D

daidokoro Küche

*__daietto__ Diät; *__daietto-shoku__ Schonkost

daigaku Hochschule; Universität

daikin-hikikae Nachnahme, per

daiku Zimmermann

*__dairekuto-*kōru__ durchwählen

dairi-ken Vollmacht; **dairi-nin** Vertreter/in; **dairi-shou** Handelsvertreter; **dairi-ten** Vertragshändler

dairiseki Marmor

dairiten Agentur

daiseidou Dom

dakara deshalb

~**dake** nur

daku umarmen

damaru schweigen

damasu betrügen

danbou Heizung; **danbou wo ireru** heizen
dannen suru aufgeben
*****dansā** Tänzer/in
*****dansu** Tanz; **dansu wo suru** tanzen
danwa-shitsu Aufenthaltsraum
darashi no nai nachlässig
dareka jemand
daremo ... nai niemand
~ de mit; **~ de aru** sein
deau begegnen
deguchi Ausfahrt; Ausgang
dekigoto Ereignis
dekimono Geschwulst
dekiru können
*****dekki** Deck
demado Erker
demo aber
denki-*konro (Elektroherd) Herd; **denki no** elektrisch; **denki-setsubi-kou** Elektriker/in; **denki-ya** Elektrohandlung
denkyuu Glühbirne
denpou Telegramm
denryuu (elektr.) Strom
densen Infektion
densensei no ansteckend
densha Zug
dentaku Taschenrechner
denwa Telefon; **denwa-bangou** Rufnummer; Telefonnummer; **denwa-*bokkusu** Telefonzelle; **denwa wo kakeru** telefonieren; **denwa wo suru** anrufen, telefonieren
denwachou Telefonbuch
*****depāto** Kaufhaus
*****derakkusu** Luxus
*****derakkusu·na** luxuriös
~ desaemo sogar
deteiku hinausgehen
~ dewanaku te sondern
*****dezain** Design
*****dezainā** Designer/in
*****dezāto** Nachtisch
*****disuko** Diskothek
do (Temperatur) Grad
*****doa** Tür; *****doaman** Portier
dodai Fundament
*****doitsu** Deutschland; *****doitsu-go** deutsch; *****doitsu-jin** Deutsche/r;

*****doitsu-*maruku** D-Mark
dokoka hokade anderswo
dokokade irgendwo
dokokae irgendwohin
doko nimo ... nai nirgends
doku Gift; **doku no aru** giftig
dokusatsu Vergiftung
dokushin Junggeselle; ledig
*****dōmu** Kuppel
donoyouni wie
don·yoritoshita diesig
~ doori mäßig
*****dorai-*kuriningu** chemisch reinigen
*****doraiā** Fön; *****doraiā wo kakeru** fönen
*****doraibā** Schraubenzieher
*****doraibu** Fahrt
*****dorama** Drama; Theaterstück
doro Schlamm
dorobou Dieb
doryoku Bemühung; Anstrengung; **doryoku suru** s. bemühen
dou Bronze; **dou-hanga** Kupferstich
dou itashimashite bitte; keine Ursache
doubutsu Tier; **doubutsu-en** Zoo
dougu Werkzeug
douhan Begleitung
doui suru einwilligen
doujini gleichzeitig
doujou Mitleid
doukoku-jin Landsmann
doukutsu Höhle
doumei Bund
dounikashite irgendwie
douro-chizu Straßenkarte
douryou Kollege, Kollegin
douyara ... rashii (adj) anscheinend
douyou ni gleich; gleichfalls

E

e Bild
~ e nach
*****eā tāminaru** Air Terminal
ebi Garnelen; Krabben
egaku beschreiben; malen; zeichnen

ehagaki Ansichtskarte
eibun-gaku Anglistik
eiga Film; **eiga-kan** Kino
eigo englisch
eigyou-jikan Öffnungszeit
eikyou Einfluß
eiyou Nahrung; **eiyou aru** nahrhaft
*__eizu__ Aids
*__ējento__ Handelsvertreter
eki Bahnhof; Station
*__ekisutora__ extra
ekitai no flüssig
*__ekonomī-*kurasu__ Economy class
endai Rednerpult
engeki Schauspiel
*__enjin__ Motor
*__enjinia__ Ingenieur/in
enjo Unterstützung
enki Aufschub; **enki suru** aufschieben; verschieben
enpitsu Bleistift; **enpitsu-kezuri** Bleistiftspitzer
enshou Entzündung
enshutsu Inszenierung; Regie
ensoku Ausflug
ensou (Konzert) Aufführung
entchō-*kōdo Verlängerungsschnur
enyou-gyogyou Hochseefischen
erabi dasu aussuchen
erabu wählen
*__erebētā__ Aufzug; Fahrstuhl
eri Kragen
eru erlangen
esa Futter
~ **e** (Richtung) zu; nach

F

*__faindā__ (Kamera) Sucher
*__fairu__ Mappe
*__fakkusu__ Telefax
*__fasshon-moderu__ Mannequin;
  *__fasshon-shou__ Modenschau
*__fasunā__ Reißverschluß
*__feā__ fair
*__fendā__ Kotflügel
*__ferī__ Fähre
*__fesutibaru__ Festival
*__firumu__ Film
*__firutā__ Filter

*__fōku__ Gabel
fuan Angst; Sorge
fuantei·na unbeständig
fubuki Schneesturm
fuchi Rand
fuchuui·na unvorsichtig
fueru zunehmen
*__fuerutopen__ Filzstift
fuiuchi Überfall
fujuubun·na ungenügend
fuka·i tief; **fukaikan** Übelkeit
·**fukai·na** übel; unangenehm
fukakai·na unbegreiflich
fukaketsu·na unentbehrlich
fukanou·na ausgeschlossen; unmöglich
fukanzen·na unvollständig
fukenkou·na ungesund
fukisoku·na unregelmäßig
fukki Rückkehr
fukou Unglück; **fukou ni au** verunglücken
fukou·na unglücklich; **fukouna kotoni** unglücklicherweise
fuku wo kiru (Kleidung) anziehen
fukugen suru rekonstruieren
fukumareteiru inbegriffen
fukumeru (inklusive) einschließen
fukumu enthalten; inbegriffen
fukuramasu aufpumpen
fukuro Beutel; Sack
fukusayou Nebenwirkungen
fukusou Kleidung
fukuyou suru (Medikament) einnehmen
fumanzoku unzufrieden
fumiireru betreten
fuminshou Schlaflosigkeit
fun Minute
funa tsukiba Anlegeplatz
funayoi seekrank
fune Schiff
funsui Brunnen
*__furaido-*poteto__ Pommes frites
*__furansu-go__ französisch
*__furawā-*dezainā__ Florist/in
~ **ni fureru** berühren
furikomi Überweisung
furikomu überweisen
furo Bad
furoba Badezimmer
furoku (Zeitung) Beilage

*furonto-*garasu Windschutzscheibe
*furoppī-*desuku Diskette
furuhon-ya Antiquariat
furui alt
furumai Benehmen
furusato Heimat
fusei Ungerechtigkeit; Unrecht
fuseikaku·na ungenau
fushinsetsu·na unfreundlich
fushitsuyou·na unnötig
fusoku Mangel
futashika·na ungewiß; unsicher
futatsu-me ni zweitens
futekitou·na ungeeignet
futon Decke; Futon
futou Kai
futoueki Frostschutzmittel
futou·na ungerecht
futsugou·na ungünstig
futsuu no normal
futsuudena·i ungewöhnlich
futotta (Mensch) dick
fuufu Ehepaar
fuukei Landschaft; fuukei-ga
Landschaftsmalerei
fuusha Windmühle
fuushin Röteln
fuushuu Brauchtum
fuutou Briefumschlag
fuyukai·na unerfreulich; unwohl
fuyuyou-*taya Winterreifen

G

~ ga aru (Dinge) es gibt; ~ ga iru
(Lebewesen); ga-ka Maler/in
gabyou Reißzwecken
*gādo shita no michi Unterführung
*gaido (Person) Fremdenführer;
Reiseleiter/in; *gaido-*bukku
(Buch) Fremdenführer; Reiseführer
gaika (Geld) Devisen
gaikoku Ausland; gaikoku-jin
Ausländer/in; der, die Fremde;
gaikoku no ausländisch; (Ausland) fremd
gaishutsu suru ausgehen
gaiyou no (med.) äußerlich
gakkou Schule

gakufu-dai Ständer
gakugyou Studium
gakusei Student/in; gakusei-ryou
Studentenwohnheim
gakusetsu (Musik) Satz
gaman Geduld; gaman dekinai
unerträglich; gaman suru ertragen; Geduld haben
*gamu Kaugummi
gan Krebs
gankyou-shi Optiker/in
*garasu (Fenster) Glas; *garasu-ya
Glaser
**gasorin Benzin; *gasorin-*kan
(benzinkanister) ; *gasorin-*sutando Tankstelle; gasorin wo ireru tanken
gasshou-dan Chor
*gasu-*konro (Gasherd) Herd
*gāze no houtai Mullbinde
gedokuzai Gegengift
geijuts-ka Künstler/in
geijutsu Kunst
geka-i Chirurg/in
geki; geki-jou Theater
gekido shiteiru wütend
gekkei Menstruation
gekkeiju Lorbeer
gekkeitai Damenbinden
gen·in Ursache; gen·in ni naru verursachen
gen·jitsu Wirklichkeit
gen·jutsu-shugi Realismus
genkan Hauseingang; genkan-
*hōru Empfangshalle
genki ni wohl
genkin Bargeld; genkin de harau
bar zahlen; genkin-waribiki
Skonto
genkou-*ra ito Abblendlicht; genkou suru abblenden
genmitsusa Genauigkeit
genryou Material
gensaku Originalfassung
genshuku·na feierlich
geri Durchfall
gesen suru ausschiffen
gesha suru aussteigen
gezai Abführmittel
*gia Gangschaltung
giji-nittei Tagesordnung
gikkuri-goshi Hexenschuß

gimu Pflicht; Verpflichtung; **gimu no nai** unverbindlich
gimuzuke rareta verpflichtet sein
gin Silber; **gin-mekki** versilbert
ginkou *(Geldinstitut)* Bank; **ginkou-bangou** Bankleitzahl
*__gipusu__ Gips
giri no ane *(ältere)* Schwägerin; **giri no ani** *(älterer)* Schwager
*__girisha__ Griechen; *__girisha no__ griechisch
gishi Ingenieur/in; Techniker/in
*__gitā__ Gitarre
gogo Nachmittag; **gogo no kouen** Nachmittagsvorstellung
gokai Mißverständnis; **gokai suru** mißverstehen
*__gokiburi__ Kakerlake
gōlu *(Spiel)* Tor, Ziel
gomi Abfall; Müll; **gomi-bako** Mülleimer; **gomi-bukuro** Abfallbeutel
*__gomu-__*__bōto__ Schlauchboot; *__gomu-nagagutsu__ Gummistiefel
goro *(ca.)* gegen
*__gorufu__ Golf; *__gorufu-jou__ Golfplatz
gosan suru s. verrechnen
goudou-jigyou Joint-venture
gouka Luxus
gouka·na luxuriös
goukei Summe; **goukei suru** zusammenrechnen
gozen Vormittag
*__gurafikku__ Graphik
*__gurafu-zasshi__ Illustrierte
*__gurasu__ Glas
*__gurūpu__ Gruppe
guuzen Zufall; **guuzen ni** zufällig
*__gyararī__ Galerie
gyokou Fischerhafen
gyoukan Vergewaltigung; **gyoukan suru** vergewaltigen
gyousei Verwaltung
gyuuniku Rindfleisch
gyuunyuu Milch

H

ha Blatt
ha Zahn; **ha-**__*burashi__ Zahnbürste;

ha-isha Zahnarzt/ärztin
haba breit
habu Nabe
*__hābu__ Kräuter
hachi Biene; Wespe
hachi Schüssel
hachimitsu Honig
hada Haut
hadaka no nackt
hae Fliege
*__hāfu-__*__taimu__ Halbzeit
haha Mutter
hai Lunge
*__hai-bīmu__ Fernlicht
*__hai-__*__sokkusu__ Kniestrümpfe
haiboku Niederlage
haien Lungenentzündung
haiiro Grau
haikikan Auspuff
*__haikingu-dou__ Wanderweg; *__haikingu wo suru__ wandern
haikyo Ruine
hairu eintreten; betreten
*__haishīzun__ Hauptsaison
haitte iku hineingehen; **haitte kuru** hereinkommen
haiyuu *(m)* Filmschauspieler; Schauspieler
haizara Aschenbecher
hajime Anfang; Beginn
hajimeni zuerst
hajimeru anfangen; beginnen
haka Grab
hakaishi Grabstein
hakari Waage
hakaru messen; wiegen
hakase Doktor
hakike Brechreiz
hakken entdecken
hakketsubyou Leukämie
hakkiri shinai unbestimmt; **hakkiri shita** klar
hakkou suru *(Briefmarken)* herausgeben; *(verlegen)* erscheinen
hakkutsu Ausgrabungen
hako Kiste; Schachtel
hakobisaru forttragen
hakobu befördern; bringen; tragen
haku erbrechen, sich
hakubutsukan Museum
hakushu Beifall
hama Strand

hamaki Zigarillo; Zigarre
hamigakiko Zahnpasta
*****hamu** *(gekocht)* Schinken
han-*zubon Hose, kurze
hana Blume; **hana-ya** Blumengeschäft
hana Nase
hanabi Feuerwerk
hanaji Nasenbluten
hanakaze Schnupfen
hanareru verlassen; weg
hanareta entfernt
hanashiai Unterhaltung
hanashiau s. unterhalten
hanasu erzählen; reden; sprechen
hanataba Blumenstrauß
hanbai Verkauf; Vertrieb; **hanbai-mou** Vertriebsnetz; **hanbai-so-kushin** Verkaufsförderung
hanbun Hälfte; **hanbun no** halb
handan suru beurteilen
*****hando-*bakku** Handtasche; *****hando-*bureki** Handbremse
*****handobōru** Handball
*****handomeido** handgemacht
*****handoru** Lenkrad; *(Zweirad)* Lenker
hane Feder; Flügel
*****hangā** Kleiderbügel
*****hankachi** Taschentuch
hanketsu Urteil; **hanketsu wo kudasu** urteilen
*****hanmā** Hammer
hantai Gegenteil; **hantai no** entgegengesetzt; umgekehrt
hanzai Verbrechen; **hanzai wo okasu** verbrennen
happa Blatt
hara wo tateru (sich) ärgern
haraikomu einzahlen
hare Schwellung; *(Wetter)* heiter
hareta geschwollen; sonnig
haretsu suru platzen
hari Nadel
harigane Draht
hasami Schere
hashi Brücke; Stäbchen
hashigo Leiter
hashika Masern
hashira Säule
hashiru laufen; rennen
hashoufuu Tetanus

hason Beschädigung; **hason suru** beschädigen
hassei suru s. ereignen
hassou Sendung; **hassou suru** absenden; *(Post)* wegschicken
hatake Acker; Feld
hatsu denki Lichtmaschine
hatsumei suru erfinden
hatsuon Aussprache; **hatsuon suru** aussprechen
hatten suru entwickeln
haya·i rasch; schnell; früh
hayaku früh
hayari Mode
hayasa Schnelligkeit
hazukashigariya no schüchtern
hebi Schlange
*****heddo-*raito** Scheinwerfer
*****hēddohōn** Kopfhörer
heijitsu werktags
heikin no durchschnittlich
heisateki·na geschlossen
heiwa Friede
heiya *(Land)* Ebene
hekiga Wandmalerei
henji Antwort; **henji suru** erwidern; **henji wo suru** antworten
henkou Veränderung; **henkou suru** umbuchen; verändern
henpeisoku Plattfuß
henpi·na abgelegen
hensai suru zurückzahlen
henshuu-sha Redakteur/in
hentousen Mandeln; **hentousen-en** Mandelentzündung
henzutsuu Migräne
*****herikoputā** Hubschrauber
nishin *(Fisch)* Hering
*****herumetto** Sturzhelm
*****heruniya** Leistenbruch
heya Raum; Zimmer
*****heyāsutailu** Frisur
hi Feuer; Tag
hibana Funke
hibiki Klang
hibiku tönen
hidari links; **hidari no** linke(r, -s)
hido·i fürchterlich; schlimm; gemein
hidoku gewaltig
hifu Haut
hifubyou Hautkrankheit

higaeri-ryokou Tagesausflug
higasa Sonnenschirm;
higashi Osten
higawari-*menyu Tagesgericht;
~menü
hige Bart; **hige wo soru** rasieren
higeki Tragödie
hihan suru kritisieren
hiji Ellbogen
hi·jitsuyouteki·na unpraktisch
hijou-*burēki Notbremse; **hijou-guchi** Notausgang
hikaku Vergleich; **hikaku suru** vergleichen
hikari Licht; **hikari wo saegiru** blenden
hikaru glänzen; leuchtend; **pikapi-ka *hikaru** blinken
hikiageru heraufsetzen
hikidasu *(Geld)* abheben
hikikae-ken Gutschein
hikikaesu umkehren
hikiniku Hackfleisch
hikisaku reißen; zerreißen
hikishio Ebbe
~ **wo hikitomeru** jdn aufhalten/s. ~
hikitsuen-sha Nichtraucher
hikitsugu übernehmen
hikiukeru übernehmen; annehmen
hikiwake unentschieden
hikiwatashi-jouken Lieferbedingungen
hikkosu umziehen
hikkuri kaesu wenden
hikou Flug
hikouki Düsenmaschine; Flugzeug
hiku ziehen
hiku·i nieder, niedrig
hima·na langweilig
himitsu ni suru verheimlichen; **himitsu no** geheim
himo Riemen; Schnur; das Band
hininyaku Antibabypille
hiningu Präservativ
hinode Sonnenaufgang
hinshitsu Qualität
hinshu Sorte
*hinto Tip
hiretsu·na gemein
hiroi *(Flächeninhalt)* weit; groß
hirugohan Mittagessen

hisho Sekretär/in
hisokani heimlich
*hitchihaikā Tramper
*hitchihaiku trampen
hitei suru leugnen
hiteiteki·na negativ
hito man; Person
hitobito Leute
hitokumi ein Paar
hitoni utsuru ansteckend
hitori de allein
hitotsu eins; **hitotsu no** ein(e)
hitsuji Schaf
hitsuyou to suru brauchen; benötigen
hitsuyou·na nötig
hitsuzen·sei Notwendigkeit; **hitsu-zenteki·na** notwendig
hiyake Sonnenbrand
hiyoke Blende
hiyou Kosten
hiza Knie
hizuke Datum
hodoku auspacken; lösen
hodou Gehsteig
hogo Schutz; **hogo suru** beschützen
hoji suru behalten
~ **no hoka** außer; **no hoka ni** außerhalb
hokano anders
hoken Versicherung; **hokenshou** Versicherungskarte; **hoken wo kakeru** versichern
*hokkē Hockey
hokori Staub
hokousha Fußgänger; **hokousha-tengoku** Fußgängerzone
homeru loben
*hōmumeido no hausgemacht
hon Buch; **honya** Buchhandlung
honbu Zentrale
hone Knochen; **sakana no hone** Gräte
honmono echt; **honmono no** Original
honou Flamme
hontou ni *(adv)* wirklich
hon·yakusha Übersetzer/in; **hon·y-aku suru** übersetzen
honyuubin Saugflasche
*hōru Halle; Saal

hoshi Stern
hoshibudou Rosinen
hoshou Garantie; **hoshoukin** Kaution; Pfand
hoso·i dünn
hossa Anfall; Ausschlag
hossorito shita schlank
***hōsu** Schlauch
***hosuto** Gastgeber/in
***hoteru** Hotel
hotondo beinahe; fast; **hotondo ~ nai** kaum
hou (Gesetz) Recht
houhou Methode; Art; Weise
houi Belagerung
houki Besen
houko Schatzkammer
houkoku Bericht; **houkoku suru** (mitteilen) melden
houkou Richtung
houmon Besuch; **houmon suru** jdn besuchen
hourensou Spinat
houritsugaku Jura
housekishou Juwelier
houshuu Belohnung; Lohn
housou Pocken
housou Packung; Verpackung; **housou suru** verpacken; **housoushi** Geschenkpapier
houtai-youhin Verbandszeug
houtaino verbinden
hoyou Kur; **hoyouchi** Kurort
hozon-kikan haltbar; **hozon suru** aufbewahren; erhalten
hunbetsu no aru vernünftig
hyakkaten Kaufhaus
hyaku hundert
hyakunichizeki Keuchhusten
hyotto shitara eventuell
hyou Hagel; Liste
hyougen Ausdruck
hyoumen-teki·na äußerlich
hyousatsu Schild
hyoushiki Wegweiser
***hyūzu** Sicherung

I

i Magen; **i-gusuru** Magenmittel
***iaringu** Ohrringe

ibiki wo kaku schnarchen
ichatsuku flirten
ichi Stellung; **ichi to nibun no ichi** anderthalb
ichiban yoi beste(r, -s)
ichido einmal
ichigo Erdbeeren
ichijiku no mi Feigen
ichijiteki·na vorübergehend
ichinichi-joushaken Tagesfahrkarte; **ichinichi-ken** Tagesspaß
ichinin-mae (eine) Portion
ichiryuu no erstklassig
ido Brunnen
ie Haus
igaku Medizin
igi Beanstandung
i·i gut
iiwake Vorwand
ijou·na außergewöhnlich
ika Tintenfisch
ikari Wut
iken Ansicht; Meinung
iki Atem; **iki wo suru** atmen
ikiru leben
ikiteiru lebend
ikkai Erdgeschoß; einmal
ikkatsu Pauschale
iku gehen
ikutsuka no einige; ein paar
ima jetzt; nun
imi Bedeutung; Sinn; **imi suru** bedeuten
imouto (jüngere) Schwester
~ inaini innerhalb
inaka (auf dem ~) Land
inazuma Blitz
ininjou Vollmacht
inki·na (düster) finster
inori Gebet
inoru beten
insatsu-butsu Drucksache; **insatsu-ki** Drucker
inshoku-ten Lokal; Gaststätte
inshou Eindruck; **inshou-ha** Impressionismus
***inshurin** Insulin
inu Hund
ippai voll
ippanteki·na allgemein
~ irai seit
iremono Behälter; Gefäß

irie Bucht
iriguchi Einfahrt; Eingang; Zugang
iro Farbe; **iro-enpitsu** Farbstift; **iro-toridori** bunt
~ ni iru s. befinden
irui Kleidung
ischa Arzt/Ärztin
ischi Arzt/Ärztin
ise-ebi Languste
ishi Stein; **ishi darake no** steinig
ishiki-fumei Ohnmacht; **ishiki-fumei no** bewußtlos
ishitsubutsu-toriatsukaijo Fundbüro
isogashi·i beschäftigt
isogi no eilig
isogu s. beeilen
isshoni gemeinsam; zusammen
isshun Augenblick
isshuu Runde
isu Stuhl
ita·i schmerzhaft
itamidome Schmerzmittel
itamu schmerzen; weh tun
itarutokorode überall
itchi shita s. einigen; **itchi suru** einig sein
ito Absicht; Faden
itoko Cousin/e
itsuka einmal; **mata itsuka** ein andermal
itsumademo stets; für immer
itsumo immer
itsuu Magenschmerzen
iu sagen; **~to iu** heißen
iwa Fels
iwashi Sardinen
iwau gratulieren
izen früher; vorher; bevor
izumi Quelle

J

jagaimo Kartoffeln
jaguchi Wasserhahn
*jakki** Wagenheber
jama wo suru stören
*jamu** Marmelade
*jānarisuto** Journalist/in
jari Kies

*jazu-*dansu** Jazztanz
jettoki Düsenmaschine
ji Hämorrhoiden
jibun de toru bedienen, sich; **jibun no** (Besitz) eigen
jibun·jishin selbst
jidai Epoche; **jidai okure no** unmodern
jidou Automatik(getriebe); **jidou-hanbaiki** Automat
jidouscha-tourokushou Kfz-Schein
jidousha-kou Automechaniker; **jidousha-kyoushuujo-shidouin** Fahrlehrer/in; **jidousha-seibi-kou** Kraftfahrzeugmechaniker/in
jidoushiki no automatisch
*jifuteria** Diphtherie
jijitsu Tatsache; wahr
jikaku shiteiru bewußt
jikan Stunde; Zeit
jikandoori no pünktlich
jiken Vorfall; Ereignis
jikkou Praxis
jiko Unfall
jikoku-hyo Fahrplan
jiku (Auto) Achse
jimaku (Film) Untertitel
jimejimeshite atsui feucht-warm; **jimejimeshite samui** feucht-kühl
jimen (Boden) Erde
jimu-sho Büro
jimukyoku Sekretariat
jin·en Nierenentzündung
jinsei Leben
jinseki Nierenstein
jinzou Niere
*jīnzu** Jeans
jiritsu shita emanzipiert
jisoku Geschwindigkeit
jissai eigentlich
jissen Praxis
jisshuu Praxis
jitensha Fahrrad; **jitensha-kyou-sou** Radrennen; **jitensha ni noru** radfahren; **jitensha-senyou-dou-ro** Fahrradweg
jitsugen suru verwirklichen
jitsuyouteki·na praktisch
jiyuu·na frei
jogen Rat; **jogen suru** raten
*jogingu** Jogging; *jogingu-*sūtsu**

Jogginganzug
*jointo-*benchā Joint-venture
jokou-eki Nagellackentferner
josei Frau; Dame; weiblich
jikken-shitsu no joshu Laborant/in
jou-ou Königin
jouba reiten; **jouba-*supōtsu** Reitsport
joudan Scherz; Witz; Spaß
jouei (Film) Aufführung
jouen (Theater) Aufführung; **jouen-yoteihyou** Spielplan
jouheki Mauer; Stadtmauer
jouhin·na (elegant) fein
jouhou-shiryou Informationsmaterial; **jouhou-shori-gaku** Informatik
jouken Bedingung
jouki-kikansha Lokomotive
joukyou Lage; Umstände; Zustand
joukyuusha Fortgeschrittener
joumu-in Besatzung; Zugpersonal
jouryuu no vornehm
jousen suru einschiffen
jousha-ken Fahrkarte
jouzai Tablette
jouzu·na geschickt
joyuu Filmschauspielerin; Schauspielerin
jukuren shita (adj) erfahren
jukushita reif
junbi suru vorbereiten
junkan-shougai Kreislaufstörung
junkanki-zai Kreislaufmittel
jun·nou suru s. akklimatisieren
juryou Annahme
juubun genug; **juubun·na** reichlich
juuden suru (Batterie) aufladen
juudou Judo
juugyouin Angestellte/r; Personal
juui Tierarzt/ärztin
juumin Bewohner; Einwohner
juusho Adresse; Wohnort
juutai Stau
juutan Teppich
juutenzai Plombe
juuyou wichtig; **juuyou dewana·i** unwichtig
juuyou·na bedeutend
juwaki (Telefon) Hörer

K

ka Mücke
~ **ka douka** ob
*kā-*rajio Autoradio
kaban Koffer; Tasche
kabe Wand
kabin Vase
kabocha Kürbis
*kābu Kurve
kachi Wert; **kachi ga aru** wert; **kachi no nai** wertlos
*kādigan Strickjacke
kado Ecke
kaeri-michi Rückfahrt; auf dem Rückweg
kaeru ändern; verändern; zurückfahren; zurückkehren
kaeshite morau wiederbekommen
kaesu wiedergeben; zurückgeben
kaettekuru wiederkommen
kafukubu Unterleib
kagaku Chemie; **kagaku-sen·i** Kunstfaser; **kagaku-sha** Chemiker/in; Wissenschaftler/in
kagami Spiegel
kagayaku glänzen; scheinen
kage Schatten
kagi Schlüssel; Verschluß; **kagi wo kakeru** verschließen; **kagi wo shimeru** zuschließen
kago Korb
kagu Möbel; **kagu-ya** Möbelgeschäft
kahei Geld
kai Etage; Mal; Muscheln; Stockwerk
kaichuu-dentou Taschenlampe
kaidan Treppe
kaidou Landstraße
kaifuku Erholung; **kaifuku suru** s. erholen
kaiga Gemälde; Malerei
kaigai Übersee; Ausland
kaigan Küste; Strand
kaigateki·na malerisch
kaigi Konferenz; Sitzung; **kaigi-shitsu** Konferenzraum
kaigou Treffen
kaihatsu Entwicklung
kai-in Mitglied; **kai-in-shou** Mit-

gliedskarte
kaika-jiki Blütezeit
kaikei Kasse; **kaikei-gakari** Kassierer/in
kaikyuu Rang
kaimono wo suru einkaufen
kairo Netz
kaisei heiter
kaisha Firma
kaishi suru anlaufen
kaisou Algen
kaisuiyoku Seebad; Strandbad
kaisuiyokujou Badeort; Strandbad
kaiteki Bequemlichkeit; **kaiteki denai** unbequem
kaitou Antwort
kaiwa Gespräch
kaiyou Geschwür; Ozean
kaizen suru verbessern
kaji Brand; *(Steuer)* Ruder
*****kajino** Spielcasino
kakaku-hyouji Wertangabe
kake-kugi Haken
kakebuton Bettdecke
kakegoto Wette
kakeru aufhängen; fehlen; hängen; rennen; wetten
kaki Austern
kakigenkin feuergefährlich
kakitome Einschreibebrief
kakitomeru aufschreiben; notieren
kako Vergangenheit
kakou Mündung
kakou suru bearbeiten
kaku schreiben
kakudo Winkel
kakujin jede(r, -s)
kakujitsu·na gewiß
kakunin-sho Bescheinigung; **kakunin suru** bestätigen
kakureru sich verstecken
kakuritsu Wahrscheinlichkeit
kakushin saseru überzeugen
kakusu verstecken
kamera Fotoapparat; *****kamera-*****man** Fotograf/in; **kamera-ya** Fotogeschäft
kami Gott
kami Papier; **kami-*****napukin** Papierservietten
kami Haar; **kami wo someru** *(Haare)* tönen; **kami wo tokasu**

kämmen; **kami wo totonoeru** frisieren
kamibukuro Tüte
kamigata Frisur
kamikizu Bißwunde
kaminari Donner
kaminoke Haar
kamisori Rasierapparat
kamome Möwe
kamotsu Fracht; Güter; Last
kamu beißen
kan der Band; Dose; Kanal; **kan-kiri** Dosenöffner
kanada-jin Kanadier
kanamono-ya Eisenwarengeschäft
kanarazu gewiß
kanari ziemlich
kanarino beträchtlich
kanashi·i traurig
kanazuchi Hammer
kanchigai wo suru s. täuschen
kanchou Behörde
kandai·na großartig
kandou suru begeistert (von)
kane Glocke
kanemochi no reich
*****kānēshon** *(Blumen)* Nelken
kangae Gedanke; Idee
ni tsuite kangaeru denken an
kangei Willkommen
kangeikai Empfang; Begrüßungsfeier
kangofu Krankenschwester
kanjiru fühlen
kan·jou-sho Rechnung
kankaku Abstand; Gefühl; Geschmack
kankei Bezeichnung; **kankei suru** betreffen; sich beziehen auf
kanki Frost; Kälte; Jubel; Lüftung
kankoku Korea; **kankoku-jin** Koreaner/in; **kankoku no** koreanisch
kankou-an·naijo Verkehrsamt
kankyaku Zuschauer
kankyou Umwelt
kanmiryou Süßstoff
kanmuri Krone
kanojo sie
kanou suru eitern
kanou·na möglich
kanouni suru ermöglichen
kanou·sei Möglichkeit

kanpeki ni vollständig
kanri-nin Portier
kanribu Direktion
kansan Umrechnung
kansatsu suru beobachten; betrachten
kansen Infektion
kansetsu Gelenk
kansha Dank; **kansha suru** danken
kanshi suru bewachen
kanshin suru bewundern
~ **ni kanshite** s. beziehen auf
kanshuu Publikum
kansou Trockenheit; Eindrücke
kansouki Wäschetrockner
kantan·na einfach
kantoku Regisseur/in
kantoku-sha Aufseher
***kanū** Kanu
kanzen ni vollkommen
kanzou Leber
kanzume Büchse; Konserven
kao Gesicht
kaori Geruch
kappatsu·na lebhaft
***kappu** Tasse
kara von; ab; aus
***kārā** Lockenwickler
karada Körper
karai *(Gewürz)* scharf, salzig
***karā-kopī** Farbkopierer
karakuchi *(Wein)* trocken
kara no leer
karashi Senf
karate Karate
kare er; **kareta koe** heiser sein
kari Probe; Schulden
karichin Leihgebühr
***karifurawā** Blumenkohl
kari no provisorisch
kariru ausleihen; mieten
***kāru** Locken
karu·i leicht
kasa Schirm
kasai Brand; **kasai-houchiki** Feuermelder
kasegu verdienen
***kasetto** Kassette; ***kasetto-rekōdā** Kassettenrekorder
kashi-*bōto Bootsverleih; **kashi-shokunin** Konditor/in

kashiko·i klug
kashitsuke Kredit
kashu Sänger/in
kasoku suru beschleunigen
kasu leihen; vermieten
kata Schulter; Form
kata·i *(Material)* hart; zäh
katamatta fest
***katarogu** Katalog
katazukeru erledigen; aufräumen
***kategorī** Kategorie
katei-youhinten Haushaltswarengeschäft
***kāten** Vorhang
***katorikku** Katholik
katsu siegen, gewinnen
katsudou Tätigkeit
katsura Perücke
katsuretsu Kotelett
katsute jemals
kau kaufen
kawa Fluß; Leder; **kawa-*jaketto** Lederjacke; **kawa-seihin-ten** Lederwarengeschäft
kawai·i hübsch, niedlich
kawakasu trocknen
kawaku trocken
~ **no kawarini** statt
kawariyasu·i wechselhaft
kayu·i jucken
kayumi Juckreiz
kazan Vulkan
kazari Schmuck
kaze Wind; Erkältung; **kaze no tsuyoi** windig; **kaze wo hiiteiru** erkältet; **kaze wo hiku** sich erkälten; **kaze wo toosu** lüften
kazoeru zählen
kazoku Familie; **kazoku-kousei** Familienstand
kazu Zahl
***kēburu** Kabel; ***kēburu-*kā** Seilbahn
***kechappu** Ketchup
kega Verletzung; **kega-nin** der, die Verletzte; **kega wo suru** verletzen
kegawa Fell, Pelz; ***kegawa-*kōto** Pelzmantel
keiba Pferderennen
keikai suru s. hüten (vor)
keikakuteki·na absichtlich
keiken Erfahrung; **keiken no nai**

unerfahren; **keiken suru** erleben, erfahren

keikoku Schlucht; **keikoku-souchi** Alarmanlage; **keikoku suru** warnen (vor)

keikotsu Schienbein

keimu-sho Gefängnis

keiren Krampf

keiri-shi Buchhalter/in

keisan suru berechnen; rechnen

keisatsu Polizei; **keisatsu-kan** Polizist/in

keishiki Form

keishoku Imbiß; Schnellimbiß

keiyaku Vertrag; **keiyaku-jouken** Vertragsbedingungen

keizai-gaku Betriebswirtschaft; **keizai-keiei-gakushi** Betriebswirt/in

*__kēki__ Kuchen; *__kēki-ya__ Konditorei

kekka Ergebnis

kekkan Ader; Fehler

kekkon Ehe; Heirat; **kekkon-shiki** Hochzeit; **kekkon shiteiru** verheiratet; **kekkon suru** heiraten; **kekkon-yubiwa** Ehering

kemuri Rauch

kenasu herabsetzen, schlecht machen

kenchiku Architektur; **kenchiku-ka** Architekt/in

kenchikubutsu Bauwerk

kengaku Besichtigung; **kengaku suru** besichtigen

kengi Verdacht

ken·in suru abschleppen

kenka Streit; **kenka wo suru** streiten

kenkai (Meinung) Ansicht

kenkou Gesundheit; Wohl; **kenkou de aru** Wohlbefinden; **kenkou-hoken** Krankenkasse; **kenkou-hoken-shou** Krankenschein

kenkou·na gesund

kenkyuu-jo Institut

kenmon-jo Grenzübergang

kenpou Verfassung

kenri Recht

kensa Untersuchung; Test; Prüfung; **kensa-kan** Kontrolleur; **kensa suru** kontrollieren; prüfen; untersuchen

kenshuu-ryokou Studienreise

ken·yaku suru sparen

keredomo jedoch

keshou wo suru sich schminken

keshi-*gomu Radiergummi

keshiki Aussicht

keshouhin-ten Parfümerie

kesseki no abwesend

kesshin Entschluß; **kesshin shita** entschlossen sein; **kesshin suru** s. entschließen

kesshite ... nai nie; keinesfalls

kesu ausmachen; löschen

*__kēsu__ Fall; Futteral

ketsueki-gata Blutgruppe; **ketsueki-kensa** Blutprobe

ketsugi suru beschließen

ketsugou Verbindung, Vereinigung

kettei suru entscheiden

ketteiteki·na endgültig

ketten Fehler

kewashi·i steil

ki Baum; Holz

kiiro Gelb

ki wo haru anstrengend; **ki wo kubaru** aufmerksam; **ki wo tsukeru** achtgeben (auf); aufpassen (auf); vorsichtig

kibishi·i streng; (Gefühl) hart

kibori Holzschnitt

kibun-soukai Erfrischung

kichigai verrückt

kichinto shita ordentlich

kieru verschwinden

kigen Laune

kigu Apparat

kigutsu Holzschuhe

kigyou Unternehmen

kiji (Zeitung) Artikel; Stoff

kikai Anlaß; Gelegenheit; Maschine; **kikai-kou** Mechaniker/in; **kikai-seisaku** Maschinenbau

kikan Dauer; Rückkehr; **kikan-shien** Bronchitis

kikanshi Bronchien

kiken Gefahr; Risiko

kiken·na gefährlich

kikinzoku-shou Juwelier

kikon no verheiratet

kikou Klima

kiku hören

kikyou Heimreise
kin Gold; kin-mekki Vergoldung; kin no golden
kinai de an Bord
kinen-butsu Denkmal; kinen-kitte Sondermarke; kinen no chi Gedenkstätte
kingaku Betrag
kini iru gefallen
kin·jo Nachbar/in
kinko Safe
kinkou Vorort, Vorstadt
kinkyuu no baai im Notfall; kinkyuu-renraku-souchi Notrufsäule
kinmu Dienst
kinniku Muskel; Zerrung
kinoko Pilze
kinou wo hakki suru funktionieren
kinpatsu no blond
kinpen Gegend; Nähe
kinshi Verbot; kinshi suru verbieten; verboten
kinu Seide
kinyuu-youshi Vordruck
kirai·na ungern
kirei·na sauber
kireini suru reinigen; aufräumen
kiri Nebel; kiri no kakatta neblig
kirikizu Schnittwunde
kirisame Nieselregen
*kirisuto Christ; *kirisuto-kyou Christentum
kiroku Aufzeichnung; Dokument; Protokoll
*kiromēta-ryoukin Kilometerpreis
kiru schneiden
kisen Dampfer
kisetsu Jahreszeit; Saison; kisetsu mae Vorsaison
kisha Journalist/in
kishi Ritter; Ufer
kishou-gakusha Meteorologe/in
kiso Fundament; Basis; Grundlage
kisoku Bestimmungen; Vorschrift; Regel
kisokuteki·na regelmäßig
kissaten Café
*kisu Kuß; *kisu wo suru küssen
kita Norden; kita no nördlich
kitai suru erwarten
kitana·i schmutzig

*kitchin Küche
kitsuen-sha Raucher; kitsuen-shitsu Raucherzimmer
kitte Briefmarke; kitte-jidou-han-baiki Briefmarkenautomat; kitte wo haru frankieren
kizu Wunde
kizuato Narbe
kizukau befürchten; besorgt sein
kizuku bemerken; merken
kizutsuku verletzen
ko Stück
kobamu s. weigern; hindern; ausschlagen; ablehnen
kobetsu Einzel; kobetsu no einzeln
kobutsu-shou Trödler
kochira e hierher; herüber
kodai Altertum; kodai-bunka Antike
kodoku Einsamkeit; kodoku·na einsam
kodomo Kind; kodomo-gutsu Kinderschuhe; kodomo-jousha-ken Kinderfahrkarte
koe Stimme
koeru überschreiten
koeta nahrhaft
kofuu·na antik; altertümlich
kogaisha Tochtergesellschaft
kogitte Scheck
kogu rudern
*kōhī Kaffee
koi dicht
*koin-*rokkā Gepäckschließfach
koishi Kiesel
kojiakeru aufbrechen
kojinteki persönlich
kokka Nation; Staat; Nationalhymne
*kokku Koch/Köchin
kokkyou Staatsgrenze
koko hier
kokochiyo·i gemütlich; bequem; angenehm
kōkoku-*kyanpēn Werbekampagne
*kokonattsu Kokosnuß
kokoro (gefühlsmäßig) Herz; kokoro no nakade innerlich
kokoro kara no herzlich
kokoromi Versuch

kokoromu versuchen
kokumin *(Volk)* Nation
kokunai Inland; **kokunai-sen** Inlandsflug
kokuritsu-kouen Nationalpark
kokusai no international; **kokusai-tsuuwa** Auslandsgespräch
kokuseki Nationalität; Staatsangehörigkeit
kokyou Heimat
kokyuu Atem; **kokyuu-konnan** Atembeschwerden
*__kōlasu__ Chor
komaka·i fein; klein; genau
komaku Trommelfell
kome Reis
*__komedī__ Komödie
komichi Pfad
komori Kinderbetreuung; Kindermädchen
komugiko Mehl
*__kōn__ Mais
kona Pulver; **kona-yuki** Pulverschnee
konchuu Insekt
*__kondishon__ Konditionen
*__kondōmu__ Kondom
kongou shita gemischt
konnan Schwierigkeit
kono diese(r, -s)
konomashi·i nach Belieben; lieb
konomi Geschmack
konomu Gefallen; Neigung; mögen, gern haben
*__konpasu__ Kompaß
*__konsāto__ Konzert
*__konsento__ Steckdose
kanshuu Publikum
*__kontakuto__ Kontakt
*__kontesuto__ Wettbewerb
kon·yaku-sha der, die Verlobte; **konyaku suru** s. verloben
*__konzerun__ Konzern
*__kopī__ Kopie; *__kopī-ki__ Fotokopierer
*__koppu__ Becher; Glas
*__korāju__ Collage
*__korekushon__ Sammlung
*__korera__ Cholera
korobu fallen; hinfallen
*__koruku-sennuki__ Korkenzieher; *__koruku wo nuku__ entkorken
koshi Hüfte

koshou Defekt, Störung; Pfeffer; **koshou-*sābisu** Pannendienst; **koshou suru** defekt
kossetsu Knochenbruch
kosshou; *__panku__ *(Reifen)* Panne
*__kōsu__ *(Essen)* Gang; Kurs; Route
*__kosuchūmu__ Kostüm
kotaeru beantworten; erwidern
*__kōto__ Mantel
koto Sache
kotoba Sprache
kotonatta verschieden
*__kōtoretto__ Kotelett
*__kotton__ Baumwolle
kottou-ichi Flohmarkt; **kottou-shou** Antiquitätengeschäft; **kottou-ya**
koudo Härte
koudou Tat
kouen Park; Vortrag
kougai Vorort, Vorstadt
kougei Kunstgewerbe
kougi Vorlesungen
~ **ni kougi suru** protestieren *(gegen)*
kouhou-katsudou Öffentlichkeitsarbeit
koui Gefälligkeit
kouishitsu (a. Umkleide); Umkleidekabine
kouiteki·na wohlwollend
kouji-genba Baustelle
koujou Fabrik; Werkstatt
kouka Geldstück; Münze; Wirkung; **kouka ga aru** wirksam; **kouka na mono** Wertsachen
kouka-daigaku Technische Hochschule
koukai no öffentlich
koukan Austausch; Wechsel; **koukan no moteru** sympathisch; **koukan suru** austauschen; tauschen; wechseln
kouka·na kostspielig
koukiatsu *(Wetter)* Hoch
koukishin no aru neugierig
kouko-gaku Archäologie
koukoku Annonce; Anzeige; Inserat; Reklame; Werbung; **koukoku wo dasu** anzeigen
koukuu-bin Luftpost; **koukuu-gaisha** Fluggesellschaft

A/Z

koukyou no öffentlich
koumu-in Beamter/Beamtin
kounyuu Kauf; **kounyuu-sha** Käufer
kouri Eis
kouri-gyousha Einzelhändler
kourin Hinterrad
kouron suru s. zanken
kouryo Rücksicht
kouryuu Untersuchungshaft; Austausch
kousaten Kreuzung
kousei-busschitsu Antibiotikum
kousei·na gerecht
kouseki *(das)* Verdienst
kousen Strahl
koushaku Fürst
koushi-mado/gaki Gitter
koushi-niku Kalbfleisch
koushiki no amtlich; offiziell
koushou Verhandlung
koushou-nin Notar/in
koushuu-denwa Münzfernsprecher
kousoku Hochgeschwindigkeit; **kousoku-douro** Autobahn; Schnellstraße
kousui Parfüm
kousuiryou Niederschlag
koutaku no aru glänzend
koutei Kaiser
koutei·tekina positiv
koutou-gakkou Gymnasium; Höhere Schule
koutsuu Verkehr
kouun Glück
kouza Konto; **kouza-bangou** Bankkonto
kouzui Flut; Überschwemmung
kowareru zerstören; zerbrechen
kowareta kaputt
koya Hütte, Häuschen
kozeni Kleingeld; Wechselgeld
kozutsumi Päckchen
kubaru verteilen
kubetsu suru unterscheiden
kubi Hals
kuchi Mund; **kuchi-beni** Lippenstift
kuchibiru Lippe
kuchi-hige Schnurrbart
kudamono Obst; **kudamono-ya**

Obsthandlung
kudaru abwärts; **yama wo kudaru** bergab
kujou Beschwerde; Beanstandung; **kujou wo iu** s. beklagen (über); s. beschweren (über); **kujou wo moushitateru** reklamieren
*****kukkī** Gebäck; Kekse
kumitate-in Monteur
kumo Wolke
kumo Spinne
kumori bewölkt
kuni *(Staat)* Land
kunren Schulung, Ausbildung
kunsei geräuchert; **kunsei no niku** Rauchfleisch
*****kūrā** Klimaanlage; Kühler
kurage Qualle
kurai Rang, Grad
kura·i dunkel
*****kurakushon** Hupe
*****kurasu** Klasse; Kategorie
*****kuratchi** Kupplung
*****kurejitto-*kādo** Kreditkarte
kurikaesu wiederholen
*****kurīmu** Creme; Sahne
*****kurīningu** Reinigung; *****kuriningu suru** reinigen; *****kuriningu-ya** Wäscherei
*****kurippu** Büroklammern
*****kurisutaru** Kristall
kuro Schwarz
*****kurōku** Garderobe
kurou *(Strapaze)* Anstrengung; Mühe
kuru kommen
kurubushi Knöchel
kuruma Auto; Wagen; **kuruma no kagi** Autoschlüssel
*****kurūzu** Kreuzfahrt
kusa·i stinken
kusari Kette
kusaru verderben; faulen
kushami wo suru niesen
kushi Kamm
*****kusshon** Kissen
kusuri Medikament; *(Arznei)* Mittel; **kusuri-ya** Apotheke; Drogerie
kutsu Schuh; **kutsu-himo** Schnürsenkel; **kutsu-shokunin** Schuhmacher; **kutsu-ya** Schuhgeschäft
kutsujoku Beleidigung; **kutsujoku**

suru beleidigen
kutsurogeru gemütlich
kutsushita Socken; Strümpfe
kutsuu Schmerzen
kuufuku Hunger
kutufuku no hungrig
kuuki Luft; **kuuki-atsu** Luftdruck
kuukou Flughafen; **kuukou-shiyo-uryou** Flughafengebühr
kuwashi·i ausführlich
kuyami Beileid
***kyabetsu** Kohl
***kyaburētā** Vergaser
kyaku Gast; **kyaku-hon** Theater-stück
***kyandoru** Kerze
***kyanpu** Camping
***kyaputen** Kapitän
***kyasshu-*kōnā** Geldautomat
kyohi suru ablehnen
kyoka sarete iru zulässig; **kyoka-shou** Erlaubnis; **kyoka suru** erlau-ben; **kyoka suru** genehmigen; **kyoka suru** zulassen
kyokenbyou Tollwut
kyori Entfernung; Abstand
kyou heute; **kyou sei suru** zwingen
kyoudai Bruder
kyoudou Kooperation; **kyoudou no** *(adv)* gemeinsam
kyoufu Angst
kyouiku Ausbildung; Erziehung; **kyouiku-sha** Erzieher/in
kyouju Professor/in
kyoukai Gesellschaft; Kirche; Ver-ein
kyoumi Interesse; **ni kyoumi ga aru** s. interessieren (für); interes-siert sein an
kyoumibuka·i interessant
kyouretsu·na gewaltig
kyousei Zwang
kyoutei suru vereinbaren
***kyūri** Gurke
kyushigai Altstadt
kyuuden Palast
kyuuji Bedienung
kyuujo-*bōto Rettungsboot; **kyuu-jo suru** retten
kyuuka Ferien; Urlaub
kyuukei Pause; Rast; **kyuukei-jo** Raststätte

kyuukyuu-sha Krankenwagen
kyuuno dringend
kyuunyuu Inhalation; **kyuunyuu suru** inhalieren
kyuuryou Lohn; Gehalt

L

***laibu** Live-
***linneru** Leinen

M

machi Ortschaft; Stadt; **machi no ikkaku** Stadtteil
machiaishitsu Wartesaal; Warte-zimmer
machigaeru verwechseln; sich ir-ren
machigai falsch; Irrtum
machigatte iru unrecht haben
mada nicht; noch immer
made bis
mado Fenster; **madogawa no za-seki** Fensterplatz
madoguchi *(Rezeption)* Schalter
mae bevor; **mae e** vorwärts; **mae ni** vorn; bevor; **maeuri** Vorverkauf; **no mae ni** vor
***mafurā** Halstuch; Schal
***māgarin** Margarine
magaru abbiegen; biegen; **migi e/ hidari e** nach rechts/links abbie-gen
mago Enkel/in
magokoro Herzlichkeit
maguro Thunfisch
mahi Lähmung
maikai jedesmal
***maiku** Mikrofon
***mainasu** minus; **mainasu no** nega-tiv
***mairudo** mild
maitoshi jährlich, jedes Jahr
***majikku-pen** Folienstift
majime·na ernst
makanai Verpflegung
***mākettingu** Marketing
makkuro·na dunkel; finster

A/Z

maku *(Theater)* Akt, Vorhang
makura Kopfkissen
mame Bohnen; Erbsen
mamonaku bald, demnächst
manabu lernen
***manga** Comic; Animation
***manikyua** Nagellack; Maniküre
man·naka Mitte
man·nenhitsu Füllfederhalter
manpuku shita satt
manuke·na blöd(e); albern
manzoku suru zufrieden
manzoku shita befriedigt
***mararia** Malaria
***maronie** Kastanien
maru·i rund
***massāgi** Massage; ***massāgi·shi**
Masseur/in; **massāgi wo suru**
massieren
***masshurūmu** Champignons
massugu gerade
masui Narkose; Betäubung
***masukara** Wimperntusche
mata wieder; und außerdem
***matchi** Streichholz; ***matchi-bako**
Streichholzschachtel
matsu Kiefer; warten
mattaku ~dewanai gar nicht
***mattoresu** Matratze
mawari michi Umweg
mawasu drehen
mayaku Rauschgift
mayonaka Mitternacht
***mayonēzu** Mayonnaise
michi ni mayou s. verirren
mayuge Augenbrauen
mazeta gemischt
mazu·i geschmacklos
mazushi·i arm
me Auge; **me ga sameru** aufwachen
megane Brille; **megane-ya** Optiker
megusuri Augentropfen
mei Nichte
meibutsu Spezialität
***meido** Zimmermädchen
meikaku·na ausdrücklich; klar und
deutlich
***mein** Hauptspeise; ***mein-*sutorī-
to** Hauptstraße
meishi Visitenkarte
meisho Sehenswürdigkeiten

meiwaku wo kakeru belästigen
meiyo Ehre
mejirushi Kennzeichen; Merkmal;
Wahrzeichen
memagurushi·i hektisch
memai Schwindel; **memai ga suru**
schwindeln; schwindlig
***memo-youshi** Notizblock
men Baumwolle; Nudeln; Gesicht;
Maske
menkai-jikan *(Krankenhaus)* Besuchszeit
menmitsu Sorgfalt
menmitsu·na sorgfältig
menshiki Bekanntschaft
***mensu** Menstruation
menyū Speisekarte
menzei-ten zollfreier Laden
***meron** Honigmelone
mesu *(Tier)* weiblich
mezamashidokei Wecker
mezurashi·i selten; ungewöhnlich
mibun-shoumei-sho Personalausweis
michi Straße; Weg
michibiku führen
michinori Strecke
michishio Flut
midokoro Sehenswürdigkeiten
midori Grün
~ no youni mieru aussehen
migi rechts; **migi no** rechte(r, -s)
mihon Muster; **mihon-ichi** Messe
mijika·i kurz
mikakeno anscheinend
mikan Mandarinen
mimawasu umsehen
mimi Ohr; ***mimi-kazari** Ohrringe; **mimi wo katamukeru** jdm
zuhören
mimi no kusuri Ohrentropfen
mimizu Wurm
minami Süden; **minami no** südlich
minarai Lehrling
minato Hafen
***mineraru-sui** Mineralwasser
***mini-*bā** Minibar; ***mini-*sukāto**
Minirock; **mini tsukeru** anziehen
miniku·i häßlich
minzoku Volk; **minzoku-buyou**
Volkstanz; **minzoku-gaku-haku-
butsukan** Volkskundemuseum;

minzoku-ishou Tracht; **minzoku-ongaku** Folkloremusik
miru anschauen; ansehen; schauen; sehen
***miruku** Milch
miryokuteki·na entzückend
miryou suru bezaubernd
***misa** Messe
mise Laden
miseru zeigen
mishiranu fremd
mitasu ausfüllen; füllen
mitorizu Grundriß
mitsukeru finden
mitsumori Kostenvoranschlag
mitsu·na dicht
mitsuyu Schmuggel; **mitsuyu suru** schmuggeln
mittsu-me ni drittens
mizu Wasser
mizubousou Windpocken
mizugi Badeanzug
mizuke no oo·i saftig
mizuumi der See
mochiageru heben
mochiiru anwenden; gebrauchen
***modan·na** modern
modemu Modem
***moderu** Modell
modoru zurückkehren
modosu zurückbringen
moeru brennen
moguru tauchen
moji Schrift; Buchstabe
mokei Modell
mokuroku Verzeichnis
mokuromu beabsichtigen
mokuteki Ziel; Zweck; Absicht; **mokuteki-chi** Bestimmungsort
mokuzai Holz
momiage Koteletten
momo Pfirsiche; Schenkel
mon Tor
monban Pförtner/in
mono Ding; Sache
morau bekommen
mori Wald
~ **moshiku wa** ~ entweder ... oder
***mōtā-*bōto** Motorboot
motenashi Gastfreundschaft; Bewirtung

motomeru verlangen
motsu haben; halten
motte iku *(Dinge)* mitnehmen; **motte kuru** mitbringen
motto mehr
mou schon; **mou ~ nai** nicht mehr
mou ippou no der, die,das andere
mouchou Blinddarm
mouchouen Blinddarmentzündung
moufu Wolldecke
mou ichido nochmal
moukeru *(Vorteil)* gewinnen; verdienen
moumoku blind
moushikomu anmelden
moushitate *(Meldung)* Angabe
moyoushi-mono Veranstaltung
moyoushimono-*puroguramu Veranstaltungskalender
moyousu veranstalten
muchitsujo Unordnung
muda·na unnütz; zwecklos
muimi·na zwecklos
mukaeni iku *(jdn)* abholen
mukaeru *(erhalten)* empfangen
mukaigawa gegenüber
mukidashi no *(Geld)* bar
mukou-gawa drüben; jenseits
mukou no ungültig
mukuiru belohnen
mune Brust; Büste
muneyake Sodbrennen
munou·na unfähig
mura Dorf
murasaki lila, violett
muruino einzigartig
muryou kostenlos; **muryou de** gratis, umsonst; **muryou no** *(kosten)* frei
mushi sasare Mückenstiche
mushiatsu·i schwül
mushiba *(im Zahn)* Loch
musubi-himo Bindfaden
musubime Knoten
musubitsukeru verbinden
musubitsuki Verbindung
keiyaku wo musubu *(den Vertrag)* abschließen; **musubu** binden
musuko Sohn
musume Tochter
muzukashi·i schwer; schwierig

muzukashisa Schwierigkeit
myaku Puls
myouji Familienname
***myūjikaru** Musical

N

nabe Kochtopf; Topf
nagagutsu Stiefel
naga·i lang
nagame Blick
~ **wo nagameru** zuschauen
nagare Strom; Strömung
nagarederu auslaufen
nagareru fließen
nagasa Länge
nageireru einwerfen
nageru werfen
naibu das Innere; **naibu de** innen
***naifu** Messer
naikaku Ministerium
naishukketsu Prellung
***naito-*kulabu** Nachtclub
naiyou Inhalt
naka de innen; **naka-niwa** Innenhof
naku weinen
nakusu verlieren
nama roh; **nama-ensou** Live-Musik; **nama-*hamu** *(roh)* Schinken
namae Name; Vorname
namakeru faulenzen
nameraka·na glatt
nami Welle
***nanbā-*purēto** Nummernschild
nanika irgendetwas
nankou Salbe
***napukin** Serviette; Damenbinden
narau lernen
~ **ni nareru** s. gewöhnen an
nareteiru gewohnt
~ **kara naritatsu** bestehen aus
naru läuten
~ **ni naru** betragen
nashi Birne
~ **nashi ni** ohne
nasu Auberginen
natsu-fuku Sommerkleid
***natto** Schraubenmutter
***nattsu** Erd
nawa Seil

nayami Kummer
~ **nitsuite nayamu** s. kümmern
um
nazenara denn; weil
nazukeru nennen
nebiki Rabatt
nebukuro Schlafsack
negai Wunsch
negau wünschen
negi Lauch
negiru feilschen
***nekkachīfu** Halstuch
nekki Heißluft; Hitze
neko Katze
***nekutai** Krawatte
nemaki Nachthemd
nemuri Schlaf
nemurikomu einschlafen
nemuru schlafen; einschlafen
nen Jahr
nenkin Rente; Pension; **nenkin-
seikatsu-sha** Rentner/in
nenrei Alter
nenza suru verstauchen
nerihamigaki Zahnpasta
nessin·na fleißig
netsu Fieber
~ **ni hanshite** *(ca.)* gegen; ~ **ni
hantai dearu** dagegen sein; ~ **ni
naru** werden; ~ **ni sansei dearu**
dafür sein; ~ **ni shiraseru** jdn verständigen; ~ **ni shitagau** folgen; ~
ni sotte entlang; ~ **ni tsuki** pro; ~
ni zokusuru gehören
nichibotsu Sonnenuntergang
nichiyou-zakkashou Haushaltswarengeschäft
nigai bitter
nigami herb, bitter
nigotta trüb
nihon Japan; **nihon-go/jin no** japanisch; **nihon-jin** Japaner/in
nijuu Doppel
nijuuno doppelt
niku Fleisch; **niku-ya** Metzgerei;
Metzger/in
~ **nimo kakarawazu** obwohl;
trotz; trotzdem
nimotsu Gepäck
ningen Mensch
ningenteki·na menschlich
ningyou Puppe

ninjin Karotten
ninkasho Lizenz; Zulassungs-
  schein
ninmei suru erneuern
ninniku Knoblauch
ninschin Schwangerschaft
ninshiki suru erkennen
ninshin shiteiru schwanger
nintai Geduld
nioi Geruch; nioi ga suru stinken
niou riechen
nise no unecht
nishi Westen; nishi no westlich
nishoku-tsuki Halbpension
nisshabyou Sonnenstich
nitchuu Tag
niteiru ähnlich; gleichen
niwa Garten; niwa-shi Gärtner/in
  ~ no baai falls; ~ no naka ni drin,
  drinnen; ~ no shita ni unter; ~
  no shusshin de aru (Person)
  stammen; ~ no tameni für; ~ no
  toki (Zeit) als
nobasu verlängern; verschieben;
  verzögern
noboru steigen; yama ni noboru
  bergauf
nodo Hals; nodo ga kawaita durstig; nodo no itami Halsschmerzen; nodo no kawaki Durst; nodo
  no kusuri Halstabletten
nogasu versäumen
nohara Heide; Feld
nokori Rest; nokori no übrig
nokosu hinterlassen; ıbriglassen
nokotte iru übrigbleiben
nomeru trinkbar
nomimizu Trinkwasser
nomimono Getränk
nomiya Kneipe
nomu (Medikament) einnehmen;
  trinken
nonoshiru beschimpfen
norikae-*basu Transferbus
norikaeru umsteigen
norikomu einsteigen; zusteigen
hikouki ni noru (Flugzeug) an
  Bord gehen
*nōto Heft
*notto (Schiff) Knoten
nou Gehirn
nouhin Lieferung; nouhin-sha Lie-

ferant; nouhin suru liefern
nouka Bauernhof
nouki Lieferzeit
noumin Bauer; Landwirt/in
nouryoku ga aru imstande sein;
  fähig sein; nouryoku no nai unfähig
noushintou Gehirnerschütterung
nousotchuu Gehirnschlag
nouyou Abszeß
nozomarete inai unerwünscht
nozomu hoffen
*nozuru Düse
*nūdoru Nudeln
nukemichi Durchgang
nuku (Zahn) ziehen
nuku ausziehen
numachi Sumpf
nureta naß
nurie-chou Malbuch
nuru schmieren
nusumu stehlen
nuu flicken; nähen
nyou Urin
*nyūsu Nachrichten; Neuigkeit
nyuujou Eintritt; nyuujou-ken
  Eintrittskarte; nyuujou-ryoukin
  Eintrittspreis
nyuukoku Einreise; nyuukoku
  suru einreisen
nyuushu dekiru ist erhältlich
nyuuyoku suru baden

O

o-cha Tee
o-kane Geld
oba Tante
obaasan Großmutter
ōbāheddo-*purojekutā Tageslichtprojektor
obasan Tante
*ōbun-*renji (kochen) Ofen
ochiaibasho Meeting Point
ochiru fallen
odayaka·na mild; ruhig; friedlich
*ōdekoron Kölnisch Wasser
odori Tanz
odoriko Tänzer/in
odoroku erschrecken; überrascht;
  s. wundern (über)

odoru tanzen
oeru beenden; enden
ohairi! herein!
oi Neffe
oikosu überholen
*****oiru** Öl; *****oiru-koukan** Ölwechsel
oitamamani shiteoku liegenlassen
oji Onkel
ojiisan Großvater
ojisan Onkel
ojousan *(Anruf)* Fräulein
oka Hügel
okaasan Mutter
okan Schüttelfrost
okane Geld
okashi Süßigkeiten; **okashi-ya**
Konditorei; Süßwarengeschäft
okashi·na lächerlich; komisch
*****ōkesutora** Orchester
okiniiri Liebling
okite iru wach
okiwasareru liegenlassen
okonai Tat
okonawareru stattfinden
okoru s. ereignen; geschehen; *(ent-stehen)* passieren
okosu wecken
*****oktan-ka** Oktanzahl
oku *(stellen)* abstellen; *(liegen)*
aufstellen; hinlegen; legen; stellen
oku hundert Millionen
okure Verspätung
okureru s. verspäten
okurimono Geschenk
okuru schenken; schicken; senden;
versenden
okyaku Kunde, Kundin
omatsuri Fest
omiyage Reiseandenken
omocha Spielzeug; **omocha-ya**
Spielwarengeschäft
omo·i *(Gewicht)* schwer
omoichigai Irrtum; **omoichigai wo
suru** s. irren
omoidasaseru jdn an etw. erin-nern
omoide Andenken; Erinnerung
omoigakena·i unerwartet
omoikitte suru wagen; sich erküh-nen
omoiyari no nai rücksichtslos
omosa Gewicht

omoshiro·i interessant; unterhal-tend
omou glauben
onaji dasselbe; gleich; identisch
onaka Bauch; **onaka ga haru** Blä-hungen; **onaka ga suku** hungrig
sein
ondo Temperatur
ondori Hahn
onegai Bitte; **onegai suru** jdn um
etw bitten
ongaku Musik; **ongaku-ka** Musi-ker/in
onna no hito Dame
onnanoko Mädchen
onsen-chi Badeort
onshirazu·na undankbar
onsui-*pūru Thermalbad/becken
oogesa·na übertrieben
oogoe no laut
ooki·i groß
ookisa Größe; Format
oosugiru zuviel
oou bedecken; zudecken
ooyoso ungefähr; etwa
oozei no zahlreich
*****opera** Oper
*****operagurasu** Opernglas
*****orenji** orange; *****orenji-*jūsu** Oran-gensaft
oreta gebrochen
*****oriento** Orient; *****oriento no** orien-talisch
*****orijinaru** Original
orimono Gewebe; **orimono-kou-jou** Weberei
oriomite gelegentlich
orite iku hinuntergehen
oroka·na dumm
orosoka ni suru vernachlässigen
ni wo orosu abladen
oru abbrechen; knipsen
*****ōru** Ruder
oshaburi Schnuller
oshieru lehren; unterrichten; infor-mieren
oshime Windeln
oso·i spät
osoraku wahrscheinlich
osore Furcht; Angst
osoreru befürchten; fürchten
osoroshi·i schrecklich; fürchterlich

A/Z

osu drücken, schieben; *(Tier)* männlich
*ōsutoria** Österreich; *ōsutoria-jin** Österreicher/in
otafuku-kaze Mumps
otera Tempel
oto Ton
otoko *(Mensch)* männlich; **otoko no hito** Herr; Mann
otona Erwachsene(r)
otousan Vater
otouto *(jüngerer)* Bruder
~ **wo otozureru** jdn besuchen
otto Ehemann
ou König
oudan Gelbsucht
oufuku-kippu Hin- und Rückfahrkarte
ouyou dekiru übertragbar
owai wo noberu Glückwunsch aussprechen
owari Ende; Schluß
owaru ablaufen
oya Eltern
oyogu schwimmen

P

*pabirion** Pavillon
*painappuru** Ananas
*paipu** Pfeife; Rohr
*paipu-*orugan** Orgel
*pairotto** Pilot/in
*pajama** Pyjama
*pākingu-*raito** Standlicht
*pāma** Dauerwelle
*pāmiru** Promille
*pan** Brot; *pan-ya** Bäckerei; Bäcker/in
*panfuretto** Prospekt
*pankushita taiya** *(Reifen)* Plattfuß
*panorama** Panorama
*pantī** Slip; *pantī-*sutokkingu** Strumpfhose
*pāru** Perle
*pāsento** Prozent
*pasokon** PC
*pasupōto** Reisepaß; **pasupōto-kensa** Paßkontrolle; *pasupōto-you-shashin** Paßbild
*pātī** Party

*paudā** Puder
*pearentsu** Herbergseltern
*pedaru** Pedal
*pēji** *(Buch)* Seite
*penchi** Zange
pendanto *(Schmuck)* Anhänger
*penshon** Pension
*perusha-jin** Perser; *perusha no** persisch
*petto** Haustiere
*pīman** *(Gemüse)* Paprika
*pīn** Stecknadel
*pinattsu** Erdnuß
*pinku-iro** Rosa
*pinpon** Tischtennis
*pinsetto** Pinzette
*pisuton** Kolben; Ventil
*poketto-ban no hon** Taschenbuch
*pokketo-*naifu** Taschenmesser
*ponī** Pony
*posutā** Plakat; Poster
*posuto** Briefkasten
*pōtā** Gepäckträger
pun Minute
*puragu** Stecker
*puraibēto** privat
*puran** Plan
*purasu** plus; **purasu no** positiv
*purasutikku** Plastik
*purēto** Platte
*purintā** Drucker
*puroguramā** EDV-Fachmann/frau
*puroguramu** Programm
*puropan-gasu** Propangas
*purotesutanto** Protestant
purotēze Prothese
*pūru** Schwimmbad; Swimmingpool

R

rādā *(Steuer)* Ruder
*ragubī** Rugby
*raisensu** Lizenz
*raitā** Feuerzeug
raiu Gewitter
*rajio** Radio
*raketto** Schläger
rakka Sturz; **rakka suru** stürzen
rakkasan Fallschirmspringen
*ramu-niku** Lammfleisch

*ranpu Lampe
*rappu Frischhaltefolie
*reberu *(Stufe)* Ebene
*rēdā-*kontorōru Radarkontrolle
rei Beispiel
reigai Ausnahme
reigi tadashii höflich; reigi tadashisa Höflichkeit
reihai Gottesdienst
reihaijo Kultstätte
*reinkōto Regenmantel
reisei·na nüchtern
reisui Kühlwasser
reizouko Kühlschrank
rekishi Geschichte
*rekkā-gaisha Abschleppdienst;
*rekkā-sha Abschleppwagen
*rekōdo Schallplatte; *rekōdo-*pu-
reiyā Plattenspieler; *rekōdo-ten
Schallplattengeschäft
*remon Zitrone
*remonēdo Limonade
renga Backstein
*renji Herd
renmei Vereinigung; Verband;
Bund
renshuu Übung; renshuu suru
ausüben; üben
*rentogen röntgen; *rentogen-
shashin Röntgenaufnahme
*renzu Linse; Objektiv
*rēru Schiene
*resepushon Empfang; Rezeption
*rēsu Rennen; Spitze
*resuringu Ringkampf
*resutoran Restaurant; Gasthaus,
Gasthof; *resutoran no *ōnā
Gastwirt/in
*rēto Wechselkurs
retsu Reihe
rieki *(Vorteil)* Gewinn
*rīfu Riff
rikairyoku Verstand; rikai suru
verstehen
riku Land
rikujou-kyougi Leichtathletik
ringo Apfel
*ringu Ring
rippuku shita zornig
ririku suru Abflug
riron Theorie
risei Verstand; Vernunft

*rīsu-gyou Leasing
*risuto Liste
ritsuzou Statue
riyuu Grund
roba Esel
robi Empfangshalle
roji Gasse
*rōpu Seil
*rōrā-*sukēto Rollschuhe
*roshia Rußland; *roshia-go rus-
sisch; *roshia-jin Russe
roshutsu-kei Belichtungsmesser
*rōsuto Braten
roudou-sha Arbeiter/in
roujin-kango-shi Altenpfleger/in
rousoku Kerze; rousoku tate
Leuchter
rusuban-denwa Anrufbeantworter
*rūto Route
ryokan Gasthaus, Gasthof
~ e ryokou suru reisen (nach);
ryokou Reise; ryokou-chuu unterwegs; ryokou-dantai Reisegesellschaft; ryokou-gaisha Reisebüro; ryokou-kaban Reisetasche;
*ryokou-koutei Reiseroute; ryo-
kou-mokutekichi Reiseziel; ryokou-sha der, die Reisende; ryokou-shuppatsu-bi Anreisetag
ryokyaku Passagier
ryou Menge
ryougae Geldwechsel
ryouhou no beide
ryoujikan Konsulat
ryoukai Einverständnis
ryoukin Gebühr; Preis; ryoukin-
hyou Preisliste
ryouri Speise; ryouri-nin Koch/
Köchin; ryouri no hon Kochbuch; ryouri wo suru kochen
ryourizumi no gekocht
ryou-shi Fischer/in
ryoushin Eltern
ryoushinteki·na gewissenhaft
ryoushuu-sho Quittung; Empfangsbestätigung
ryoushuusho wo kaku quittieren
*ryukkusakku Rucksack
*ryūmachi Rheuma
ryuukan Grippe
ryuukou Mode
ryuushutsu suru *(Flüssigkeit)* ab-

laufen
ryuuzan Fehlgeburt

S

saba Makrele
sabi Rost
sadamerareta festgelegt; bestimmt
sadameru festsetzen
*****sādin** Sardinen
*****sadoru** Sattel
sāfin surfen
sagan Sandstein
sagasu suchen
sageru *(Preis)* herabsetzen
sagi Betrug; **sagi-shi** Schwindler
saiban-kan Richter/in; **saiban-sho** Gericht
saidan Altar
*****saifu** Geldbörse
saigo no letzte(r, -s)
saigoni zuletzt
saihou-dougu *(Nähzeug)* Flickzeug
saikai suru wiedersehen
saiken suru wiederaufbauen
saiketsu Blutprobe
saikoro Würfel
saikou höchstens
*****sain** Unterschrift
saisho Anfang; **saisho no** erst
saishoku-shugi vegetarisch
saisho ni zunächst
saiteiru *(Blumen)* blühen
*****saizu** Format; Maß
sakaeru *(Geschäft)* blühen
sakai Grenze
sakan Maurer
sakana Fisch; **sakana-ya** Fischgeschäft
*****sākasu** Zirkus
sakaya Spirituosengeschäft
sakebu schreien
sakerare nai unvermeidlich
sakeru vermeiden
saki Spitze
sakidatte im voraus
sakka Schriftsteller/in
*****sakka** Fußball; **sakkā-jou*** Fußballplatz
*****sakkyoku-ka** Komponist/in

sakotsu Schlüsselbein
sakuhin Werk
sakuranbo Kirschen
*****sākuru** *(Genosse)* Runde
sakyuu Düne
samatageru hindern; verhindern
samonaito sonst
samu·i kalt; kühl; frieren
samuke Schüttelfrost
san *(Anruf)* Frau; Herr
*****san-*oiru** Sonnenöl; *****san-*rūfu** Schiebedach
*****sanatoriumu** Sanatorium
sanba Hebamme
sanban-me dritte(r, -s)
sanbun no ichi ein Drittel
*****sandaru** Sandalen
sango Koralle
*****sangurasu** Sonnenbrille
sangyou-mihonichi Fachmesse; Industriemesse
sanka suru teilnehmen (an)
sankyaku Stativ
sanmyaku Gebirge
sanpo Bummel; Spaziergang; **sanpo wo suru** spazierengehen
sansei suru zustimmen
sanshoku-tsuki Vollpension
sanson Bergdorf
santou-senshitsu Zwischendeck
sara Teller
*****sarada** Salat
*****saradawo mazeru** *(Salat)* anmachen
*****sarami** Salami
*****sarumonera-kin** Salmonellen
~saseru lassen
sashidashi-nin Absender
sashie Illustration
sashikizu Stich
sashikomi Steckdose
sashikomu stechen
sashiosae beschlagnahmen
sasori Skorpion
sasu Stich
sasuyou na itami Seitenstechen
sate nun
satou Zucker
satsuire Brieftasche
*****sauna** Sauna
sawagashi·i unruhig; laut
schaljō-bangō *(Zug)* Wagennum-

mer
schinkin-kousoku Herzinfarkt
sebiro Sakko; Anzug
sebone Rückgrat; Wirbelsäule
sei Sex; Geschlecht
seibi-kou Schlosser/in
seibutsu-gaku Biologie; **seibutsu-gakusha** Biologe/in
seibyou Geschlechtskrankheit
seichou suru wachsen
seifu Regierung
seigaku-ka Sänger/in
seihin Produkt
seiji Politik; **seiji-gaku** Politikwissenschaft
seijitsu·na treu
seika Ergebnis
seikaku·na genau; korrekt
seiketsu·na sauber
seiki Geschlechtsorgane; Jahrhundert
seikou Erfolg
seikyuu-sho Rechnung
seimei Leben
seinen-gappi Geburtsdatum
seisan Produktion; **seisan-butsu** Erzeugnis; **seisan-sha** Hersteller; **seisan suru** erzeugen; s. verrechnen
seishoku-sha Geistlicher
seishun-jidai/ki Jugend
seito Schüler/in
seiton Ordnung
seitou berechtigt
seizu-kou Technische(r) Zeichner/in
sekai Welt
seki Husten; Sitz; **seki dome-gusuri** Hustensaft; **seki wo suru** husten
sekinin Verantwortung; Schuld; **sekinin ga aru** schulden; verantwortlich; **sekinin-sha** Leiter/in
sekitan Kohle
sekiyu-*ranpu Petroleumlampe
sekken Seife
sekki-jidai Steinzeit
sekkotsu *(Knochen)* Bruch
***sekkusu** Sex
sekkyou Predigt
sema·i schmal; eng
sen Drüse; Linie

senaka Rücken
senden Werbung; Reklame; **senden suru** werben
sen·in Matrose
senjitsu neulich
senkou Studienfach
senkyo Wahl
senmendai Waschbecken
senmenjo Waschraum
senmon-i Facharzt/ärztin
sen·nuki Flaschenöffner
senpuuki Ventilator
sensai·na zart
senscha Wagenwäsche
sensei Dozent/in; Lehrer/in
senshitsu Kajüte
senshuken Meisterschaft
sensou Krieg
sensui-fuku Taucheranzug
sentaku Auswahl
sentakuki Waschmaschine
sentakumono Wäsche
sentsū Kolik
senzai Spülmittel; Waschmittel
***sēringu** segeln
serofan-*tēpu Tesafilm
***serori** Sellerie
***serufu-*sābisu** Selbstbedienung; ***serufu-*taimā** Selbstauslöser
***sērusu-man** Außendienstvertreter
sesshoku Berührung
***sētā** Pullover
setchakuzai Klebstoff
setsubi Einrichtung; Anlage; Ausstattung; **setsubi-kouji-shi** Installateur/in
setsumei suru erklären
setsuzoku Anschluß
settoku suru überreden
sewa wo suru verschaffen
shageki *(Waffe)* Schuß
shain Angestellte/r
shajiku *(Auto)* Achse
shakai *(Welt)* Gesellschaft; **shakai-gaku** Soziologie
shakkin Schuld; **shakkin ga aru** schulden
shako Garage
shamen *(Berg)* Hang
***shanpū** Haarwaschmittel; Shampoo
sharei Honorar

sharin Rad
shashin Foto; Fotografie; **shashin-ka** Fotograf/in; **shashin wo toru** fotografieren
shashitsu *(Zug)* Abteil
shashou Schaffner
shatai Karosserie
*__shatsu__ Hemd
*__shattā__ *(Kamera)* Verschluß
*__shawā__ Dusche
shazai Entschuldigung; **shazai suru** *(sich)* entschuldigen
shi Tod
shiageru vollenden
shiai Wettkampf
shiawase Wohl; Glück
shiawase·na glücklich
shibafu Rasen
shibaraku no aida eine Zeitlang
shibumi herb
shichaku suru anprobieren
shichou Bürgermeister/in
shichou suru behaupten
shichousha Rathaus
shidou Führung; Leitung; **shidou-sha** Führer; Leiter/in
shidou-souchi Anlasser; **shidou suru** anspringen; anlaufen
shigai-chizu Stadtplan; **shigai-kyokuban** Vorwahlnummer
shigeki suru reizen
shigemi Busch
shigoto Arbeit; **shigoto wo suru** arbeiten
*__shigunaru__ Signal
shihai-nin Geschäftsführer/in
shiharai Zahlung; **shiharai-jouken** Zahlungsbedingungen; **shiharai-sashizusho/kawase** Zahlungsanweisung
shiharau auszahlen; bezahlen; zahlen
shihei Geldschein
shiji Hinweis; Angabe; **shiji suru** anweisen
shijou; ichiba *(Wirtschaft)* Markt
shika-gikou-shi Zahntechniker/in
shikai Sicht
shikake-dokei Glockenspiel
shikakukei no viereckig
shikan Krone
shikashi aber

shiken Test; Prüfung
shiki Leitung; **shiki-sha** Dirigent
shikichi Gelände; Grundstück
shima gestreift; Insel; **shima-meguri** Inselrundfahrt
shimai Schwester
shimatte iru geschlossen; zu
shimeru einenPlatz belegen; verschließen; zumachen
shimetta feucht
shimi Fleck
shinai Innenstadt; **shinai-*basu** Stadtbus; **shinai-kankou** Stadtrundfahrt; **shinai-tsuuwa** Ortsgespräch
~ **shinakereba naranai** müssen
shinbou Geduld; **shinbou zuyoi** geduldig
shinbun Zeitung
shindaiken Liegewagenkarte; Schlafwagenkarte
shindan Diagnose; **shindan-jikan** *(Arzt)* Besuchszeit; **shindan-sho** ärztliches Attest
shinde iru tot
shingaku Theologie
shingouki Ampel
shinjirarena·i unglaublich
shinjiru glauben
shinjitsu Wahrheit
shinju Perle
shinkei Nerv; **shinkei shitsu no** nervös
shinken·na ernst
shinkirou Fata Morgana
shinkoku Anmeldung; ernst
shinnen Glaube; Überzeugung
shinnyuu Überfall
shinpai Sorge; **shinpai suru** besorgt; sorgen für, s. ~ um
shinpan Schiedsrichter
shinpo Fortschritt
shinpu Priester
shinri-gaku Psychologie; **shinri-gakusha** Psychologe/in
shinrin-kanri-sha Förster/in
shinryou-jo *(Arzt)* Praxis
shinsatsu-jikan Sprechstunde
shinseinaru heilig
shinseki no verwandt
shinsen frisch
shinsetsu Freundlichkeit; Gefällig-

keit; Liebenswürdigkeit; Herzlichkeit

shinsetsu·na freundlich; lieb; liebenswürdig; nett

shinshitsu Schlafzimmer; Wohn-Schlafraum

shinu sterben

shin·you Vertrauen; **shin·you dekiru** zuverlässig; ~ **wo shin·you suru** vertrauen auf

shin·youshinai mißtrauen

shinzō-kekkan Herzfehler

shinzou Herz; **shinzou-hossa** Herzanfall; **shinzou-senmoni** Herzspezialist

shio Salz

shiraberu prüfen; nachprüfen; nachsehen; untersuchen

shirarete inai unbekannt

shirare Nachricht; Mitteilung

shiraseru Bescheid geben; informieren; mitteilen

shiriau kennenlernen

*__shirindā__ Zylinder

shiringu Schilling

shiro Burg; Schloß; Weiß

shirokuro-*firumu Schwarzweiß-Film

*__shirubā__ Silber; *__shirubā no__ silbern

shirushi Zeichen

shisan Reichtum

shisen Blick

shisho Bibliothekar/in

shishutsu Ausgaben; **shishutsu suru** ausgeben

shisshin Ohnmacht; **shisshin suru** ohnmächtig

shita Zunge

shita ni unten; unterhalb

shitabirame Seezunge

shitagau befolgen

shitashiku suru befreundet sein

shitataru tropfen

shitate-ya Schneider/in

shiten Filiale

*__shīto-*beruto__ Anschnallgurt

*__shītoberuto wo shimeru__ anschnallen, sich

shitsubou shita enttäuscht

shitsugyou arbeitslos

shitsumon Frage

shitte iru wissen; kennen

shitumon wo suru fragen

shiyakusho Rathaus

shiyou Anwendung; Gebrauch; Verwendung; **shiyou-chuu** besetzt; **shiyou-ryou** Benutzungsgebühr; **shiyou suru** gebrauchen; verwenden

shizen Natur; **shizen-hogo-kuiki** Naturschutzgebiet; **shizen no na-türlich; **shizen-ryouhou** Naturheilverfahren

shizuka·na leise; ruhig; still

shizuke sa Ruhe

shizuku Tropfen

*__shīzun__ Saison

shoen Premiere

shohousen Rezept

shokki Gedeck

shoku Beruf; Stelle; **shoku-nin** Handwerker/in

shokubutsu Pflanze; **shokubutsu-en** Botanischer Garten

shokuchuudoku Lebensmittelvergiftung

shokudou Speiseröhre; Speisesaal; Restaurant; **shokudou-sha** Speisewagen

shokugyou Beruf; **shokugyou-gakkou** Berufsschule

shokugyougara beruflich

shokuhin Lebensmittel; Nahrungsmittel; **shokuhin-ten** Lebensmittelgeschäft

shokuin Personal; Angestellte/r

shokuji Essen; Mahlzeit; **shokuji no mae ni** vor dem Essen; **shokuji wo suru** essen

shokuji-kou Setzer/in

shokumotsu Nahrung

shokuyoku Appetit; **shokuyoku-fushin** Appetitlosigkeit

shomei Unterschrift; **shomei suru** unterschreiben

*__shōru__ Schal

shorui Papiere; Dokument; **shorui-kaban** Brieftasche

shoshinsha Anfänger/in

*__shōto__ Kurzschluß

*__shōtsu__ Shorts; Slip

shou Ministerium

*__shou__ Show

shou-nin Zeuge

shoubai Geschäft
shoubou-sho Feuerwehr
shouchou Symbol; Wahrzeichen; **shouchou-shugi** Symbolismus
shoudaku suru zusagen
shoudoku-eki Desinfektionsmittel; **shoudoku suru** desinfizieren
shougakkou Grundschule
shougo Mittag
shougyou-gakkou Handelsschule; **shougyou-toshi** Handelsstadt
shouhi Verbrauch; **shouhi suru** verbrauchen
shouhin *(Waren)* Artikel; Ware
shouhizei Mehrwertsteuer
*****shōuindou** Schaufenster
shouka Verdauung; **shouka-furyou** Verdauungsstörung
shoukai Vorstellung; **shoukai suru** vorstellen
shoukaki Feuerlöscher
shouko Beweis
shoukou-netsu Scharlach
shoukyaku Verbrennung
shoumei Beleuchtung; **shoumei-sho** Ausweis; Zeugnis; **shoumei suru** bescheinigen; beweisen
shounen Junge
shounimahi Kinderlähmung
shounyuudou Tropfsteinhöhle
shourai Zukunft; **shourai no** zukünftig
shouri Gewinn; Sieg
shousai Einzelheiten
shousetsu Roman
shoutai Einladung; **shoutai suru** einladen
shoutotsu Zusammenstoß
shoyuu Besitz; **shoyuu-sha** Besitzer; Eigentümer; **shoyuu suru** besitzen
shudan Mittel; Art und Weise
shuei Pförtner/in
shufu Hausfrau
shujin Gastgeber/in; Wirt/in
shujutsu Operation; **shujutsu wo suru** operieren
shukketsu suru bluten
shukkoku Ausreise; **shukkoku suru** ausreisen
shukujitsu Feiertag
shumi Hobby

shumino waru·i *(Stil)* geschmacklos
shunkan Moment
*****shunōkeru** Schnorchel
shuppatsu Abfahrt; Abreise; **shuppatsu-jikan** Abfahrtszeit; **shuppatsu suru** abfahren; abreisen (nach)
shuppi Unkosten
shuppin-sha Aussteller
shurui Sorte; Art
shussei Geburt; **shussei-chi** Geburtsstadt
shusseki shiteiru anwesend
shuto Hauptstadt; *****shūto** *(Fußball)* Schuß
shuu Woche; **shuu goto ni** wöchentlich
shuuchaku-eki Endstation
shuudouin Kloster
shuudoujo Nonne
shuufuku suru restaurieren
shuugeki Überfall; **shuugeki suru** überfallen
shuui Umgebung
shuukai Treffen
shuukaku Ernte
shuukan Gewohnheit
shuukyou Religion
shuu·nyuu *(der)* Verdienst
shuuri Reparatur; **shuuri-dougu** Flickzeug; **shuuri suru** reparieren; flicken
shuuryou fertig
shuushuu-hin Sammlung
shuuyuu Rundfahrt; **shuuyuu-ken** Netzkarte; Rundreisefahrschein
shuyaku Hauptrolle
*****sīdī** CD/Compactdisc
*****sītsu** Bettlaken
soba wo tooru vorbeikommen
sobo Großmutter
sode Ärmel
soegi Schiene
sofu Großvater
*****soketto** Steckdose
*****sokkusu** Strümpfe
soko da; dort; **soko e** dorthin
soko Boden
sokoku Vaterland
sokutatsu Eilbrief
solo Solist/in

songai Schaden; **songai-baishou** Schadenersatz; **songai wo ataeru** schaden
sonkei Verehrung; Achtung
sono aida ni inzwischen; **sono hoka ni** außerdem; **sono-youna** solch; **sono-youni** so
sonoato danach
sonotameni dazu
sonshitsu Verlust
sora Himmel
soredemo jedoch
soredokoroka sogar
soreirai seitdem
soretomo oder
soreyueni daher; deshalb
sori Schlitten
* **sōsēji** Wurst
* **soshiaru-*wākā** Sozialarbeiter/in
soshiki Gewerbe
soshite dann; und
sosogu münden; gießen
* **sōsu** Soße
sotchuu Schlaganfall
soto draußen
sou-dairinin Generalvertreter; **sou-dairiten** (Generalvertretung
soubi Ausstattung
soudan suru konsultieren
soufuuki Gebläse
sougaku Pauschale
souji Reinigung; **souji suru** putzen
soukin *(Geld)* Überweisung
souon Geräusch; Lärm
shitsunai-soushoku-ka Dekorateur/in
soutouna beträchtlich
souzouteki·na kreativ
su Essig
subarashi·i herrlich; wunderbar
subekide aru sollen
suberidai Rutschbahn
subete alle
* **suchuwādesu** Steward/eß
* **suchuwādo** Steward
sudeni bereits; schon
~ **sugiru** *(mit adj)* zu
sugisaru vergehen
sugite vorbei; vorüber; ~ **wo sugite iku** vorbeigehen
sugosu verbringen
suguni gleich; sofort

sugureta ausgezeichnet
suiei Schwimmen; **suiei-senshu** Schwimmer/in; **suiei suru** baden; schwimmen
suika Wassermelone
suiminyaku Schlaftabletten
suiro *(Wasser)* Kanal
suisen Empfehlung
suisoku Vermutung; **suisoku suru** vermuten
* **suisu** Schweiz; * **suisu-furan** Schweizer Franken; * **suisu-jin** Schweizer/in
* **suitchi** Auslöser; Lichtschalter; Schalter; * **suitchi wo ireru** einschalten
suitei suru schätzen
* **sukāto** Rock
suketchi Zeichnung
* **sukēto-gutsu** Schlittschuhe
* **sukī** Ski; * **suki-*zubon** Skihose
sukimakaze Luftzug
suki·na mögen
* **sukkecchi-*bukku** Zeichenblock
sukoshi ein bißchen; wenig
sukuna·i gering
sukunakutomo mindestens; wenigstens
sumai Wohnung
sumasu beenden
sumomo Pflaumen
sumu wohnen
suna Sand; **suna darake no** sandig
sunaji no sandig
sunda klar
* **sunō-*taiya** Winterreifen
* **sūpā-māketto** * Supermarkt
* **supagettī** Spaghetti
* **supāku-*pulagu** Zündkerze
* **supana** Schraubenschlüssel
* **supea** Ersatz
* **supīdo** Schnelligkeit
* **supīkā** Lautsprecher
* **suponji** Schwamm
* **supōtsu** Sport; * **supōtsu-*man** Sportler/in; * **supōtsu-youhin** Sportartikel
* **supōtsu-*shūzu** Turnschuhe
suppa·i sauer
* **sūpu** Suppe; * **sūpu-zara** Suppenteller
* **supūn** Löffel

A/Z

*supurē Haarspray
*suraido Dia
  *suranpu Flaute
suri Taschendieb
*surippa Hausschuhe
suru machen; tun
surudo·i spitz
susuki (Fisch) Barsch
susumeru empfehlen
susumu vorgehen
*sutajio Studio
*sutando Ständer
*sutanpu Stempel
*sutāto Start; *sutāto suru starten
suteki·na hübsch; prima
*sutekki Stock
*sutōbu Ofen
*sutorobo Elektronenblitz
*sūtsu Anzug
suugaku Mathematik
suwaraseru setzen
suwaru s. hinsetzen; sitzen

T

*T-*shatsu T-Shirt
*tabako Tabak; Zigarette; *tabako wo suu (Zigarette) rauchen; *tabako-ya Tabakladen
taberareru eßbar
taberu essen
tabi ni deru verreisen
tabidachi Abreise
tabidatsu abreisen (nach)
tabun vielleicht
tachiagaru aufstehen
tachidomaru stehenbleiben
tadade gratis; kostenlos; umsonst
tadashi·i recht haben; richtig
tagaini einander
taichou ga i·i fit
taido Benehmen
taiho suru verhaften
taion-kei Fieberthermometer
taira·na eben; flach; glatt
tairiku Festland
taishikan Botschaft
taishou Gegenstand
taishuu-engeki Volksstück
taisou Gymnastik; Turnen
taitou ni gleichwertig

*taiya Autoreifen; Reifen
taiyou Sonne
taizai Aufenthalt
taka·i hoch; teuer
takasa Höhe
taki Wasserfall
takkyuu Tischtennis
takoage Drachenfliegen
*takomētā Tachometer
takumashi·i kräftig
takusan no viel; zahlreich
*takushī Taxi; *takushi-*doraibā* Taxifahrer/in; *takushi-noriba Taxistand
takuwae Vorrat
tamago Ei
tamanegi Zwiebel
~ no tameni wegen; zugunsten
tamerau zögern
tameshi Versuch
tamesu probieren; versuchen
tango Wort
tani Tal
tanjou-bi Geburtstag
tankikan no kurzfristig
tannou Gallenblase
tanoshimi Genuß; Spaß; Vergnügen; Lust
tanoshimu s. amüsieren; genießen
*tanpon Tampons
tansho Nachteil
tansu Schrank
tantou zuständig; tantou-sha Ansprechpartner
*taoru Badetuch; Handtuch; Tuch
tarinai fehlen; nicht ausreichen
taru Faß
tasai·na farbig
tashikana sicher; bestimmt
tassuru erlangen; erreichen
~ wo tasukeru jdm helfen
tataku anklopfen; klopfen
tatemono Gebäude
tateru (Plan) aufstellen; bauen
tatoe Beispiel
tatsu stehen
tawamure Flirt
tazuneru s. erkundigen; besuchen; fragen
te Hand; te-bouki Handfeger; te ni hairu erhältlich; te wo furu winken

teashi *(Hände und Füße)* Glieder
tebukuro Handschuhe
*****tēburu-*kurosu** Tischtuch
tegami Brief
teian Angebot; Vorschlag; **teian
  suru** vorschlagen
teido Standard; Grad
teiji suru vorzeigen
teiki-koukuubin Linienflug
teikiatsu *(Wetter)* Tief
teikyou *(anbieten)* Angebot; **teikyou suru** anbieten; bieten
teinei·na höflich
teineisa Höflichkeit
teiryuu-jo Haltestelle
teisei suru richtigstellen; verbessern
teko Hebel
ten Punkt; **ten-in** *(im Laden)* Ver-
  käufer/in
tenbou-dai Aussichtspunkt
tengoku Himmel; Paradies
tenimotsu Handgepäck; **tenimot-
  su-hassou-*kauntā** Gepäckabfertigung; **tenimotsu-hikiwatashijo**
  Gepäckausgabe
*****tenisu** Tennis
tenji-hin Ausstellungsmaterial;
  tenji-kai Ausstellung
tenjou Decke
tenjou-in Reisebegleiter/in
tenka Zündung
tenkan Epilepsie
tenkeiteki·na typisch
tenki Wetter; **tenki-yohou** Wetter-
  vorhersage
tenmondai Sternwarte
tennou Kaiser
tenraku Sturz; **tenraku suru** stürzen
tensou suru nachsenden
tenteki Infusion
*****tento** Zelt; *****tento wo haru** zelten
*****tēpu** das Band
terasu Bestrahlung; *****terasu** Terrasse; Balkon
*****terebi** Fernseher; *****terebi-shitsu**
  Fernsehraum; *****terebi wo miru**
  fernsehen
*****terehon-*kādo** Telefonkarte
*****terekkusu** Telex
teru scheinen

tesuuryou Provision
*****tetanusu** Tetanus
tetsu Eisen
tetsudau helfen
tetsudou Eisenbahn; **tetsudou-in**
  Eisenbahner
tetsugaku Philosophie
tezukuri no handgemacht
*****tisshu** Papiertaschentücher
  ~ **to** mit; und; ~ **to shite** als
tobidatsu abfliegen; vorspringen
tobu fliegen; springen
tochi *(Erde)* Grund; Kastanien;
  tochi no einheimisch
todana Schrank
todokede Anmeldung; Meldung;
  Anzeige
todokederu anzeigen; melden
todokeru überbringen
todoku reichen; erreichen
todomaru bleiben
*****toire** Toilette
*****toiretto-*pēpā** Toilettenpapier
tojikomeru einsperren; einschließen
tojiru schließen
tokei Uhr; **tokei-ya** Uhrmacher/in
  ~ **no tokoro** bei
tokorode übrigens
toku lösen
tokubetsu·na Sonder-; speziell;
  tokubetsu ni extra
tokuni besonders
tokusei Eigenschaft; Sonderanfer-
  tigung
tokushu na Sonder-; speziell
tomare! halt!
tomaru halten; stehenbleiben;
  übernachten
*****tomato** Tomaten
tomegane Haken
tomeru abstellen; anhalten
tomodachi Freund/in
tonarino hito Nachbar/in
*****ton·neru** Tunnel
ton·ya Großhändler
too·i *(fern)* weit
tooku ni fort
toori nukeru Durchfahrt; **toori
  sugiru** vorübergehen
toppatsu-jiken Zwischenfall; Vorfall

toppuu Bö; Windstoß

*__toraberāzu-__*__chekku__ Reisescheck

*__torakku__ Lastwagen

*__toranpu__ Karte; Spielkarten

*__toreirā__ (Auto) Anhänger

*__torēningu__ Schulung

tori Vogel; **tori ageru** wegnehmen; **tori-niku** Hähnchen

toriaezu vorläufig

toriatsukai Behandlung; Handhabung

toriatsukau behandeln

toride Festung

torihiki Geschäft; **torihiki-kankei** Geschäftsbeziehungen; **torihiki wo suru** handeln

torikaeru wechseln; ersetzen; umtauschen; vertauschen

torikesu abbestellen; stornieren; zurücknehmen

torini iku (Dinge) holen

torisaru abnehmen

torishimariyaku Geschäftsführer/in; Direktor/in

torishimari Kontrolle

toriwake hauptsächlich; besonders

toru (Telefon) abheben; nehmen

toshi Alter; Jahr

toshokan Bibliothek; **toshokan-in** Bibliothekar/in

*__tōsutā__ Toaster

*__tōsuto__ Toast

totemo sehr

totetsumona·i unwahrscheinlich

totonoeru (Ordnung) ausrichten

totsuzen no plötzlich

totte Griff

tou Turm

touchaku Ankunft; **touchaku-jikan** Ankunftszeit; **touchaku suru** ankommen; eintreffen

toudai Leuchtturm

touge (Gebirge) Paß

tougei Töpferei

tougi Diskussion

tougyuu Stierkampf

touji damals; Wintersonnenwende

toujiki Keramik- und Porzellanwaren

toujou-ken Bordkarte

touketsu Frost; **touketsu shita** Glatteis

touki Keramik; Porzellan

toumorokoshi Mais

tounan Diebstahl

tounyou-byou Diabetes; **tounyou-kanja** Diabetiker/in

touyu Petroleum

touzen no logisch; selbstverständlich; berechtigt

tozan Bergsteigen

*__tsuā__ Tour

tsuchi (Boden) Erde

tsugi no nächste(r, -s)

tsugou no yo·i günstig; passend

tsuika-hiyou Nebenkosten; **tsuika no** zusätzlich

tsuini endlich

~ **ni tsuite** über

tsukaeru bedienen; dienen

tsukamaeru fangen

tsukamu ergreifen

tsukareru anstrengend

tsukareta erschöpft; müde

tsukau benutzen

tsukeawase (Essen) Beilage

tsukeru einschalten; anmachen; **hi wo tsukeru** anzünden

tsuketasu hinzufügen

tsuki Monat; Mond; **tsuki zuki** monatlich

tsukisoi-nin Begleiter

tsukisou begleiten

tsuku stoßen

tsukue Schreibtisch

tsukuru bilden; schaffen; machen

tsuma Ehefrau

tsumarana·i langweilig

tsumari also; nämlich

tsumaru verstopft

tsumatta gefüllt; überfüllt; gestopft

tsumayouji Zahnstocher

tsume Nagel; **tsume-kiri** Nagelschere

tsumemono Füllung

tsumeru Dichtung; packen

tsumeta·i kühl; kalt

tsumi Schuld; **tsumi no nai** unschuldig

tsumikomu aufladen

tsuneni immer

tsureni iku (Person) holen

tsurete iku (Person) mitnehmen; **tsurete kuru** mitbringen

tsuri Angel
*__tsūrisuto__ Tourist/in
tsuru fischen; angeln
tsutaeru *(Grüße)* ausrichten
tsutsumi Paket
tsutsumu einpacken; einwickeln;
verpacken
tsuuchi Mitteilung; **tsuuchi suru**
benachrichtigen
tsuujou normalerweise; **tsuujou
no** üblich
tsuuka Währung; **tsuuka suru** passieren; durchfahren
tsuukou-ryoukin Autobahngebühren; Straßenbenutzungsgebühr
tsuuwa Telefongespräch
tsuuyaku Dolmetscher/in
tsuuyou suru gelten
tsuyo·i stark
tsuyosa Stärke
tsuyu Regenzeit
tsuzukeru fortsetzen; weiterma-
chen
tsuzuku dauern; folgen
tsuzuri Buchstabierung
tuujou no gewöhnlich

U

uchi Haus; **uchi e kaeru** nach Hause gehen; **uchi ni iru** daheim
uchiawase suru zusammenschlagen
ude Arm; **ude-doke·i** Armbanduhr
udewa Armband
ue oben; **ue e** aufwärts
uēbu o tsukeru *(Haare)* legen
*__ueitā__ Kellner; Ober
ugoki Bewegung
ugoku bewegen; funktionieren
*__uinkā__ Blinker; Warnblinker
ukairo Umleitung
ukeire Aufnahme
ukeireru aufnehmen
uketori ni iku *(etw.)* abholen; **uketori-nin** Empfänger
uketoru *(erhalten)* annehmen;
empfangen; erhalten
uketsuke Rezeption
ukkari suru aus Versehen
uma Pferd; **uma ni noru** reiten

~ **umare** gebürtig aus
umareru geboren werden
umi Eiter; Meer; die See; **umi no
jōsu** Seegang
unagi Aal
unchin Fahrpreis
undou-jou Sportplatz
unga Kanal
unpan-nin Träger
unten-menkyo-shou Führerschein; **unten-sha/shu** Kraftfahrer; **unten-shu** Chauffeur; Fahrer/
in; **unten-souchi** Getriebe; **unten
suru** fahren
uraji *(Stoff)* Futter
ureshi·i froh
ureyuki Absatz
uriage zei Umsatzsteuer
urikire Ausverkauf
uriko *(im Laden)* Verkäufer/in
uritsukushi Ausverkauf
uru verkaufen
*__ūru__ Wolle
urusa·i laut
ushi Kuh
~**no ushiro ni** hinter; **ushiro e**
rückwärts; **ushiro ni** hinten
uso Lüge
usu·i dünn; hell
uta Gesang; Lied
utagai Zweifel
utagainashi ni zweifellos
utagau an etw zweifeln
utagawashi·i zweifelhaft
utau singen
utsu schießen; Schlag; schlagen
utsukushi·i schön
utsukushisa Schönheit
utsurikawari Übergang
uwagi Jacke

V

v-beruto Keilriemen

W

*__wādo-__*__purosessā-__*__shisutemu__
Textverarbeitungssystem
*__wain__ Wein

*waipā Scheibenwischer
waka·i jung
wakare Abschied; wakare wo tsugeru s. verabschieden
wakareru trennen
wakeme Scheitel
wakeru teilen; verteilen
wakimichi Nebenstraße
wan Bucht
*wanpīsu Kleid
warau lachen
wareru (Geschirr) Bruch; zerbrechen
wareyasu·i zerbrechlich
wariai Prozentsatz
waribiki Ermäßigung; Rabatt
warimashi-ryoukin Zuschlag
waru·i schlecht; böse
wasureru vergessen
wata Watte
watashi ich; watashi no tameni
meinetwegen
watashitachi wir; watashitachi no
unser, unsere
watasu abgeben; übergeben; geben
*watto Watt
wazuka no gering
wazurawashii lästig
*wōkuman Walkman

Y

yachin (Haus) Miete
yado Unterkunft
yagai-gekijou Freilichtbühne
yaita geröstet; gebraten
yakaifuku Abendkleid
yakedo-gusuri Brandsalbe
yakiniku Braten
yaku braten; backen
yakugaku Pharmazie
yakunitatsu zweckmäßig; nützlich
yakunitatanai nutzlos
yakunitatsu nützlich
yakusho Amt; Behörde
yakusoku Termin; Verabredung;
Versprechen; yakusoku wo suru
versprechen; verabreden
yakusou Kräuter
yakuzai-shi Apotheker/in
yama Berg

yamakaji Waldbrand
yameru aufhören
yamome no verwitwet
yane Dach
yanefuki-shokunin Dachdecker/in
yanushi Hausbesitzer
yao-ya Gemüsehändler
yappari doch
yari-nage Pfeilwerfen
yasai Gemüse
yasashi·i nett; zärtlich; einfach
yasei Wild; yasei no wild
yaseta mager; schlank
yasui billig
yasumu s. ausruhen; ruhen; Pause
machen
yawaraka·i weich; zart; sanft
yoake (am Abend) Dämmerung
yobi-buhin Ersatzteile; yobi-*taiya
Reservereifen
yobidashi-on Freizeichen
yobidasu ausrufen
yobikakeru aufrufen
yobi*taiya Ersatzrad
yobou-seschu-techou Impfpaß;
yobou-sesshu wo suru impfen
yobousesshu Impfung
yobu rufen
*yōdo Jod(tinktur)
*yoga Yoga
yogore Schmutz
*yōguruto Joghurt
yo·i gut
yokan Ahnung
yokei·na überflüssig
~ no yoko neben
yokogiru quer durch; überqueren
yokotawatte·iru liegen
yoku häufig; oft; yoku tsukawareru gebräuchlich
yokushitsu Badezimmer
yokusou Badewanne
yomu lesen
yonbun no ichi ein Viertel
yopparatta betrunken
yopparau s. betrinken
yori ijou mehr; ~ yori mae ni eher
yoriyoi besser
yorokobashi·i froh; erfreulich
yorokobi Freude; Lust
yorokonde gern
yorokonde iru erfreut (über)